AF521901

The College History Series

Winthrop University

Dedication

*For Dr. Arnold Shankman and Dr. J. Edward Lee,
Winthrop faculty members who have played an instrumental role
in the Winthrop University Archives' growth and success.*

The College History Series

WINTHROP UNIVERSITY

RON AND MAGDALENA CHEPESIUK

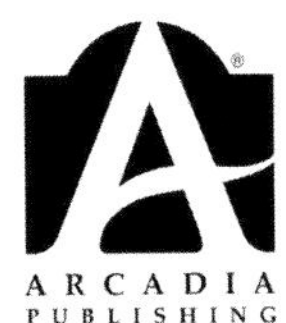

ARCADIA PUBLISHING

Copyright © 2000 by Ron and Magdalena Chepesiuk.
ISBN 978-0-7385-0550-3

Published by Arcadia Publishing
Charleston, South Carolina

Printed in the United States of America

Library of Congress Catalog Card Number: 99-069534.

For all general information contact Arcadia Publishing at:
Telephone 843-853-2070
Fax 843-853-0044
E-Mail sales@arcadiapublishing.com
For customer service and orders:
Toll-Free 1-888-313-2665

Visit us on the Internet at www.arcadiapublishing.com

About the Authors

Ron Chepesiuk has been head of the Winthrop University Archives since 1973. He is the author of 12 books and close to 2,000 articles. From 1996 to 1999, he was the editor-in-chief of *International Leads* newsletter, the international arm of the American Library Association, and he currently serves as a contributing editor to *American Libraries*. In 1999 he received the Humphry-OCLC-Forest Press award for "significant contribution to international librarianship."

Magdalena Aranda Chepesiuk is a native of Bogota, Colombia. A freelance journalist and photographer who specializes in covering historical subjects and current affairs, she currently works as a plant supervisor at the Wilton Connor Packaging Company in Charlotte. Magdalena and Ron have been married 13 years.

Contents

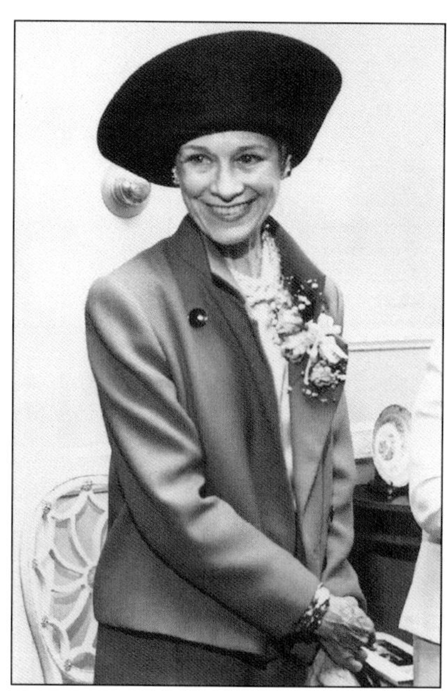

The Winthrop Tradition: A Personal View

In the Crawford family, it was an absolute—the three girls would go to Winthrop and the boy to Clemson. At these state colleges, we would be "protected" under strict discipline and be equipped to "make a living and lead an educated life." College life did indeed have a vital influence on us and truly "gave us a Life."

Our college years were critical years in the nation's history: the end of the Great Depression, the beginning of World War II. Winthrop—in fact, the whole world—was changing. We dealt with rationing coupons for food and gasoline, and students who married had to move out of the dorms and find apartments. Many new opportunities opened up for women. It was the years of Rosie the Riveter, of joining the Wacs and Waves, or finding jobs in the military and civilian life.

Eventually Winthrop became co-ed, uniforms were abolished, traditions modified. But for us, the Winthrop Clock marked the passage of days, and the attitude of the faculty stayed stable and grew. Dedicated professors continued to search to find out what was special in each of us. Their confidence made us feel strong—capable of filling the needs of the world as well as our own dreams. The faculty encouraged us, really gave us permission, to be the very best and to live our lives to the fullest.

Some of the college staff will never be forgotten: Mr. Blankenship, the college cop who was a substitute father; Mr. Hollis, who ran the laundry (I loved running to an early class between the laundry and dining room and remembering the rising steam, the smell of soaps, starch, and hot irons); dorm mothers who took care of us with a patience at which to marvel; and Mrs. McBryde, the dietitian. The smell of baking rolls in the afternoon, the crunch of grapenut ice cream from the College Farm—these are her legacy.

Every meal started with a Blessing, some of which are still pasted on my refrigerator. I cherish the feelings they evoke and visualize the Sunday Supper with the setting sun streaming through cathedral-like windows, its shimmering rays touching the bent heads of Winthrop students.

The Blue Line was a Winthrop tradition, but its vivid memory is shared with Rock Hillians. We wobbled down Oakland Avenue in our Nellie Don blue dresses, blue hat, high heels, and white gloves—all the while trying to keep stockings seams straight and garter belt in place. The local boys cruised the line, and we flirted back (many found their future husband walking the Blue Line).

We learned Latin, history, and how to roll up pajama legs to make it to breakfast on time. We swam in non-fit swimsuits and played field hockey in droopy parts and gym suits. But we looked very Ginger Rogers-esque for tennis in crisp, white shorts, shirt tied in front to leave just enough skin showing to feel chic and risque.

Today, the magnolia trees in front of Tillman stand strong, linking my years on the campus with today. The campus survived the fury of Hugo and is a symbol of the relationships and friendships made at Winthrop. They grow deep and strong like the tree. Just as the tree's branches reach out to each new generation of students, our arms reach out and encourage each other and the students to come.

Winthrop women—and now also men—have made and still are making history as this book vividly shows. Winthrop has survived storms from within and without, but the Winthrop relationships and friendships have never been shattered. And so it will remain.

Thank you, Winthrop. You have given me a beautiful life filled with laughter, loving and lasting friendships. The continuing need to learn that you kindled in me and to other graduates still grows strong. And to your future students, Winthrop University continues to promise—"The best is yet to come!"

—Ida Crawford Stewart, Class of 1943

INTRODUCTION

What is past is prologue.
—William Shakespeare

In 1886, David Bancroft Johnson, the superintendent of the Columbia City School System, journeyed to Boston, Massachusetts, to see Robert C. Winthrop, chairman of the Peabody Education Board. Dr. Johnson's objective was to secure money from the board to start a teacher training institution for women. Columbia, like most cities in South Carolina at the time, was plagued with a shortage of teachers, and Johnson believed that the problem could be alleviated by educating women to be teachers. After a short interview, Winthrop promised the young educator that the Peabody Board would give him $1,500 to help him launch his dream.

On November 15, 1886, the Winthrop Training School was formerly opened with 19 students under the tutelage of one teacher, Mary Hall Leonard. After securing the money from Winthrop, Johnson had gone personally to Bridgewater, Massachusetts, to obtain Miss Leonard's services for the fledgling institution. The school was named in honor of its benefactor, Robert C. Winthrop.

And so Winthrop College was born, modestly and in the service of the state. More than 113 years later, Winthrop is no longer an academic institution struggling to make its mark on the world. Today, it is a thriving university with 5,000-plus students and a myriad of programs designed to serve the diverse needs and interests of the modern American citizen.

This book chronicles the remarkable Winthrop saga. Through images and information from the university's archives, readers will learn about the events and people who have helped make something no one who had watched the birth of Winthrop in 1886 thought possible.

Winthrop University is a celebration of an institution's remarkable history as it enters the new millennium. The book highlights Winthrop's rich history, diverse programs, and central themes, while showing that the university has always been true to its central mission: providing quality education to Americans so that they can better serve South Carolina and the Republic. The authors are honored to publish this photographic history for the many alumni, faculty, administrators, and friends of Winthrop, who, through the decades, have made the institution what it is today. We hope you enjoy it.

Acknowledgments

The authors wish to thank the individuals who helped make this book possible. First, Gina Price White, the Winthrop assistant archivist, read the manuscript and provided valuable suggestions. Her work in the Winthrop Archives has also been a big reason for the department's growth and success. Dr. Edward Lee, Winthrop professor and historian, read the manuscript and provided valuable editorial suggestions. Dr. Lee's support of the Winthrop Archives during his tenure at Winthrop has been an important factor in its continued development. Dr Mark Herring, dean of the Dacus Library, provided support and encouragement throughout the project, which was extremely appreciated.

The late Dr. Arnold M. Shankman played an instrumental role in the early growth of the Archives, and we miss his support and friendship. Martie Curran and Nan Mitchell of the Winthrop Alumni Relations Office were helpful in the book's production. Sonnie Bennett and Judy Knowles in the University Relations Office were extremely helpful with photos and background research, and they are always a joy to work with. Winthrop photographer Joel Nichols took several photos used in our book, and we appreciate his support. We would also like to thank the many donors, many of whom have been alumni, who have given photos, scrapbooks, diaries, and other materials to the Archives. The authors have used images from those donations, and we appreciate their support of Winthrop University.

One

Movers and Shakers

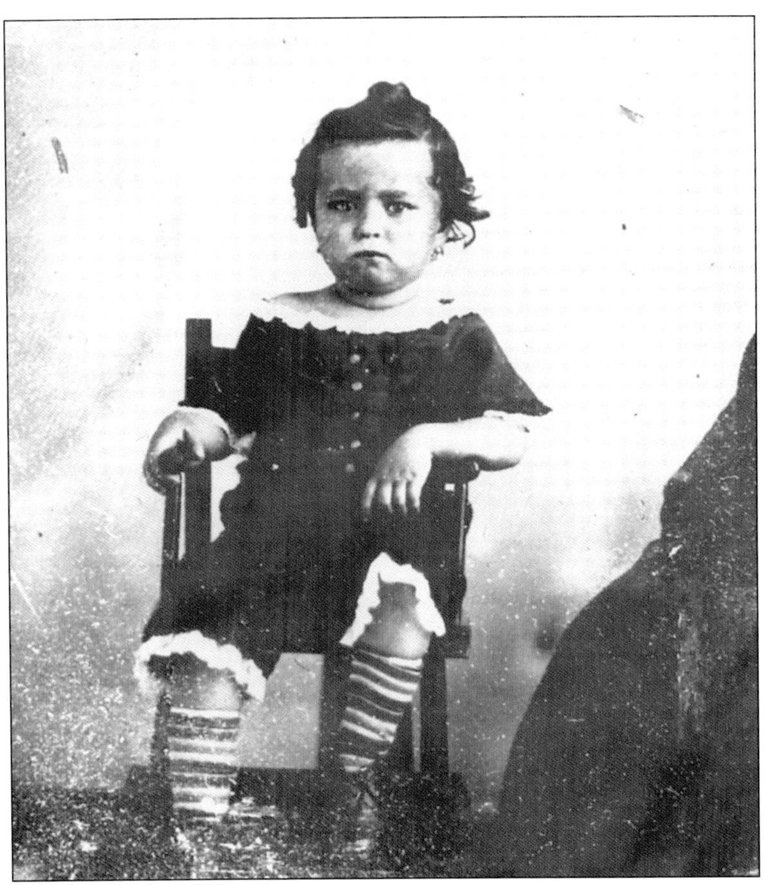

Winthrop President David Bancroft Johnson (1856–1928) was born in a dormitory of La Grange Female College in La Grange, Tennessee, on December 10, 1856. His father, David Bancroft Johnson Sr., was founder and president of the institution. In 1864, the young boy lost his arm after it was crushed in a fall from a moving freight train. As a child, D.B. showed the determination that would later exhibit itself in establishing Winthrop College.

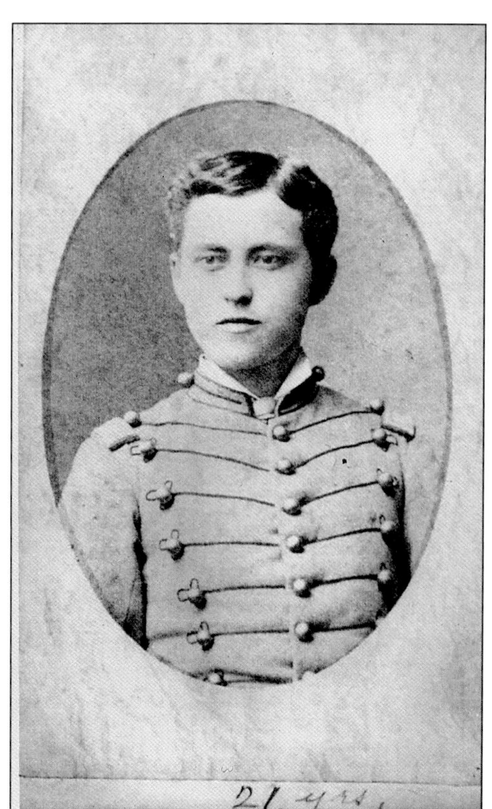

This portrait captures a young D.B. Johnson as a student at East Tennessee University (later renamed the University of Tennessee) in Knoxville. Johnson graduated with honors.

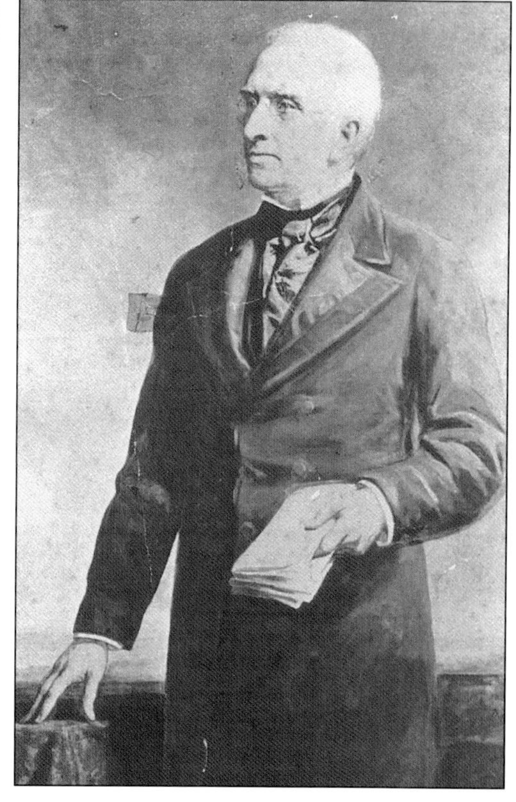

Robert C. Winthrop (1809–1894) is the namesake of Winthrop University. A member of the distinguished Winthrop family of New England, Robert C. Winthrop was regarded as "the unofficial statesman of Massachusetts." Winthrop was chairman of the Peabody Board, which set up the Peabody Education Fund during Reconstruction to help Southern education get back on its feet after the devastation of the Civil War. An initial grant of $1,500 from the fund started Winthrop, and, according to legend, Robert C. Winthrop gave $50 out of his pocket toward establishing the school.

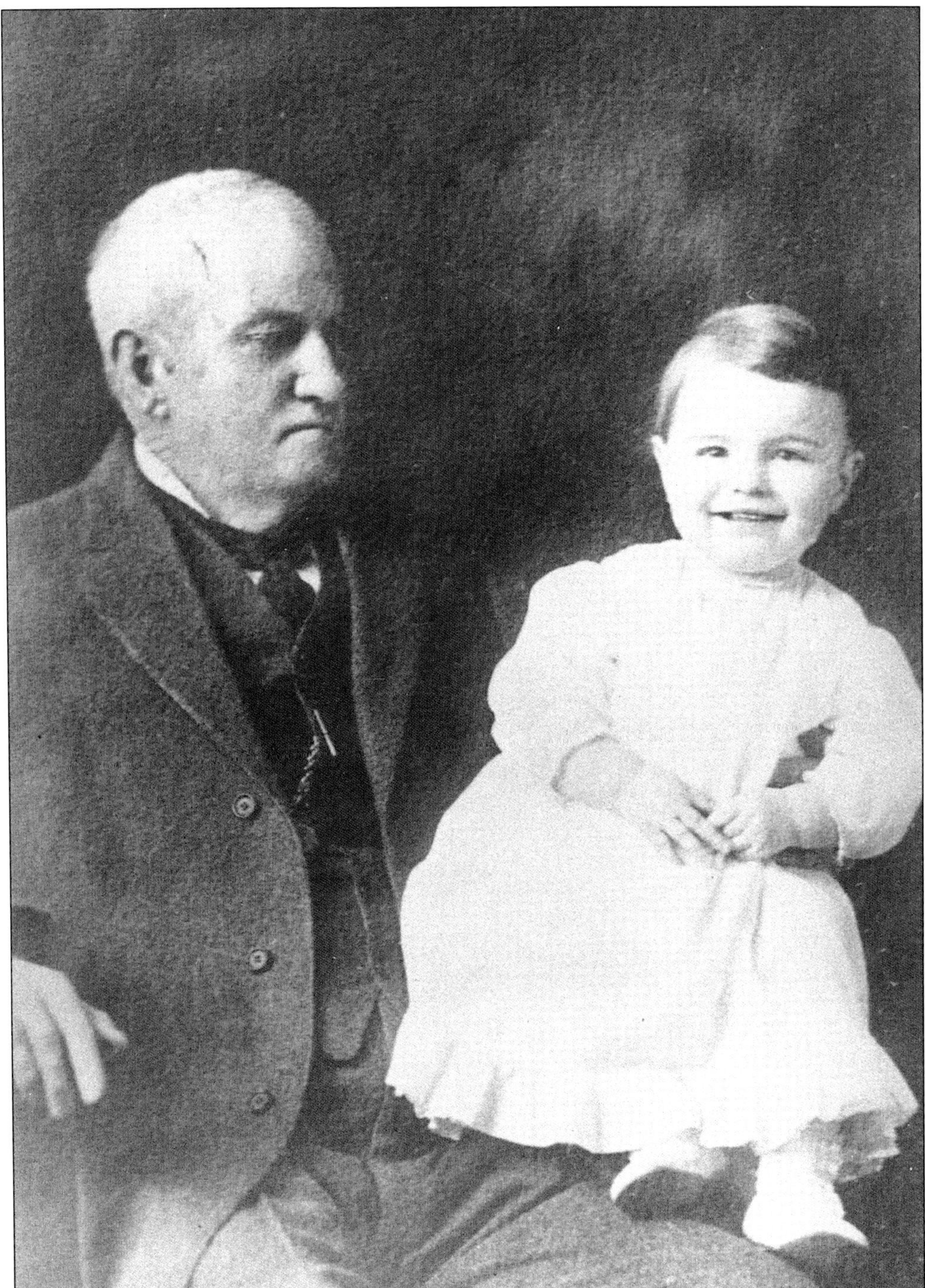

"Pitchfork" Ben Tillman (1847–1918), one of South Carolina's most colorful and influential politicians, promoted the establishment of Winthrop College as a state institution even before he held public office. He was named "Pitchfork" for his fiery style as South Carolina governor from 1891 to 1894. Tillman secured state funds for Winthrop College's construction and was a member of the Winthrop Board of Trustees from 1891 to 1918.

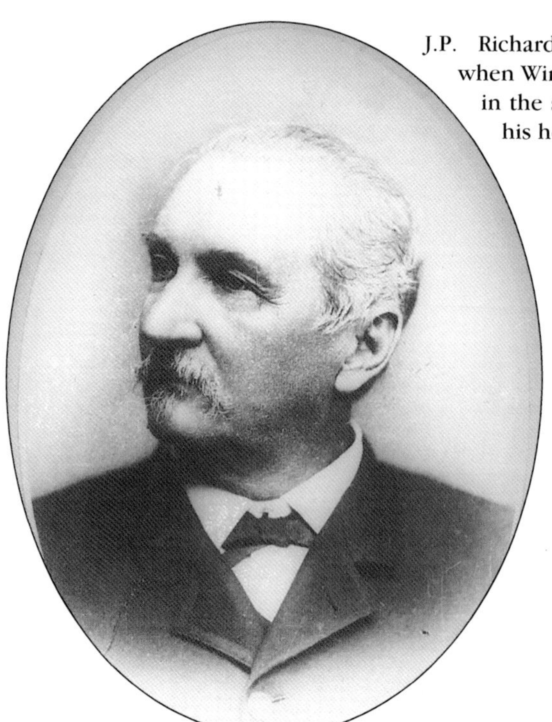

J.P. Richardson, the governor of South Carolina when Winthrop was founded, took an active interest in the school. Richardson Dormitory is named in his honor.

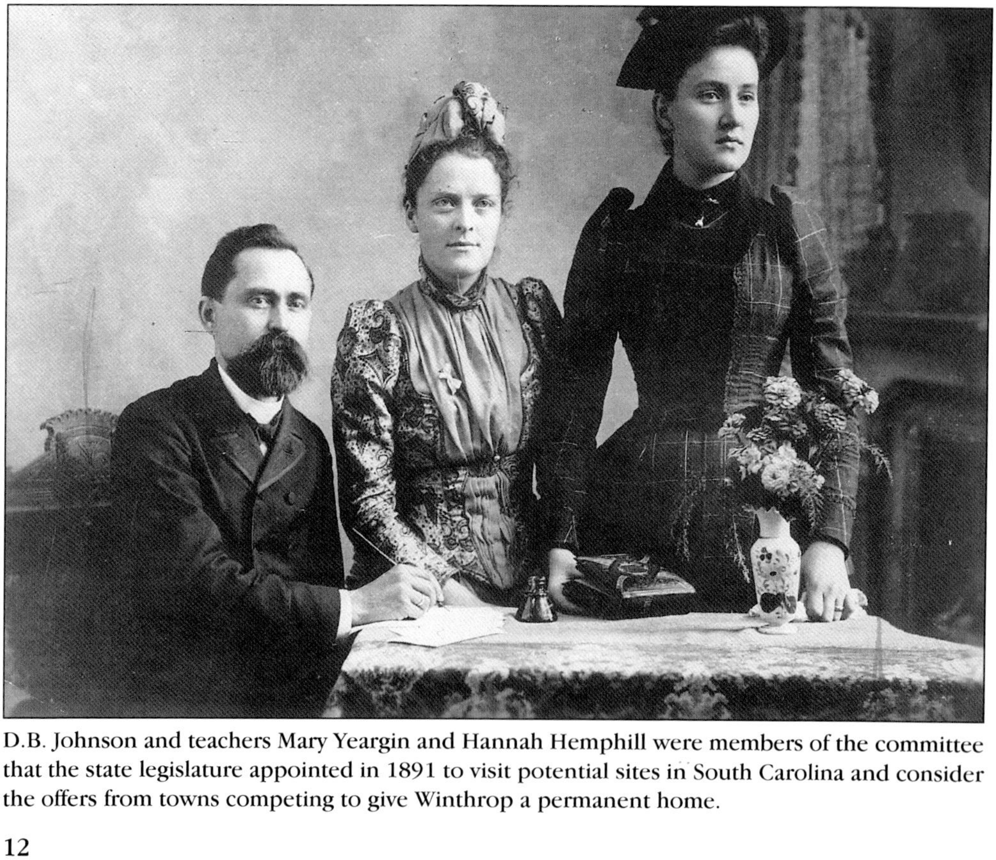

D.B. Johnson and teachers Mary Yeargin and Hannah Hemphill were members of the committee that the state legislature appointed in 1891 to visit potential sites in South Carolina and consider the offers from towns competing to give Winthrop a permanent home.

The infirmary, like Tillman Hall, was constructed with convict labor in 1896 at a cost of $5,000. The facility included the most modern features in hospital design at the time and included a pharmacy, sanitary examining rooms, quarters for the resident physician and nurse, adequate ventilation of wards and a special kitchen. The Infirmary was later named for Dr. Thomas A. Crawford, an internationally known physician and original member of the Board of Trustees.

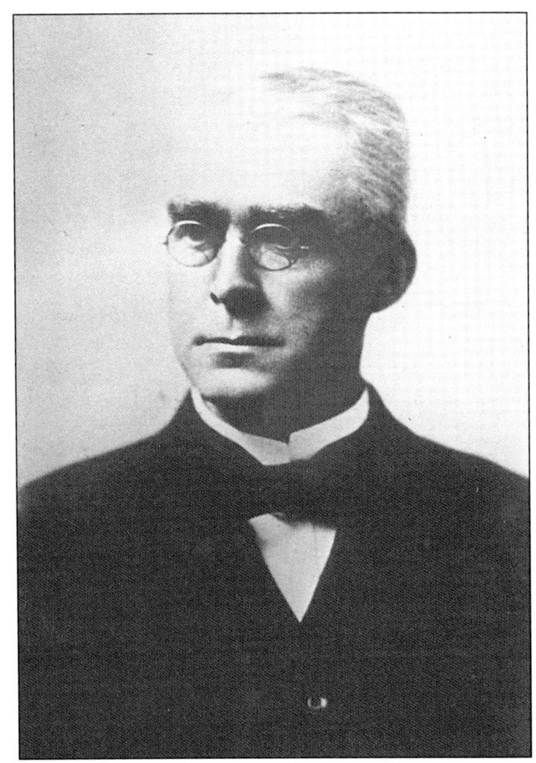

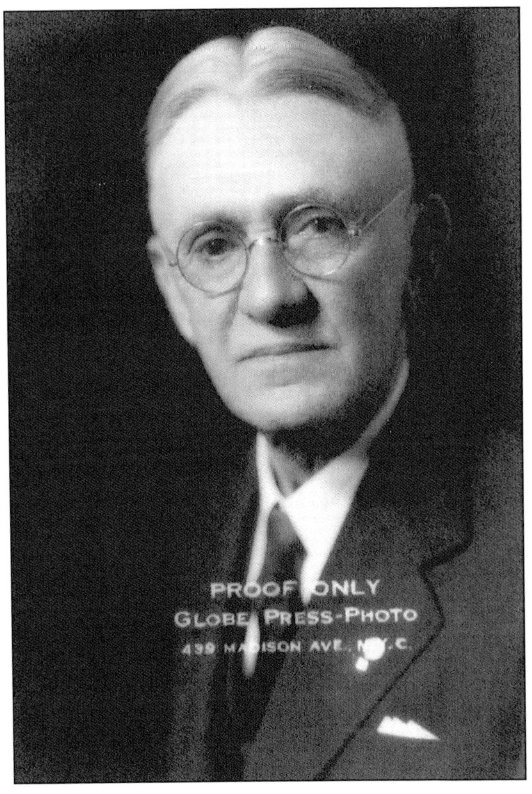

Rock Hillian W.J. Roddey was instrumental in the early development of Winthrop College. He served as a member of the Winthrop College Board of Trustees from 1893 to 1945, during which time, he was a state legislative representative backing industry and education.

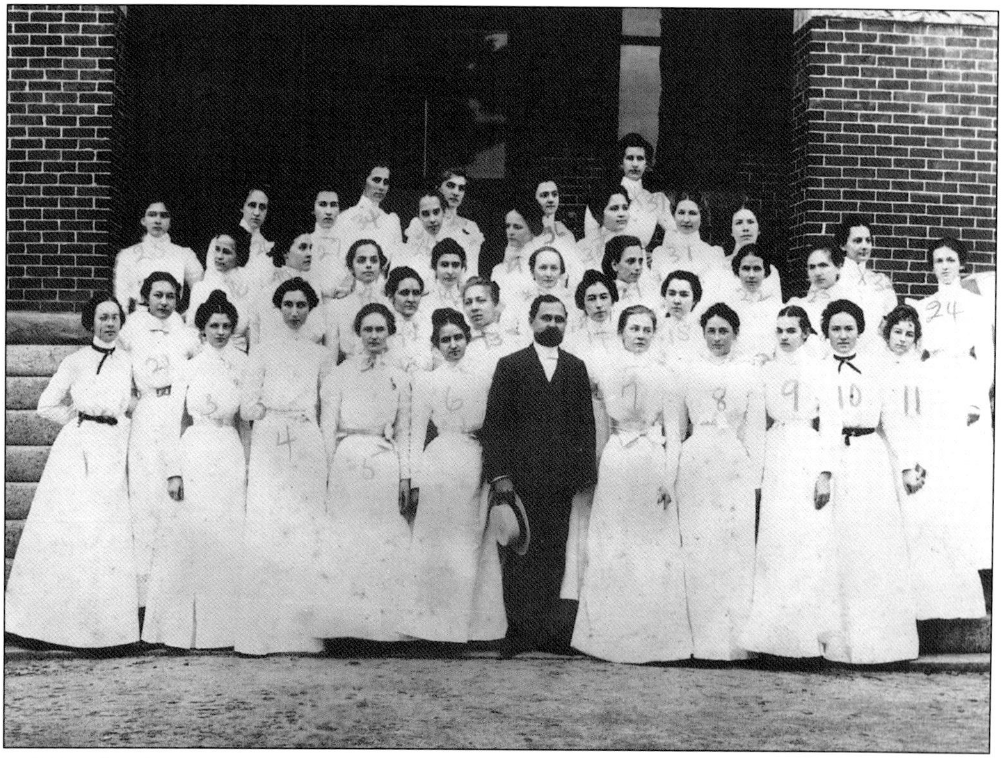

D.B. Johnson and members of the Class of 1900 look smart in their uniforms as they pose in front of Tillman Hall, then known as Main Building. Winthrop was founded as a college for white women. By 1900, Winthrop's enrollment had topped 500.

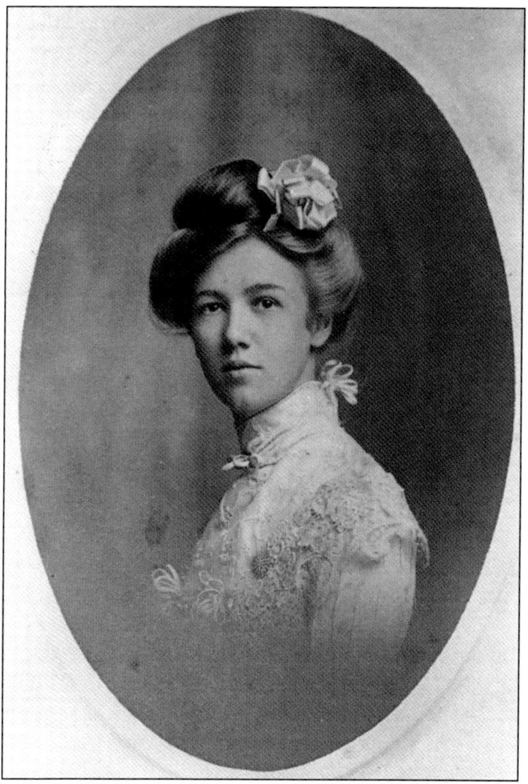

This is a 1902 portrait of Mai Rutledge Smith Johnson, the wife of President D.B. Johnson and Winthrop's first lady. Born into a distinguished South Carolina family, her great-great-grandfather, Edward Rutledge, signed the Declaration of Independence and was the state's first governor. Until the age of 91, she worked as an associate librarian at Winthrop, often six days a week.

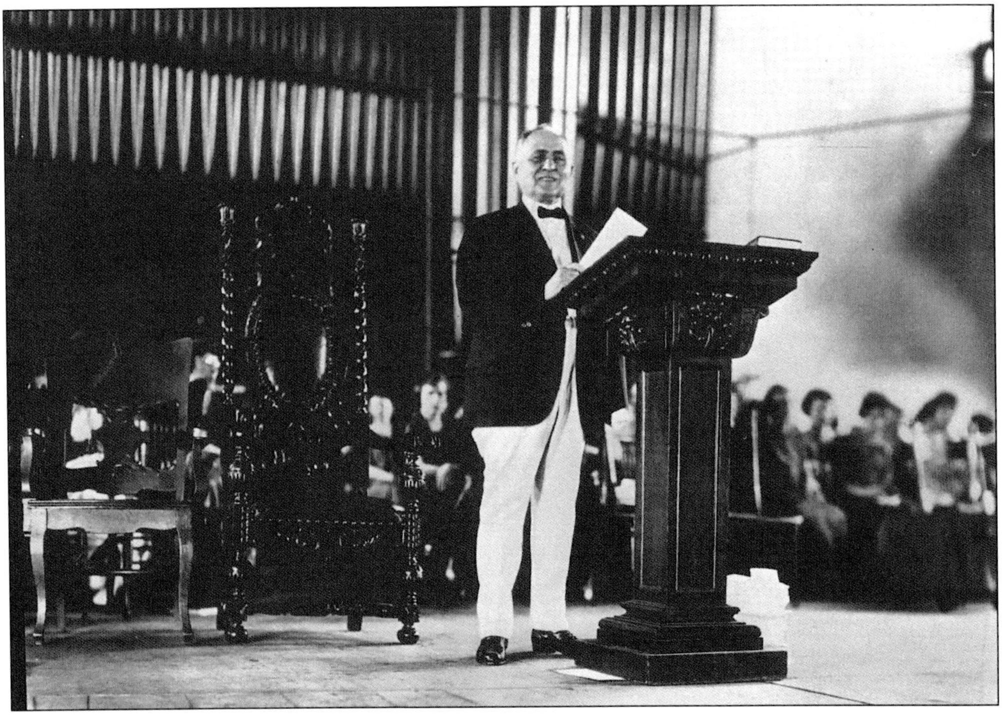

D.B. Johnson is giving a *c.* 1920s address to Winthrop students. As the records in the Winthrop Archives show, Johnson was a tireless worker on behalf of the college. Many of Winthrop's buildings still in use today were built during his tenure as president. Johnson died on December 26, 1928. The following year, the Winthrop Board of Trustees presented a report to the South Carolina General Assembly that showed Winthrop had 2,601 graduates certified to teach in South Carolina. The college with the next highest in the state had 396.

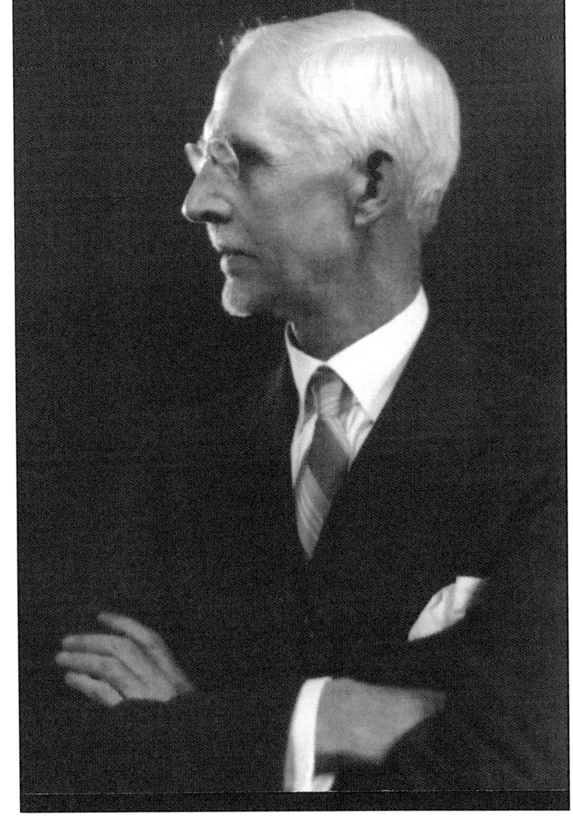

James Pinckney Kinard (1864–1951), Winthrop's Dean of the College, succeeded Johnson and served Winthrop ably as president until 1934. Kinard had graduated from The Citadel in 1886 as a member of the first class to graduate from the school after the Civil War and went on to receive his Ph.D. from John Hopkins University. Kinard came to Winthrop College as a professor of English in 1895.

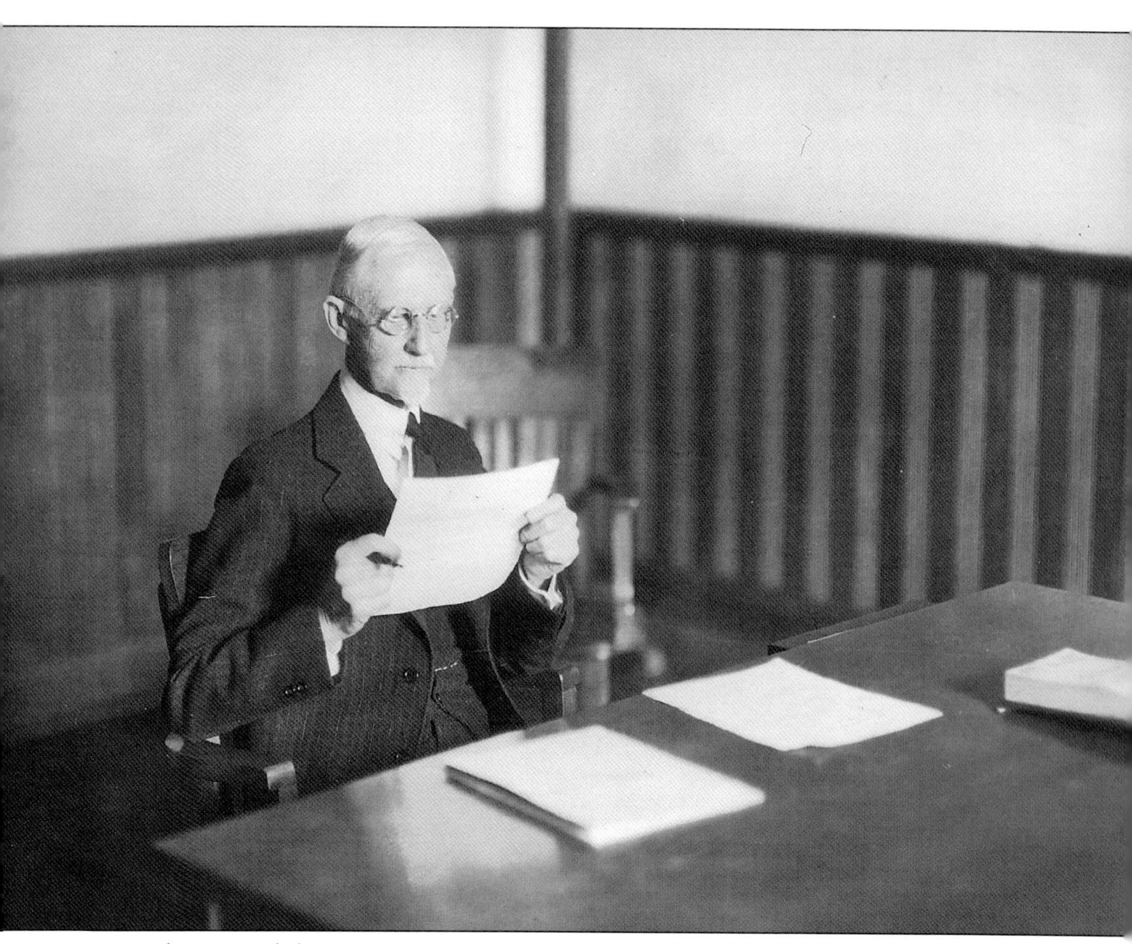

Kinard's accomplishments included the expansion of the college's library, the planning of the amphitheater, the securing of accredited membership in the Southern Association of Colleges and Secondary Schools, and the construction of Kinard Building (named in his honor) in 1929 to accommodate most of Winthrop's classes.

Dr. Shelton Phelps (1883–1948), Kinard's successor, served as Winthrop president from 1934 to 1943. Born in Nevada, Missouri, Phelps received a Ph.D. from George Peabody College for Teachers and was formerly dean of the graduate school at George Peabody College.

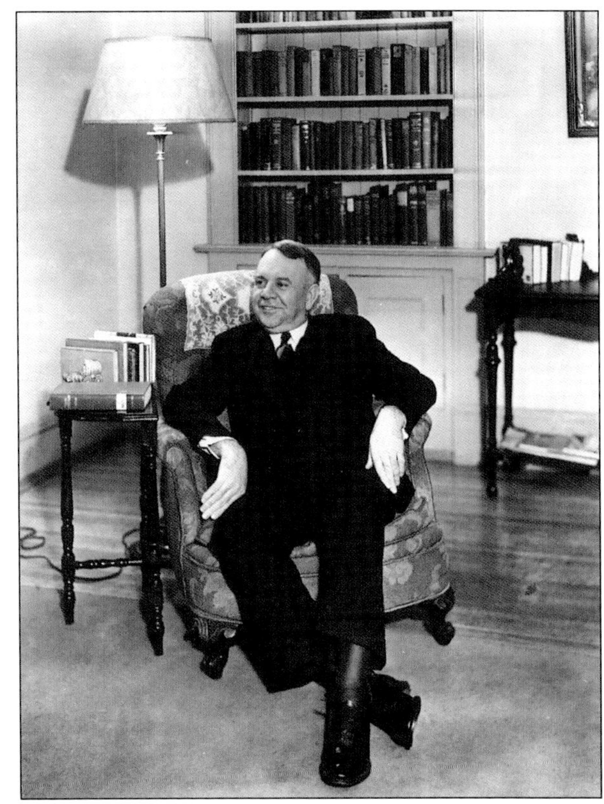

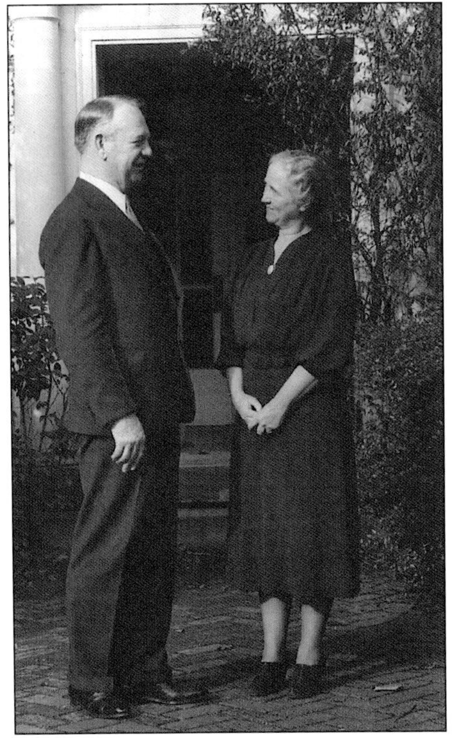

President Phelps and his wife pose for this charming picture in 1939. Under Phelps's leadership, the college quickly began to recover from the economic woes of the Depression. He worked hard to improve the quality of the faculty and encouraged faculty to obtain advanced training. Byrnes Auditorium and Thurmond Hall were both built during his administration.

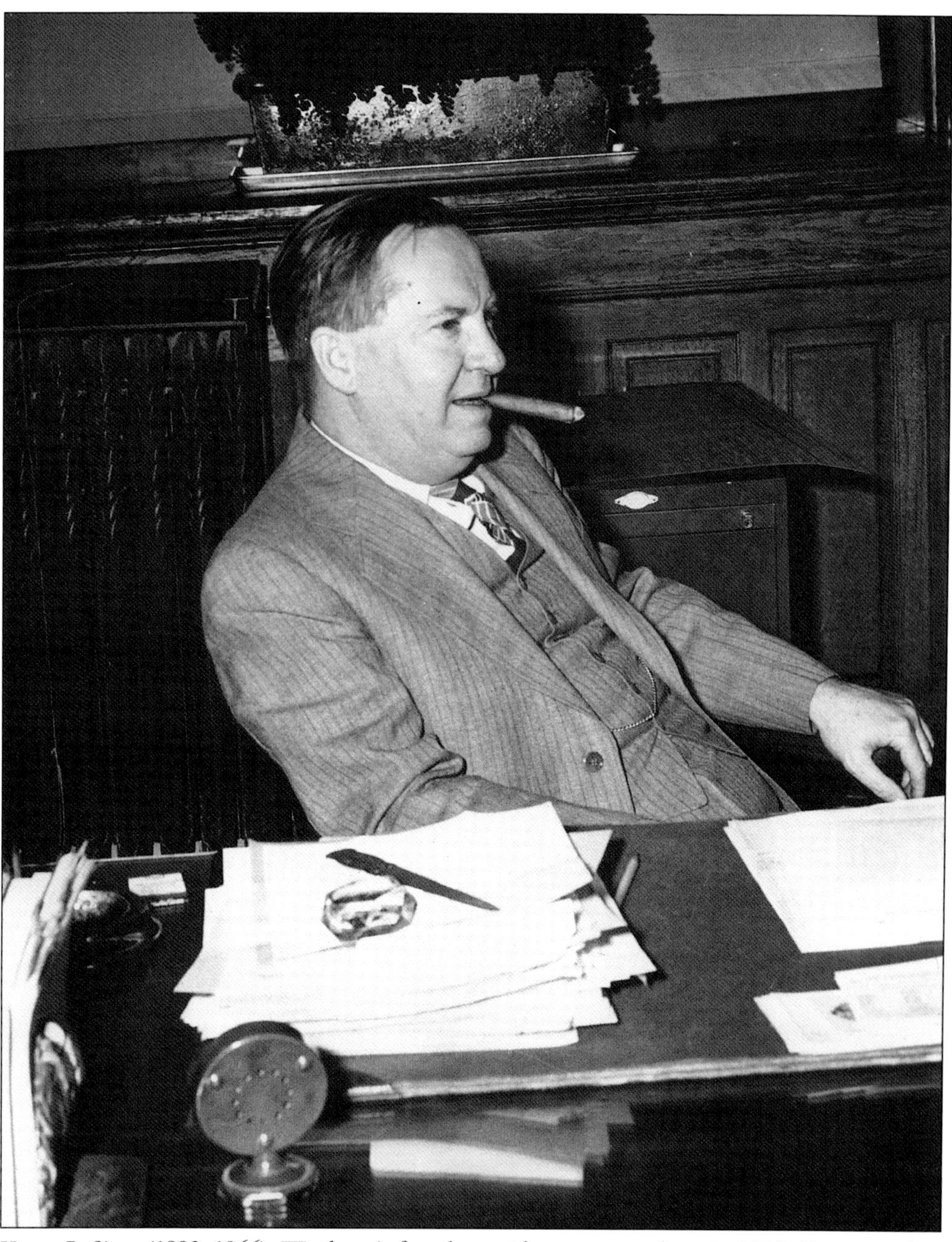

Henry R. Sims (1893–1966), Winthrop's fourth president, appears here in 1950. Sims served as an attorney, editor of the *Orangeburg Times and Democrat*, and a state senator before becoming Winthrop's president in 1944.

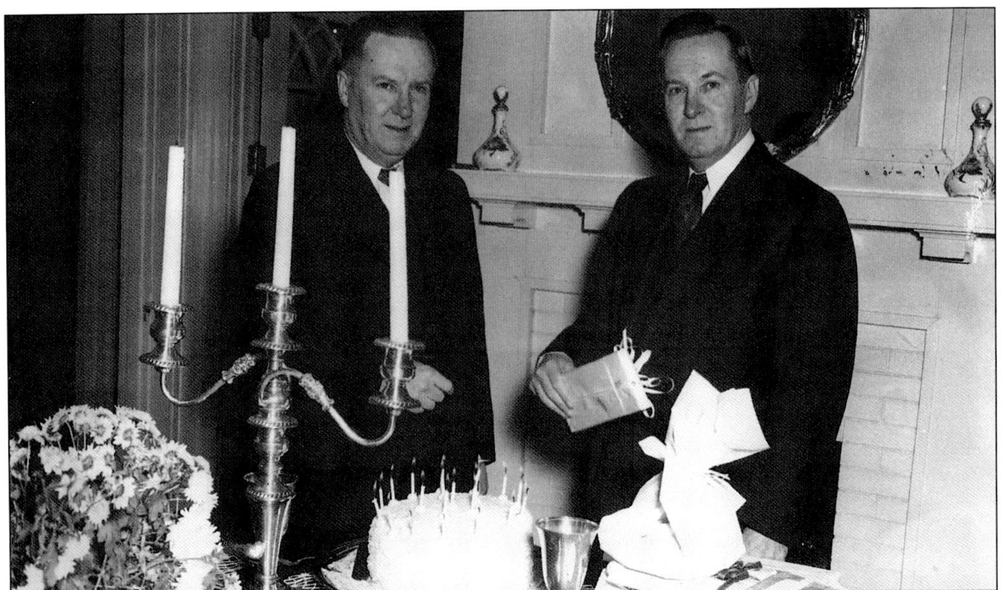

Winthrop President Sims (left) poses with his twin brother, Hugo, in the Winthrop president's home. Sims served as president until 1959. During his term, Sims had several accomplishments, including strengthening the college's academic program by establishing entrance examinations for freshmen and introducing college board examinations as an admission requirement. He also used his considerable political skills to increase the college's financial base nearly tenfold.

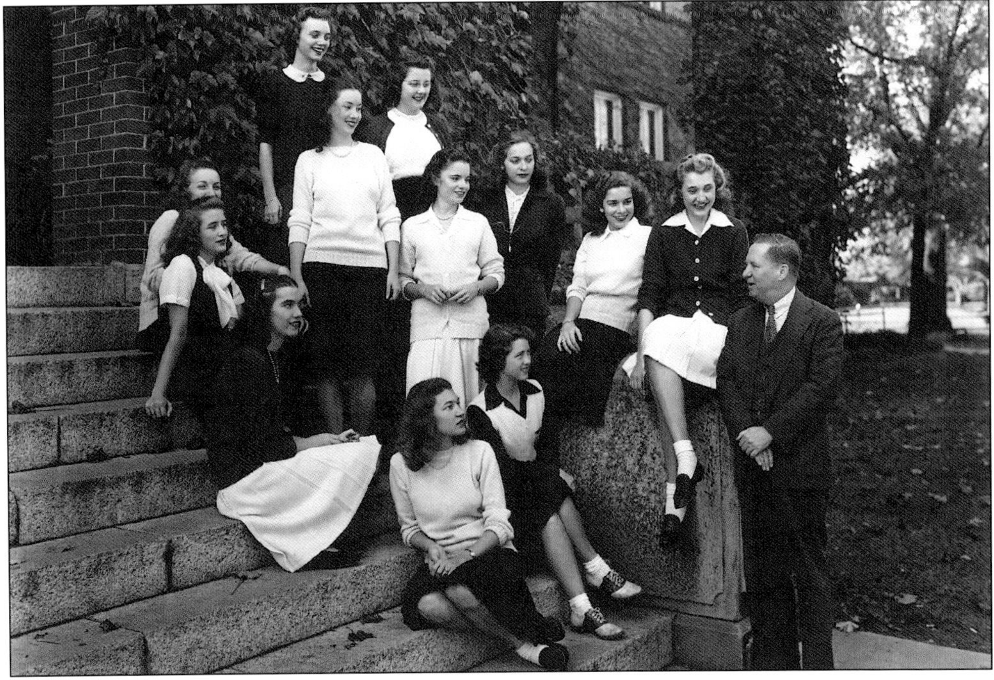

Members of Winthrop's Senior Order are pictured with President Sims on the steps of Tillman Hall in November 1946. They are, from left to right, as follows: (seated) Betty Masters, Mary Stanley, Ella V. Goudelock, Mary Lay Ewing, and Bette Stribling; (standing) Edith McCallum, Pat Nicklin, Mary Ellen Jackson, Mary Staples, Jean Crouch, Peggy Funderburk, and Hilda Brockman.

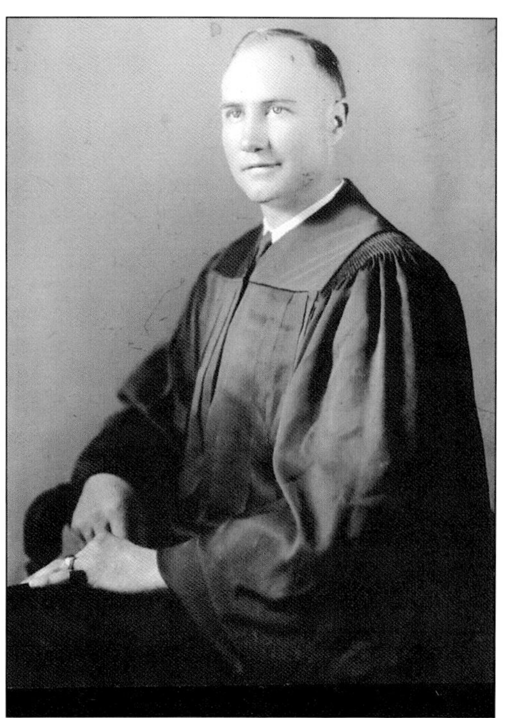

Longtime South Carolina politician Senator Strom Thurmond has been a strong supporter of Winthrop throughout his lifetime. His first wife, Jean Crouch Thurmond (Class of 1947), and three sisters were Winthrop graduates. As governor of South Carolina, Thurmond served as ex-officio member of Winthrop's Board of Trustees from 1947 to 1951.

This photograph captures the faculty procession leading up to the inauguration of Dr. Charles S. Davis, Winthrop's fifth president, in 1960. Davis served as president from 1959 to 1973. He had come to the post from Florida State University, where he had served as Dean of the Faculty. Under his guidance, Winthrop's enrollment almost doubled to more than 4,000.

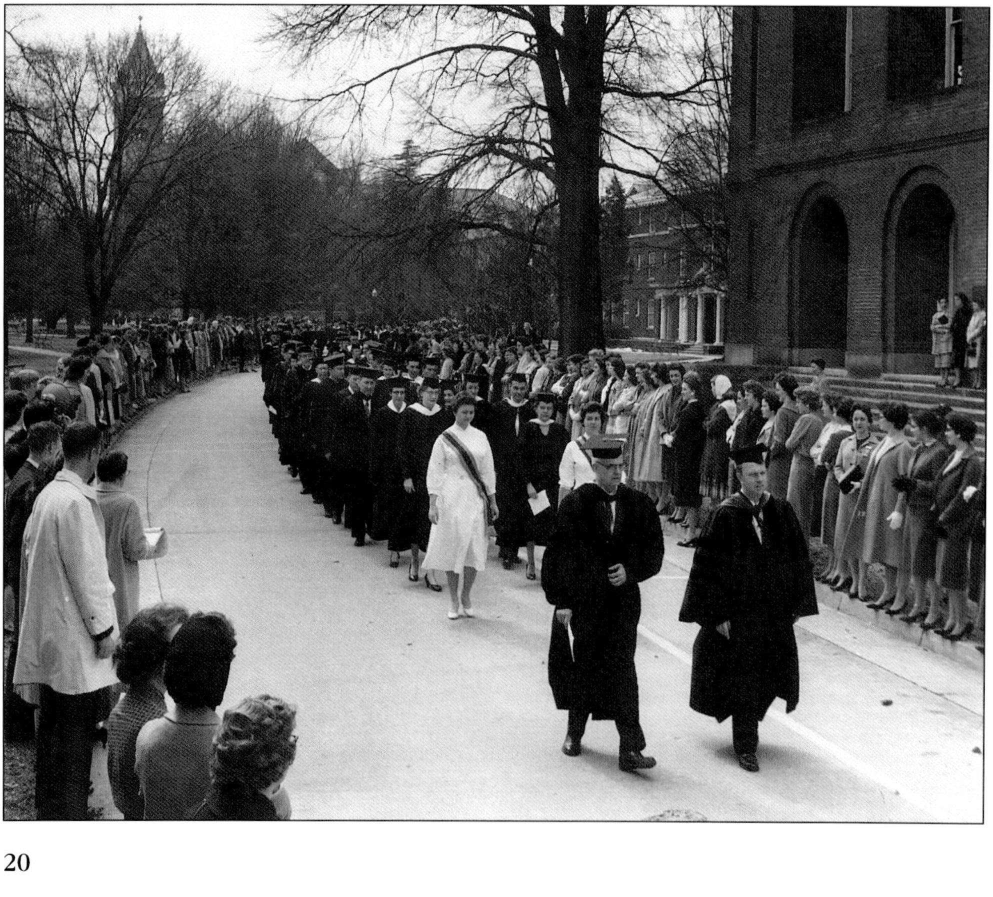

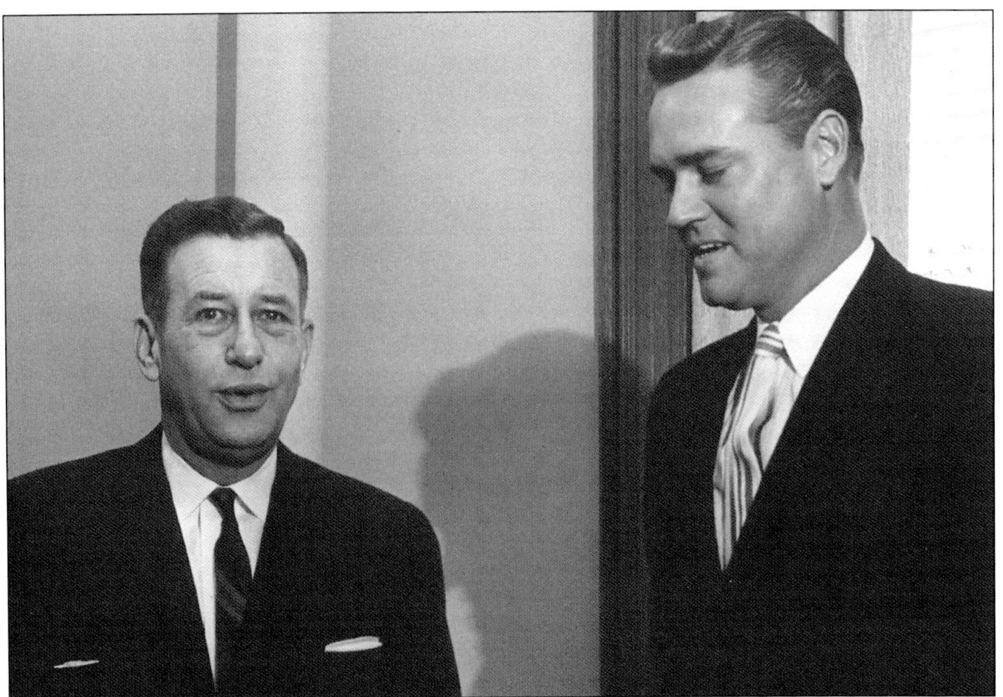

Dr. Davis (left) is pictured here at his inauguration with longtime South Carolina senator and then governor, Ernest "Fritz" Hollings.

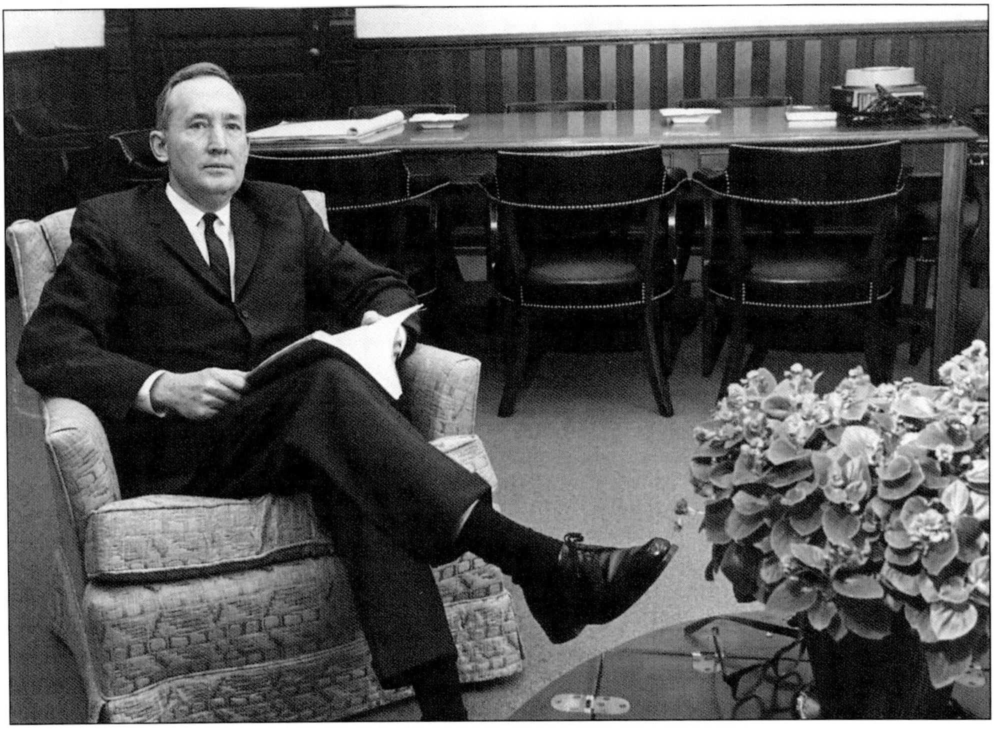

During Dr. Davis's administration, Dr. Walter Douglas Smith played an important role as Dean of the College, serving in that capacity from 1959 to 1968. This photo was taken in January 1968.

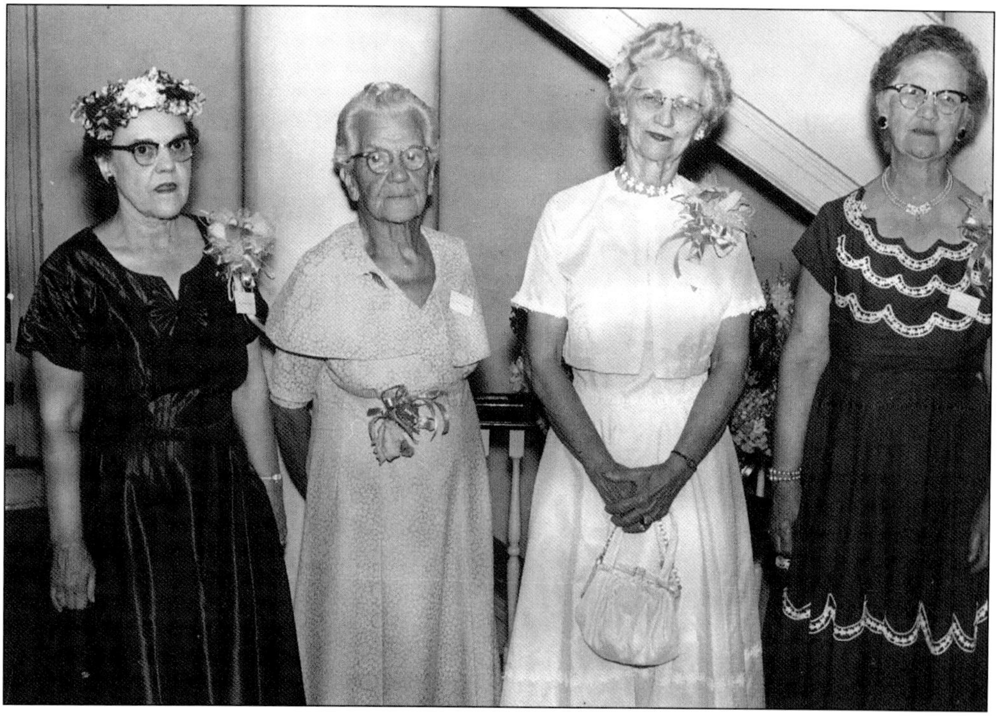

In this unusual 1962 photograph appear the wives of four Winthrop presidents. From left to right are Mrs. Henry R. Sims, Mrs. James P. Kinard, Mrs. Shelton S. Phelps, and Mrs.D.B. Johnson.

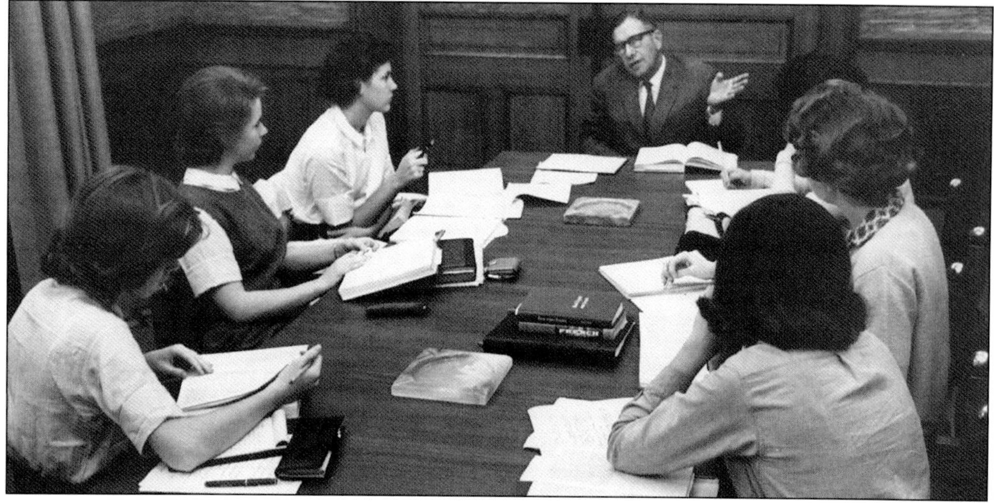

Dr. Davis talks with students in this 1964 photograph. A number of administrative and curricular changes took place during Dr. Davis's 13-year tenure. Most importantly, he played a major role in securing the South Carolina General Assembly's passage of the 1972 partial coeducation bill. Because of his careful attention, Winthrop grew in many ways. The college started four new masters degree programs. Enrollment rose from 1,351 to 4,068, while the faculty increased from 130 to 212. President Davis was instrumental in strengthening the library collection. To accommodate the increasing student body, he convinced the legislature to build two new dormitories: Richardson and Wofford. Also completed during the Davis years were the Dacus Library and Dinkins Student Center.

Two longtime Winthrop supporters, William H. Grier and Howard Burns, appear in this May 26, 1962 photo. Both Grier and Burns served as members of the Winthrop Board of Trustees.

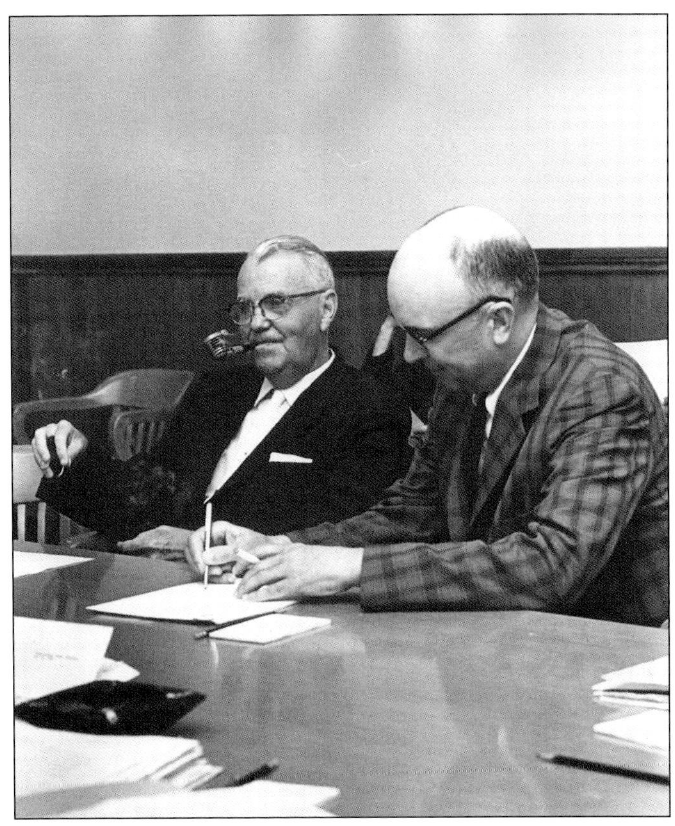

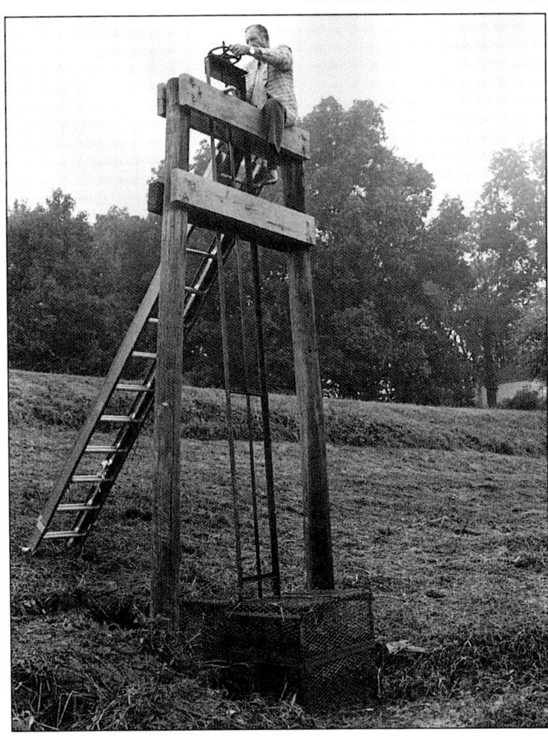

President Davis appears in this interesting photograph at the opening of the College Lake in September 1972.

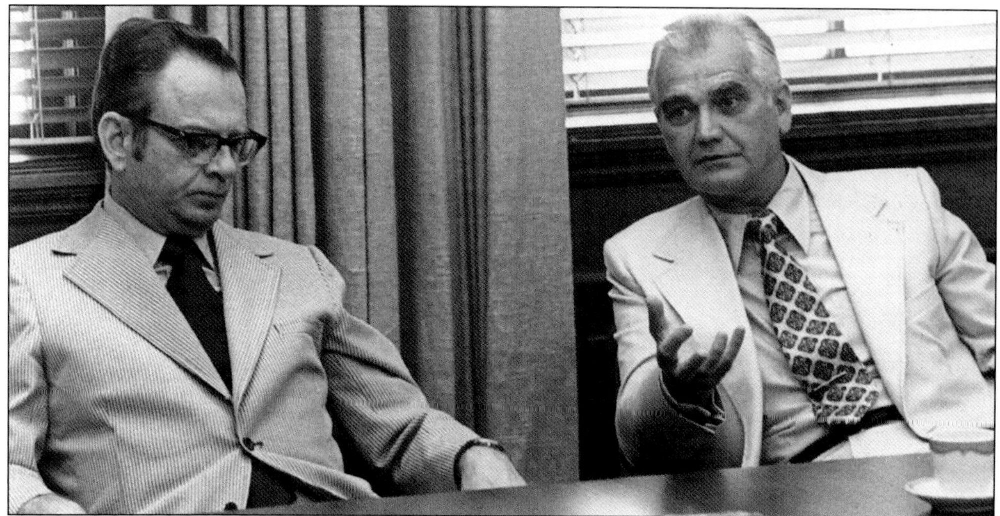

President Charles B. Vail and General William Westmoreland are seen in this July 1973 photograph. A native of Bessemer, Alabama, Dr. Vail earned his Ph.D. degree in physical chemistry from Emory University. In 1968, he was appointed Dean of the School of Arts and Sciences at Georgia State University and remained in that post until coming to Winthrop in July 1973.

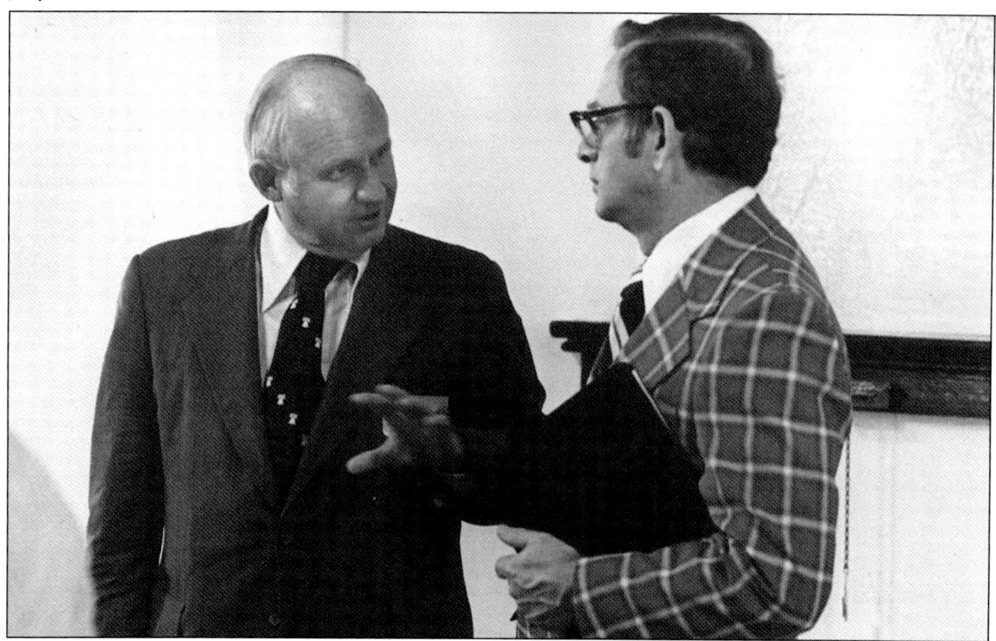

President Vail appears with South Carolina governor John C. West in September 1974. Under Dr. Vail's leadership, Winthrop experienced significant change. Perhaps most significantly, Winthrop became a co-educational institution in 1974. Vail also started many outreach programs, including Joynes Center for Continuing Education and the Human Development Center. Other programs instituted by Dr. Vail included a faculty exchange program, an educational consortium encompassing Winthrop and school districts in surrounding counties, the Small Business Advisory Center, the summer band camp, which brought thousands of high school students to Winthrop, and the organization of men's intercollegiate athletics.

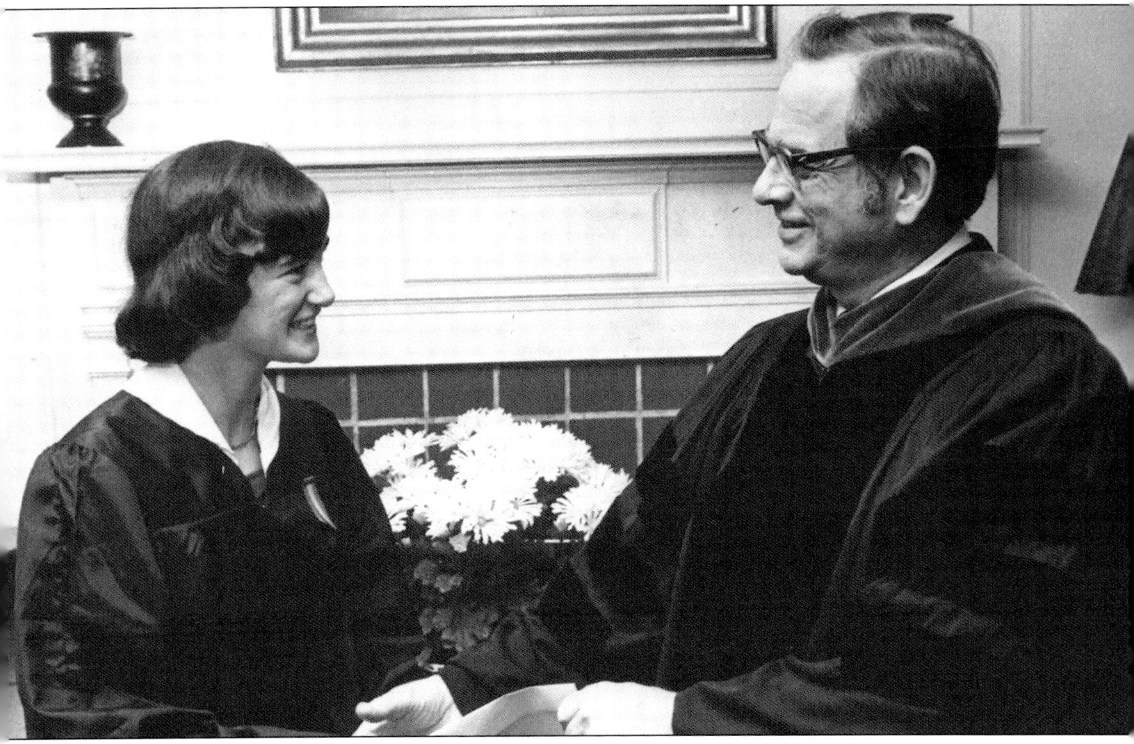

On April 30, 1977, during commencement exercises, Vail presented the Tillman Award to Sheri Durham MaCaulay of Lexington, South Carolina. The Tillman Award, established by the Tillman Memorial Commission, is presented each year to the Winthrop graduate having the best grade point average. Dr. Vail stepped down as Winthrop's sixth president in June 1982.

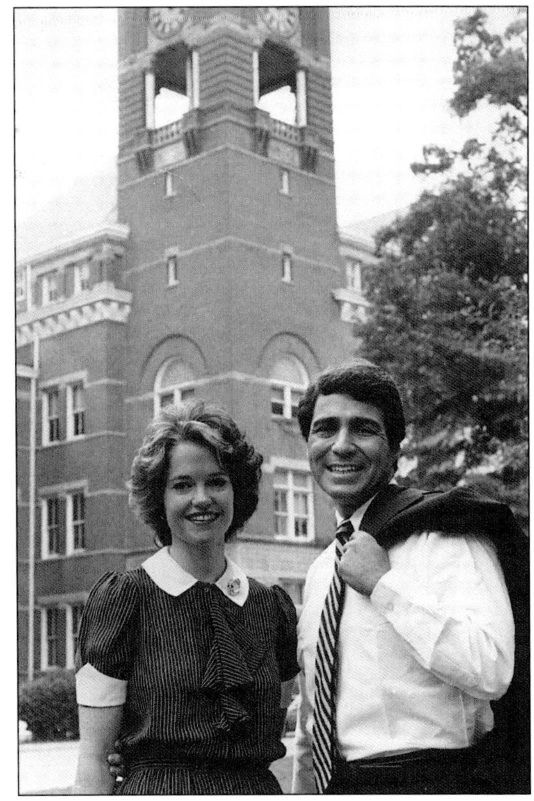

Phil Lader, Winthrop's seventh president, is seen here with his wife, Linda, in May 1983. A Harvard- and Oxford-trained lawyer and a former Sea Pines Company executive, Lader served as Winthrop president from August 1983 to December 1985. During his brief term, Lader moved to honor Winthrop's tradition while expanding its horizons.

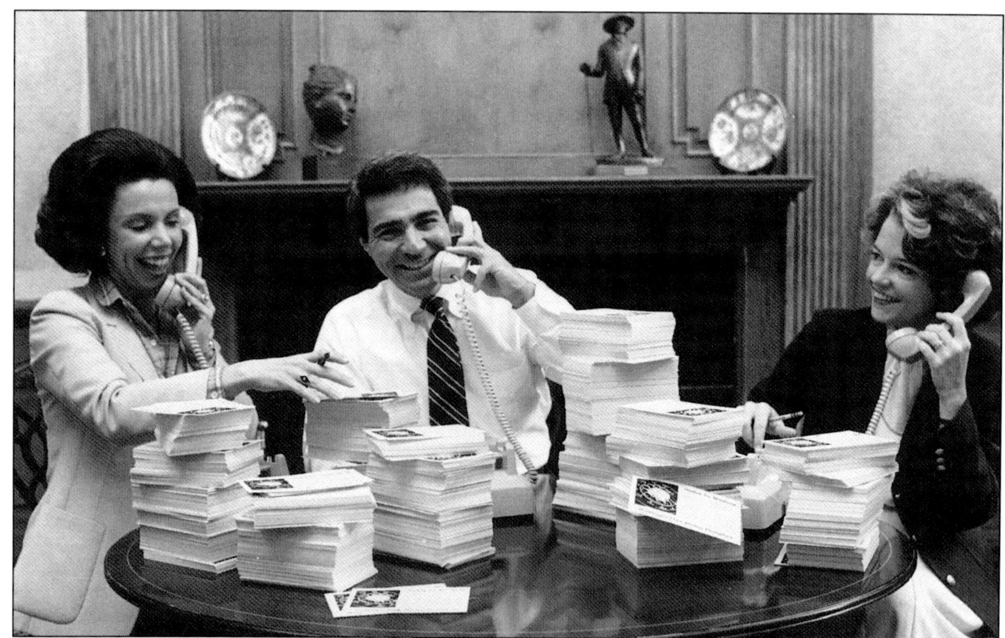

Phil Lader appears with Martie Curran (Winthrop director of Alumni Relations) and Linda Lader (right). Among his many accomplishments, Lader brought back the Convocation and Blue Line traditions, which were events that began the school year; introduced the cultural events program; established an International Center/Study Abroad Program; pushed the college to become a member of the National Collegiate Athletic Association (NCAA); and welcomed prominent national figures to the campus.

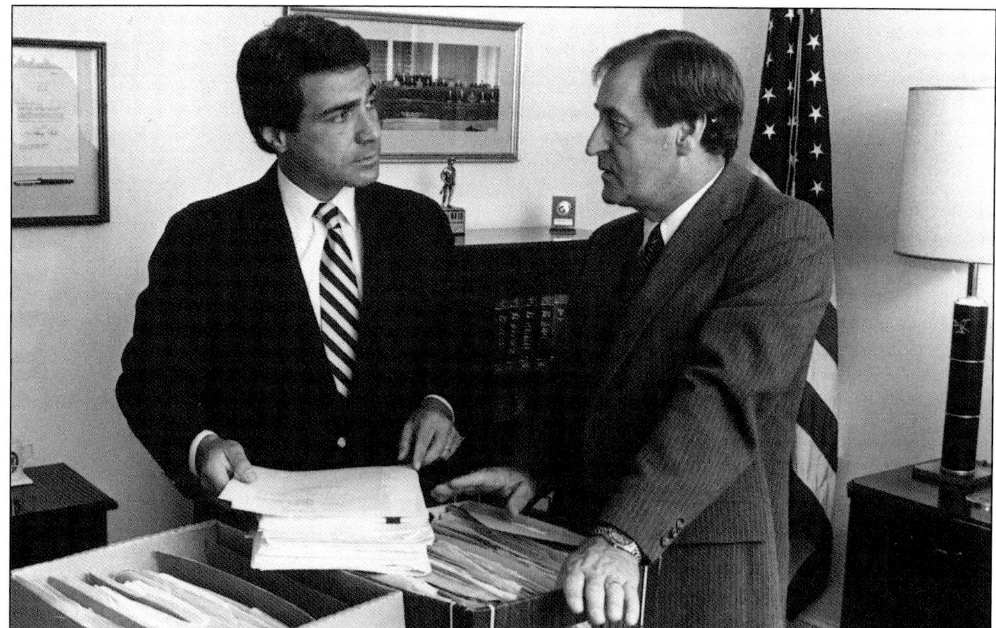

President Lader examines the records of former U.S. Congressman Ken Holland, which were donated to the Winthrop Archives in September 1983. In 1997, Lader became U.S. ambassador to Great Britain.

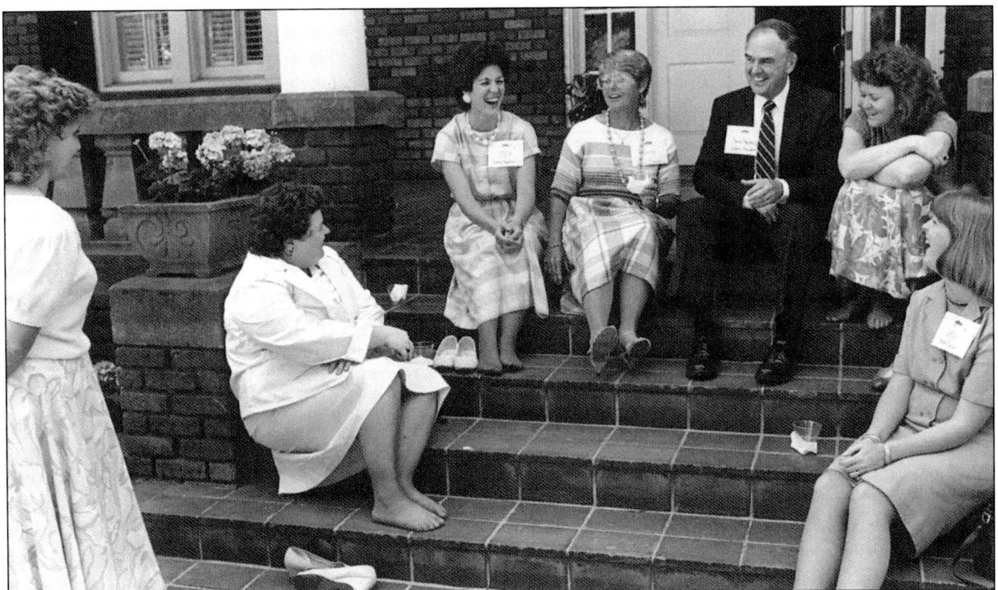

After Phil Lader left Winthrop, Dr. Marcus Newberry became Winthrop's interim president. Dr. Newberry is pictured here with Winthrop alumni during the university's Alumni Weekend. To come to Winthrop, Dr. Newberry took a leave from his position as vice president of Academic Affairs and professor of internal medicine at the Medical University of South Carolina. Dr. Newberry served as Winthrop president until May 1986. In recalling his tenure, Newberry later said, "I've had a good time here. I don't think I've has such a good time in years."

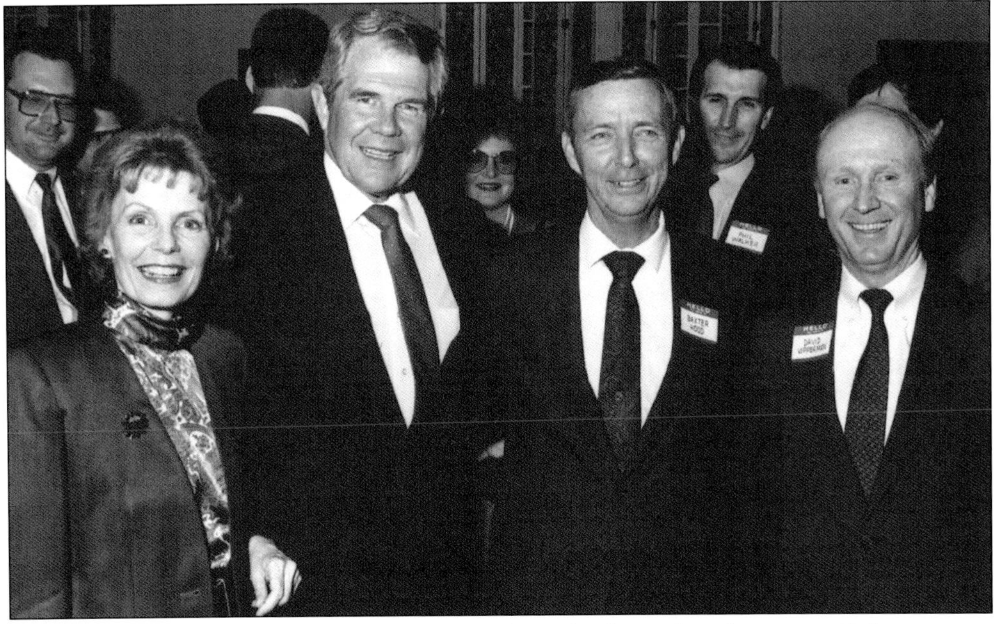

President Martha Kime Piper appears with Winthrop faculty and students at a Christmas party in 1986. On June 2, 1986, Dr. Piper became Winthrop's first woman president. Prior to her appointment, she had been serving as chancellor of the University of Houston's Victoria campus. Dr. Piper had many Winthrop family ties. Her grandmother worked at Winthrop, and her mother and sister were educated there.

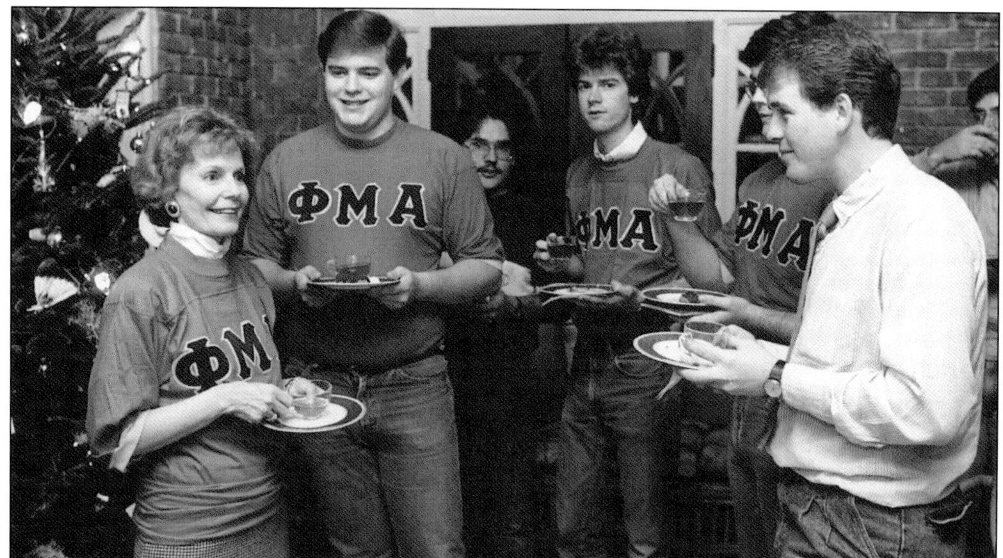

President Piper poses, from left to right, with Christian evangelist Pat Robertson, York Technical College President Baxter Hood, and local civic leader Dave Vipperman. Dr. Piper died in office in1988 at age 56. During her tenure, Winthrop became the nation's first college to sign a NCAA fair share agreement encouraging the promotion of minorities and the use of minority businesses. Dr. Piper introduced the Executive Masters of Business Program, implemented the state's first Master of Liberal Arts degree, and had 20 buildings constructed between 1894 to 1943 listed on the National Register of Historic Places.

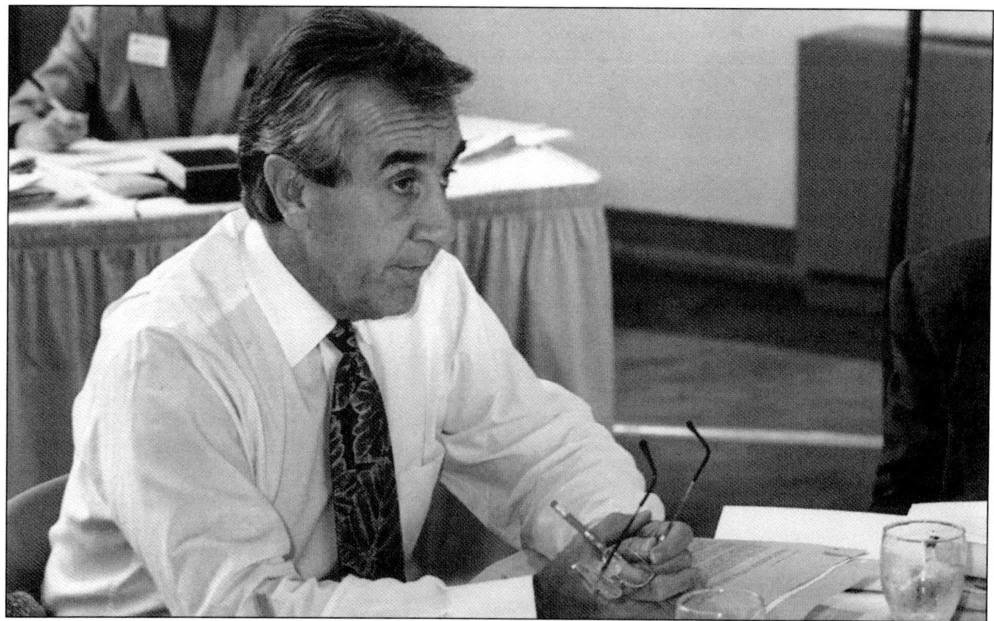

Dr. Anthony DiGiorgio, Winthrop's eighth president, is seen here at a Winthrop Board meeting in October 1992. Before coming to Winthrop, Dr. DiGiorgio was vice president of Academic Affairs at Trenton State College in Trenton, New Jersey. Dr. DiGiorgio earned a bachelor's degree in English from Gannon College (now University) in Erie, Pennsylvania, in 1963 and a Master's degree and doctorate in counseling psychology from Purdue University.

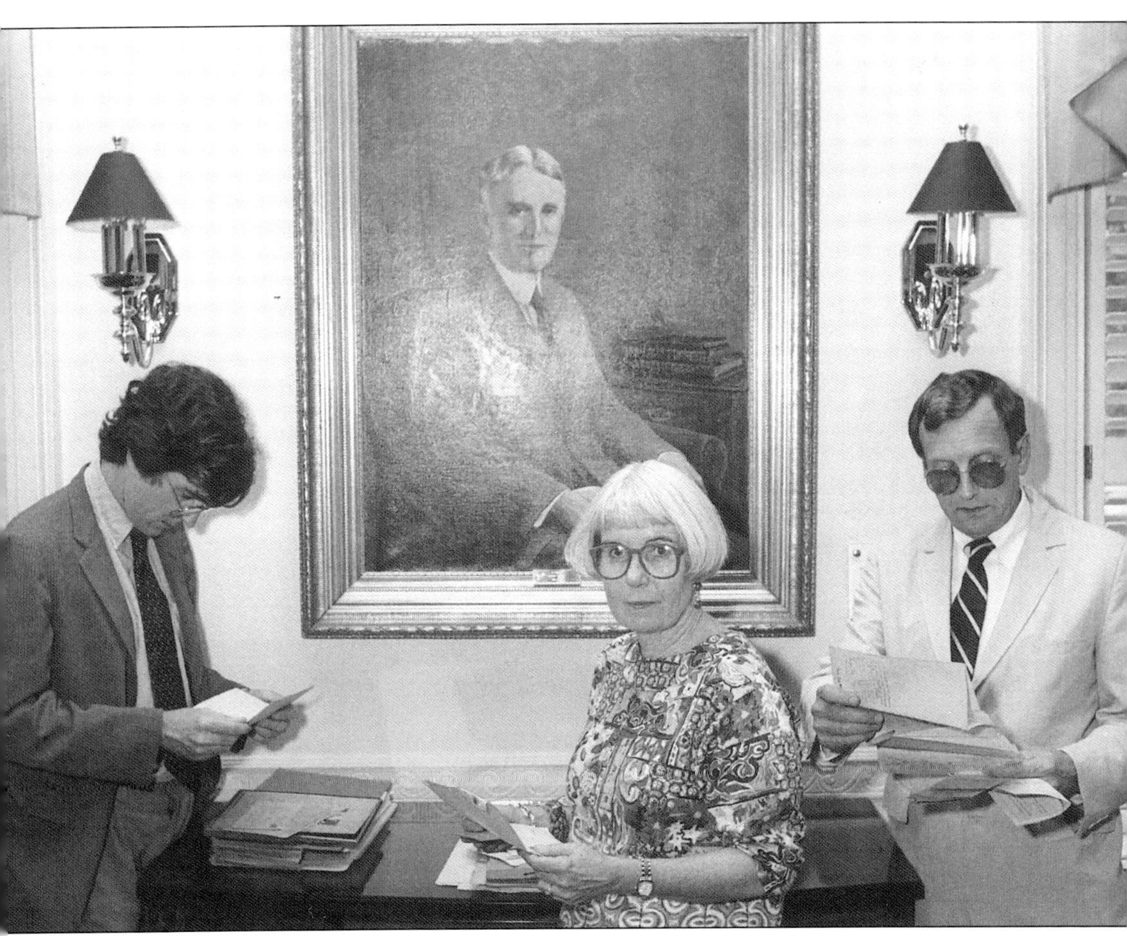

George W. Dunlap (1912–1989), Rock Hill civic leader and president of Home Federal, founded the Winthrop College Foundation and helped to establish the Dunlap-Roddey Trustee Room in Johnson Hall in 1991. A few months prior to Mr. Dunlap's death, Home Federal announced the establishment at Winthrop of a $10,000 George W. Dunlap Scholarship in Banking and Finance. Pictured here, from left to right, are as follows: John Holder, Angela Roddey Holder, and Winthrop Trustee member David White. They are examining papers of John T. Roddey, which were donated to the Winthrop Archives, in the Dunlap-Roddey Trustee Room.

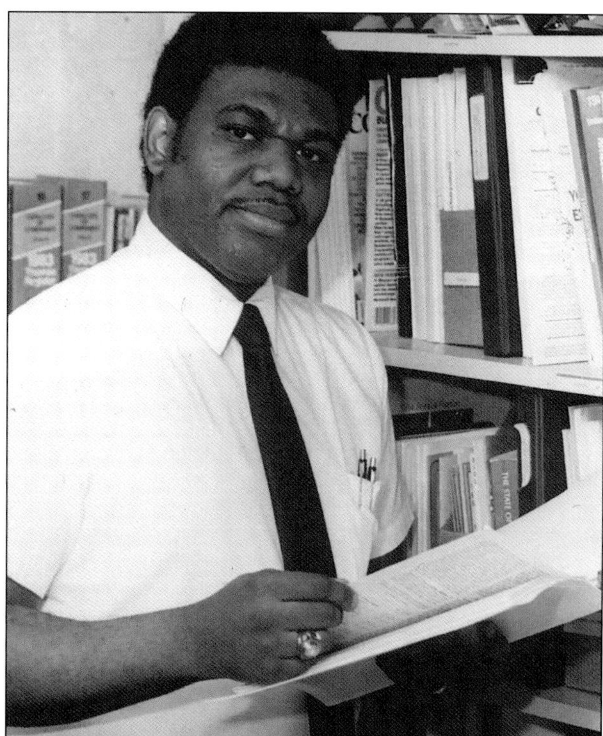

Larry Durham, a Winthrop Board of Trustees member, appears here in 1985. A native of Rock Hill, Mr. Durham has a long association with Winthrop. A 1987 graduate of Winthrop, he was director of the school's Small Business Administration center from 1987 to 1988 and an instructor in the School of Business Administration from 1987 to 1988. Appointed to the Winthrop Board of Trustees in 1999, Durham is currently an independent businessman with State Farm Insurance in Lancaster, South Carolina.

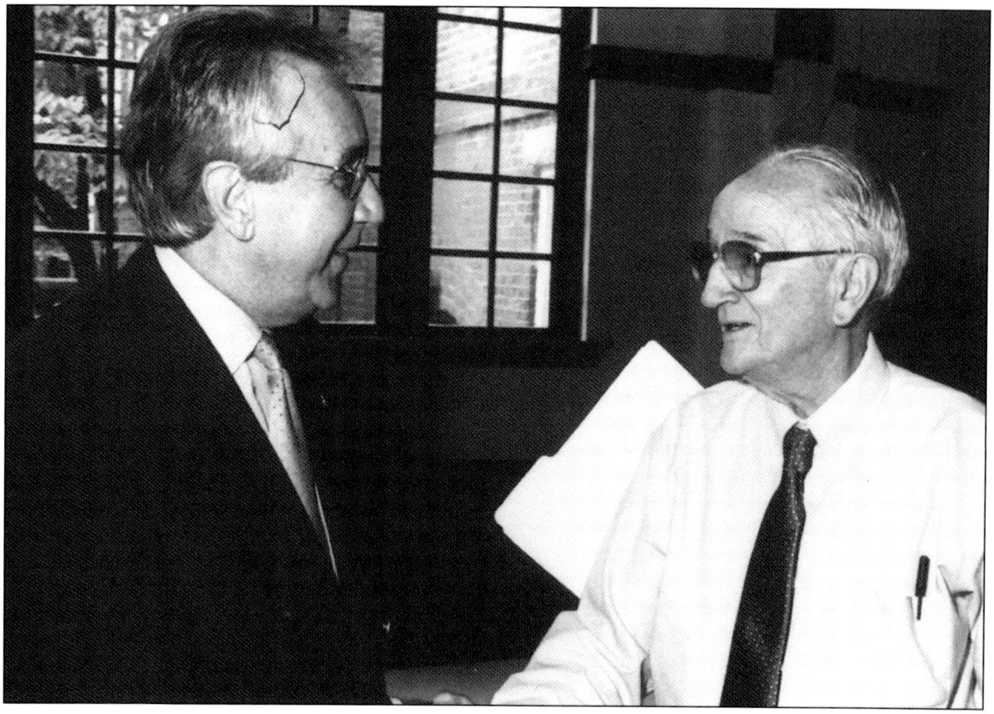

President DiGiorgio and Winthrop Board of Trustees member Tom Crowson exchange pleasantries in 1998. Mr. Crowson served as a Winthrop history professor for 30 years before retiring in 1984. He was elected to the Board of Trustees in 1998.

Two

Campus Life

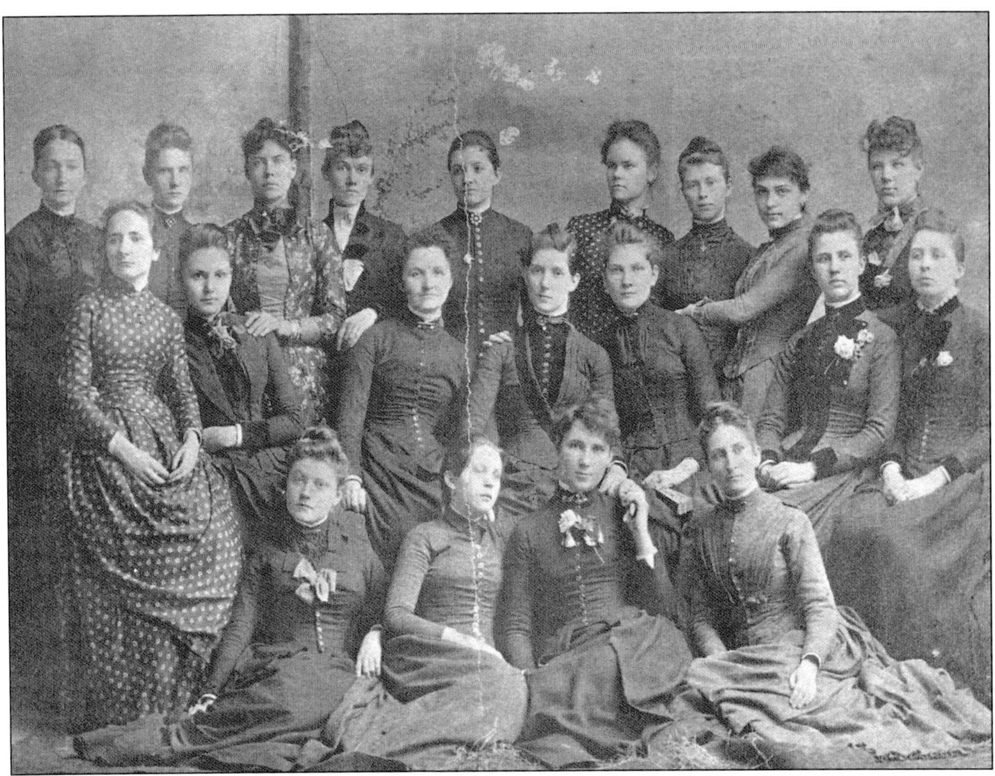

Students at the Winthrop Training School (as Winthrop was initially known until 1895) pose for a photo in 1889. The school at the time was located in Columbia.

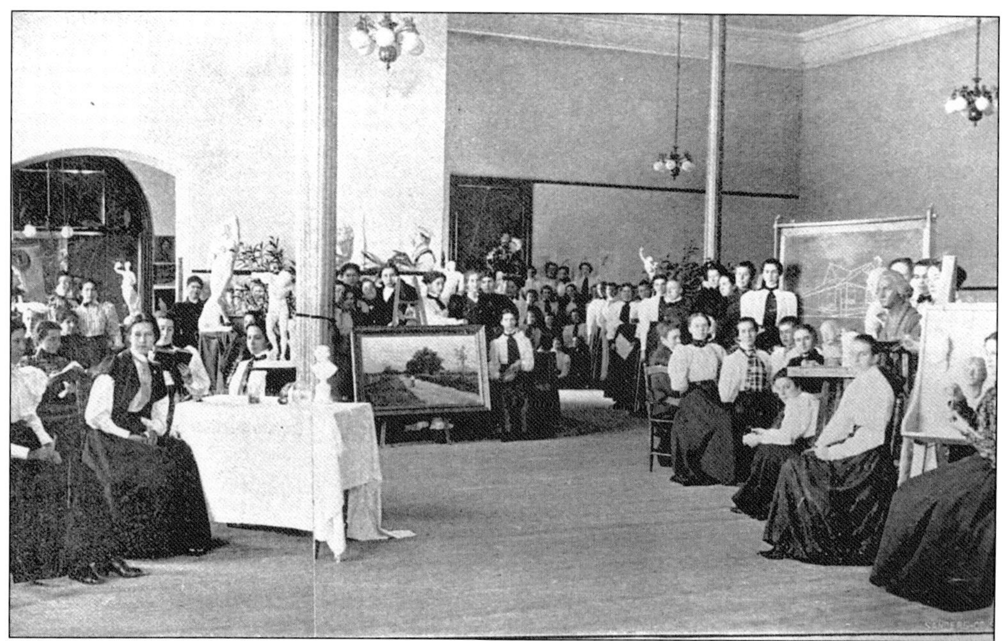

This picture shows an art classroom in Main Building (later Tillman Hall) soon after the college moved from Columbia to Rock Hill in 1895.

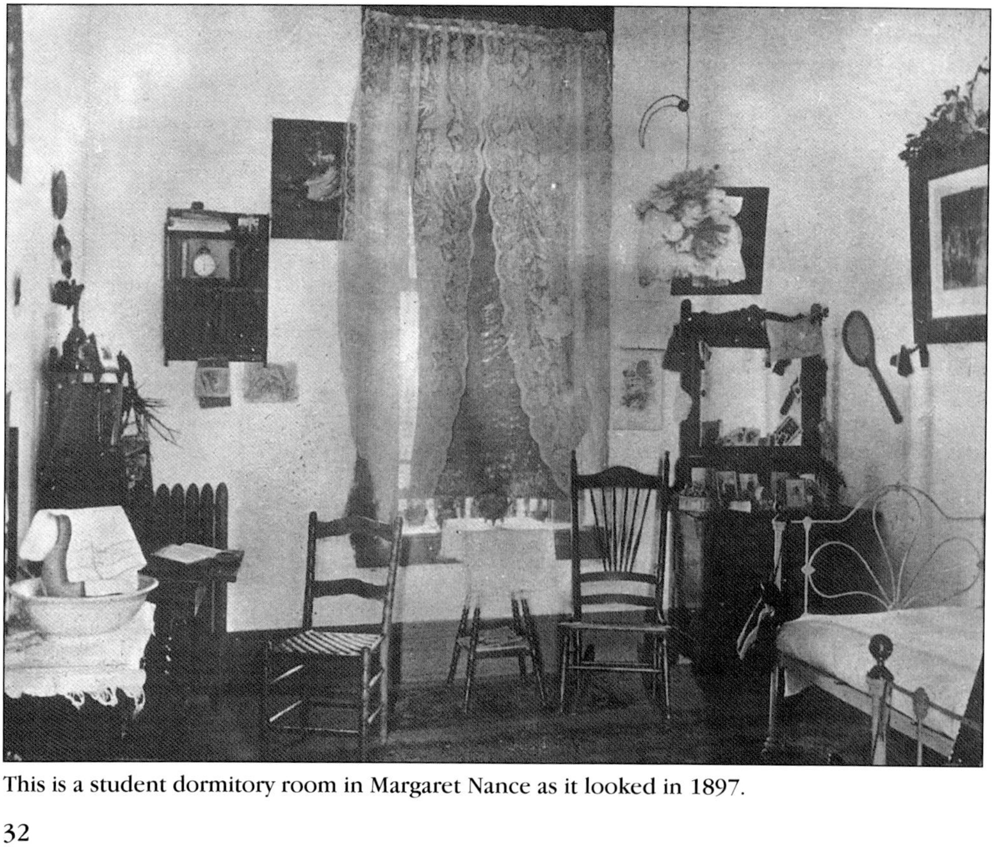

This is a student dormitory room in Margaret Nance as it looked in 1897.

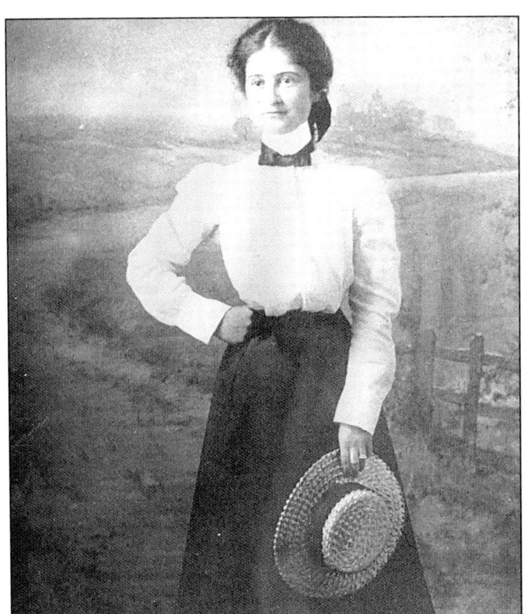

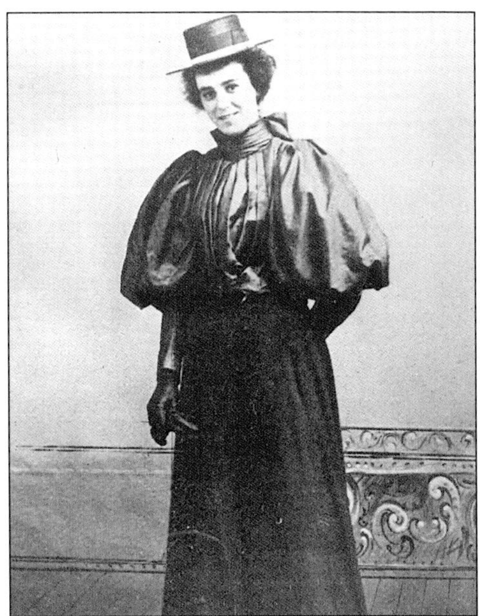

These are two students from the late 1890s wearing their school uniforms. Beginning in 1895, all students, without exception, had to wear uniforms. The reasons for the regulations were practical and egalitarian: to promote economy and to do away with any class distinctions that might exist so that "the richest girl in the school cannot be distinguished from the poorest." For $30, the student received a serge coat and shirt, jacket, cloak, six shirtwaists, two hats, a commencement uniform, and a gym suit.

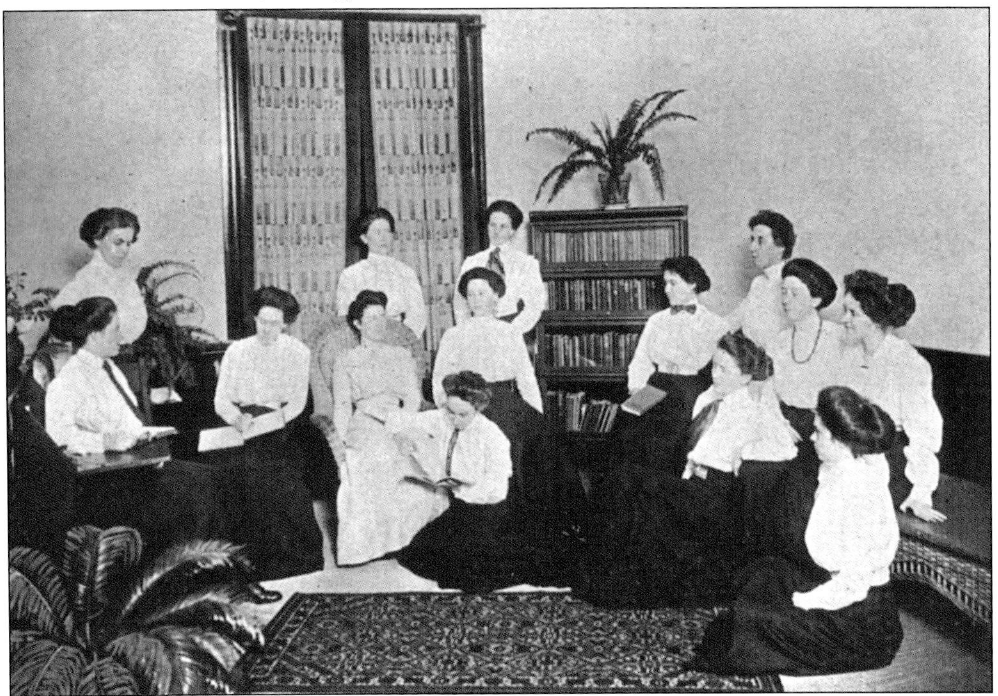

This 1902 photograph shows the editorial staff of the first issue of *The Winthrop Journal*, the student literary publication.

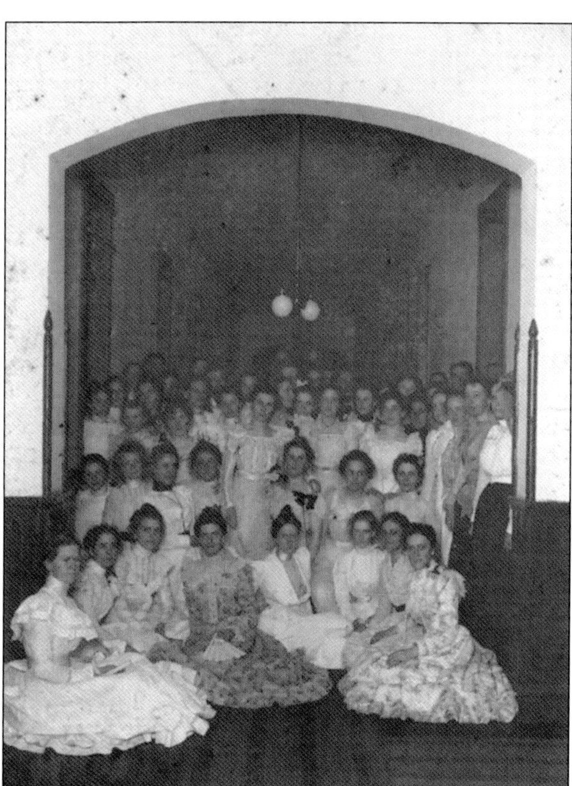

Students and teachers pose for a photo during Winthrop's first summer school in 1898.

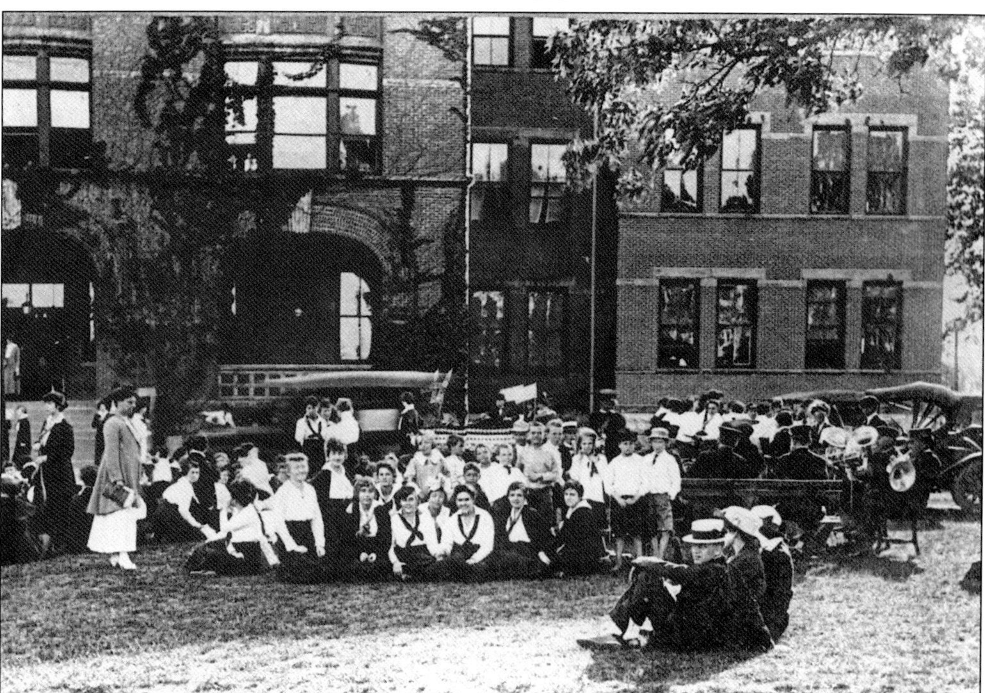

A group of students and members of the Rock Hill community gather in front of Main Building in the 1910s.

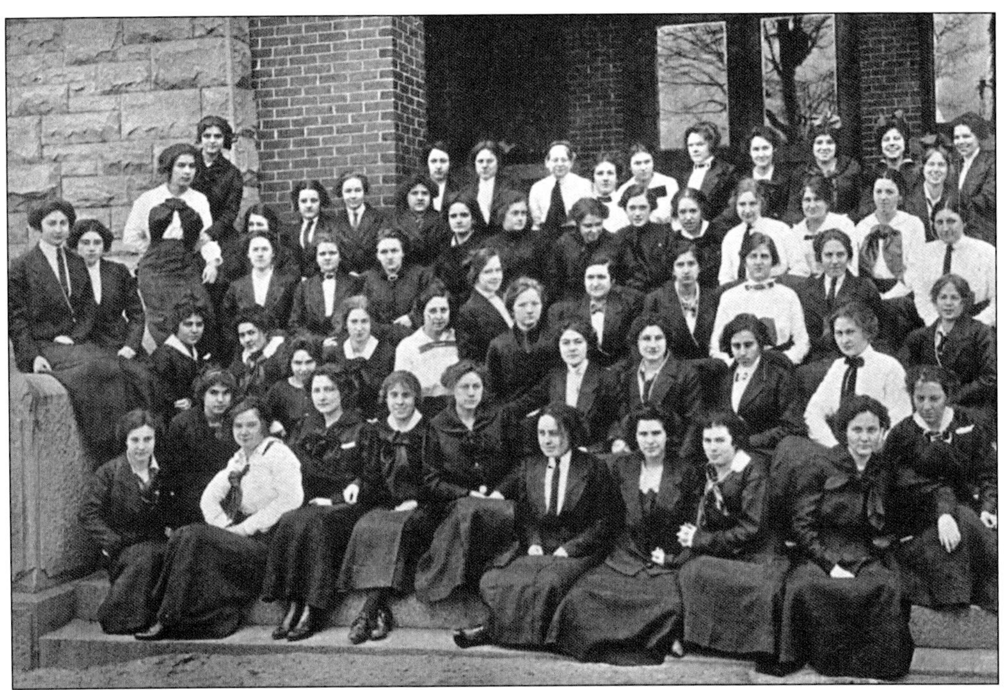

The junior class of 1913 poses for this photograph on the steps of Main Building.

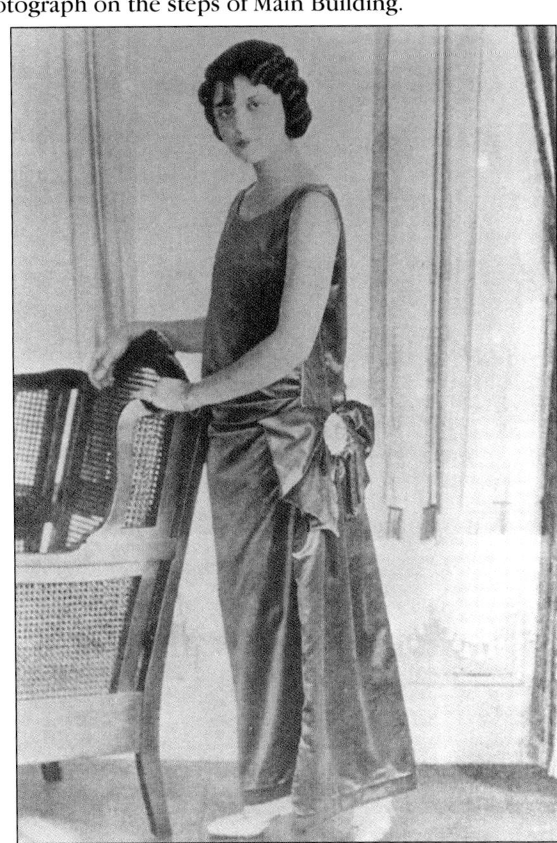

In 1924, Jesse Mathews, shown here in the latest fashion, was voted "Most Attractive" by her classmates.

Winthrop Normal and Industrial College

DINING HALL RULES

1. Students must assemble promptly during the ringing of the five minutes bell and remain in their places until the blessing is asked.

2. There must be perfect quiet during the blessing.

3. No loud talking, laughing, or boisterous conduct allowed in the dining-hall.

4. No food taken from the tables without permission from the housekeeper.

5. No dishes or silver shall be taken from the dining-hall.

6. No changing of seats in the dining-hall without permission from the proctor.

7. No young lady except the waitress must leave the table for food.

8. The waitress on duty must take the dishes off the trucks.

9. The waitress must remain in position and receive food from the trucks and deposit soiled dishes, and not run to meet trucks.

10. The waitress must be in the dining-hall five minutes before the last bell rings.

11. Students are not allowed in the kitchen except when waiting on tables.

12. No permission must be given to speak to students at other tables except through the house-keeper.

13. No young lady is allowed to leave dining-hall without permission from the one in charge of the table and then only to go to the Infirmary. The students at each table will be dismissed in a body.

14. All students who desire friends to dine with them will register at the Secretary's office one-half hour before the meal.

15. Hereafter, students will invite only parents or guardians to take meals with them in the dining-hall unless exception is made by special permission of the President.

16. No waiting for friends in corridors outside dining-hall doors.

17. Chairs are to be left in position at tables when not in use.

VIRGINIA T. BELL,
Housekeper.

Approved: D. B. JOHNSON,
President.

September, 1915.

The rules for the college's dining hall show that in September 1915 discipline at Winthrop was strict during the college's formative years.

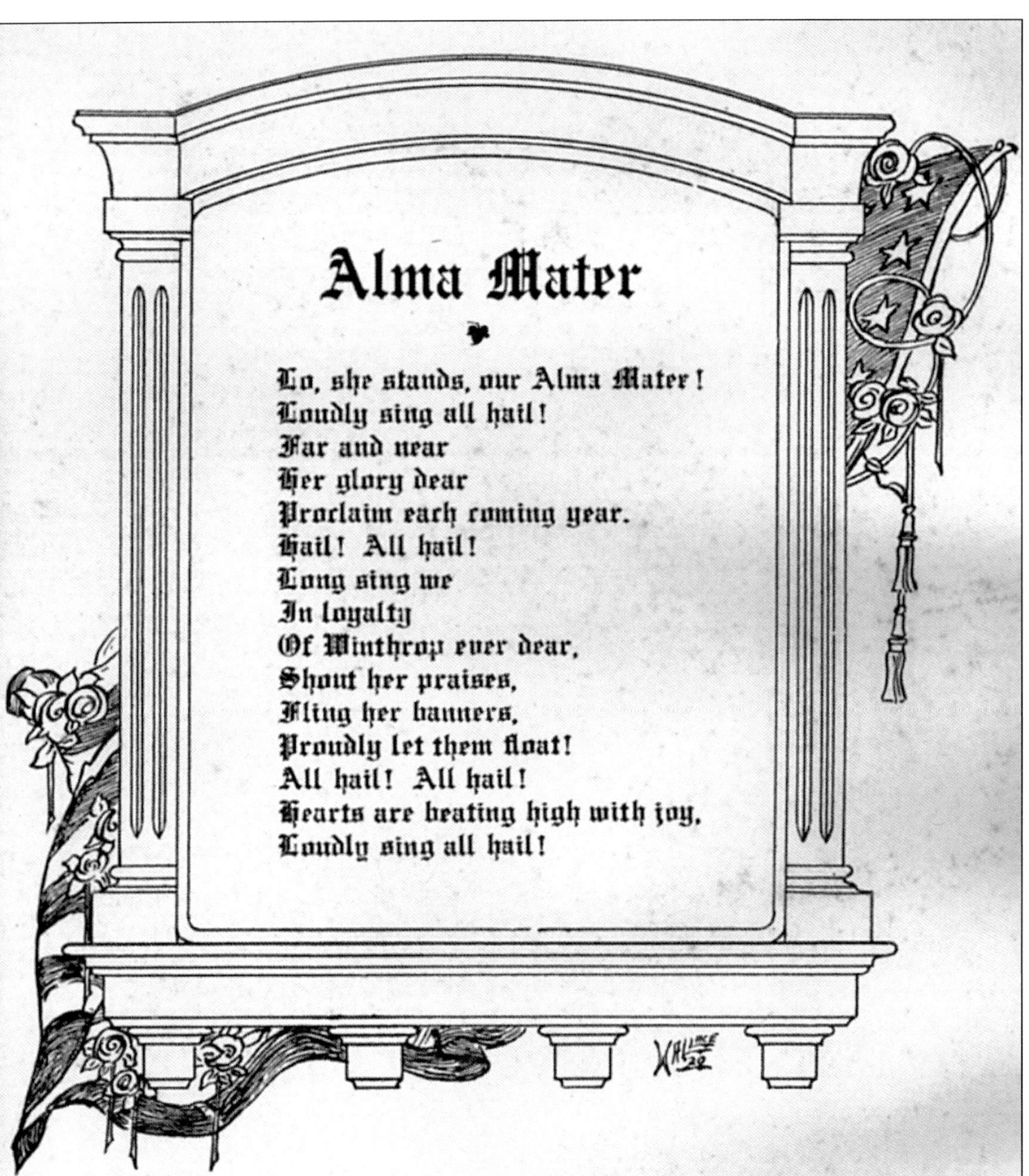

This is the Winthrop College song as it appeared in the 1920 *Tatler*, the student yearbook.

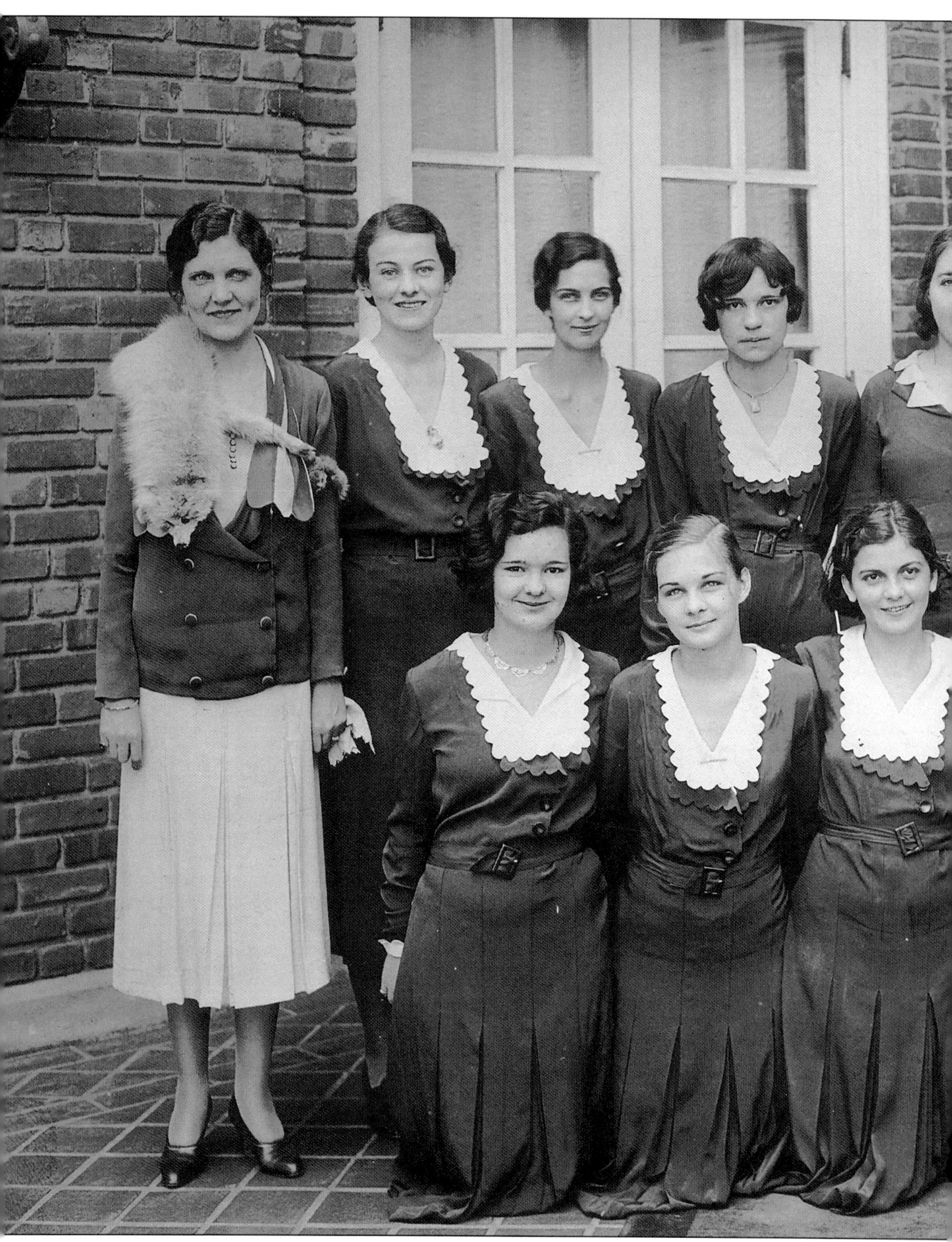

The Baptist Student Union Council gather at Johnson Hall in 1932. They are, from left to right, as follows: (front row) Sara Carson, Billie Kirwen, Louise Cleland, Frances Bradford, Omera Mincey, Evelyn Cochran, and Louise Thackston; (back row) Ludie Mitchell, Mary Nance Daniel,

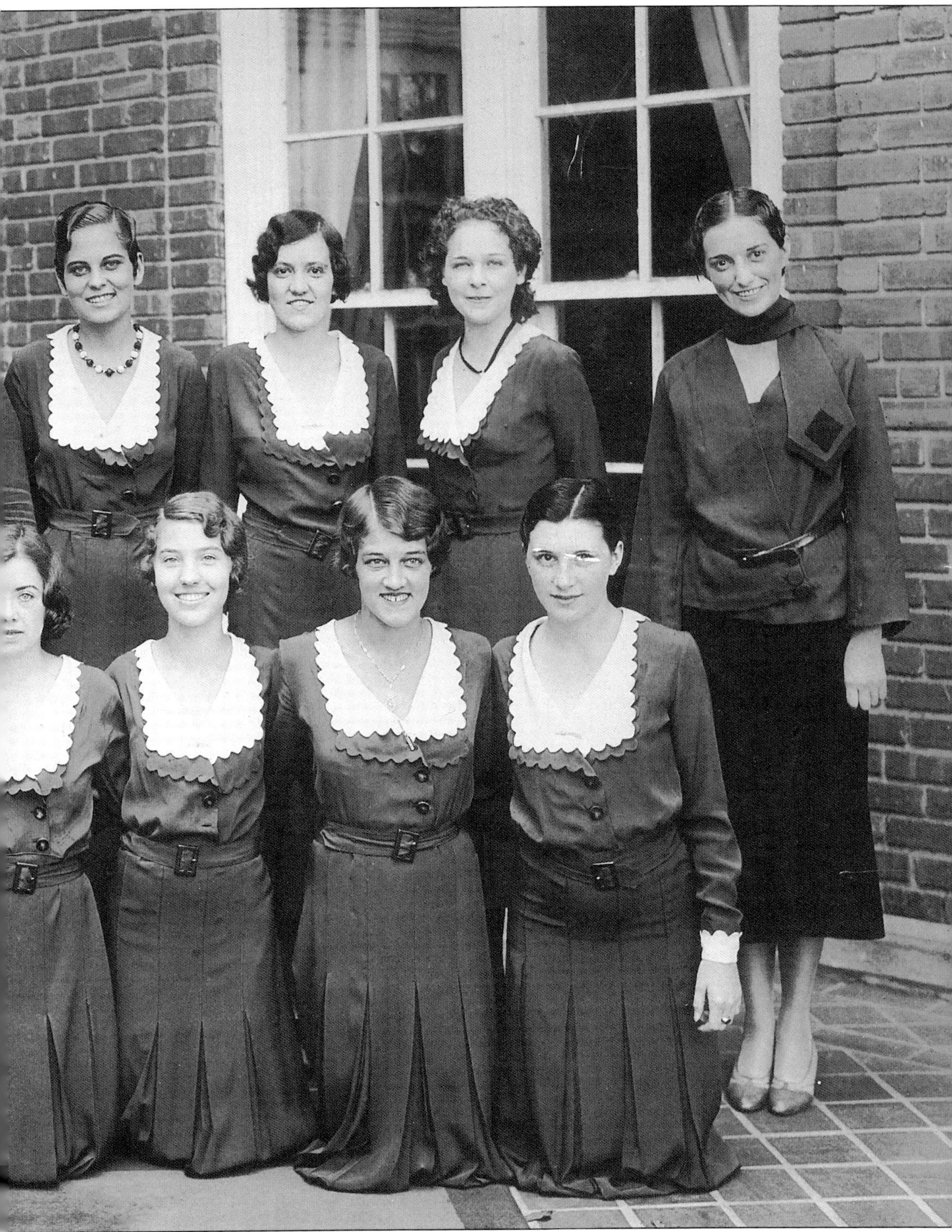

Elizabeth Stowe, Verna Carter, Ramona Brock, Isabel Etheridge, Phoebe Lawton, Bobby Carter, and Zana Wilson.

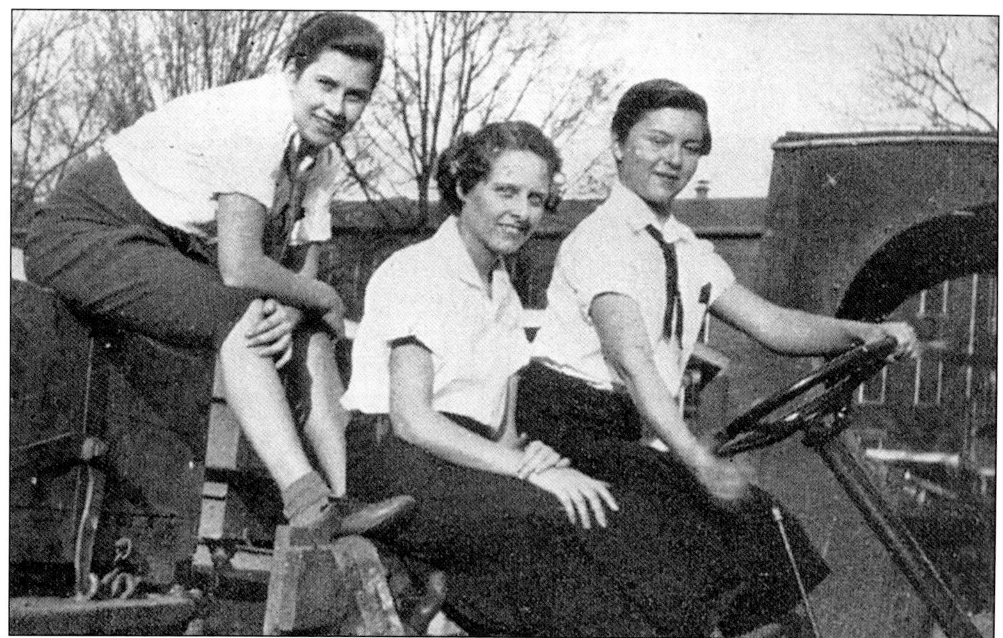

Looking smart in their uniforms, these three Winthrop students get ready for a day out on the town during the 1930s.

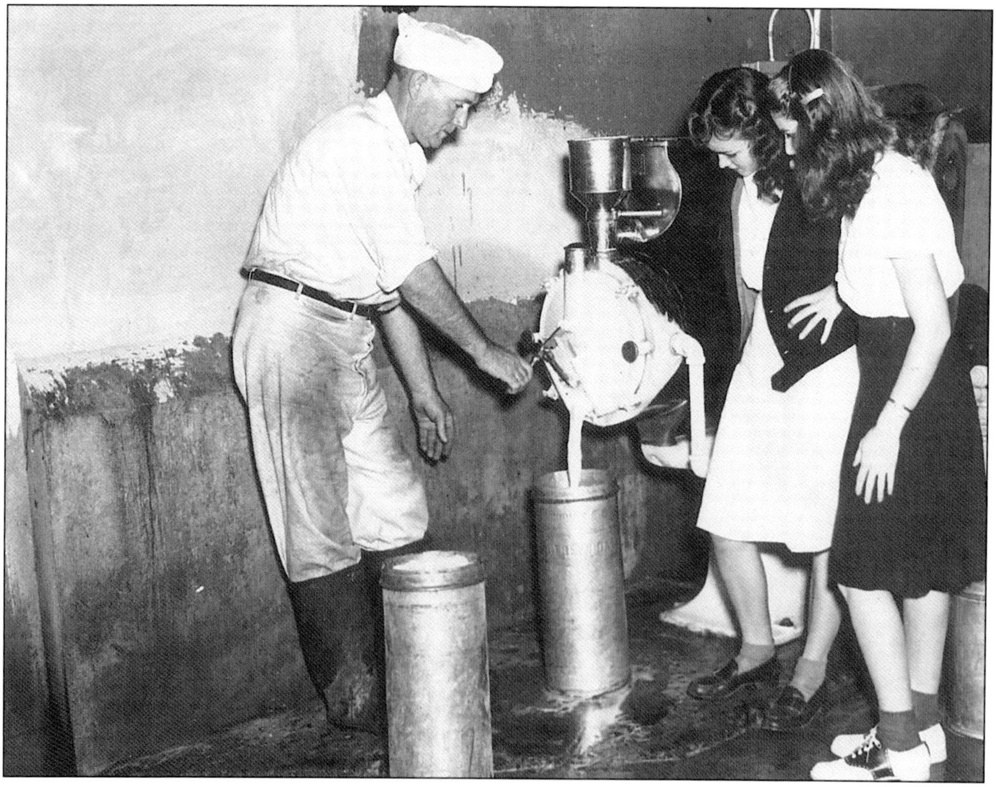

Students visit the dairy at the "College Farm" in 1947. In the late 1940s, the College Farm continued to produce vegetables, dairy, and poultry products for the college.

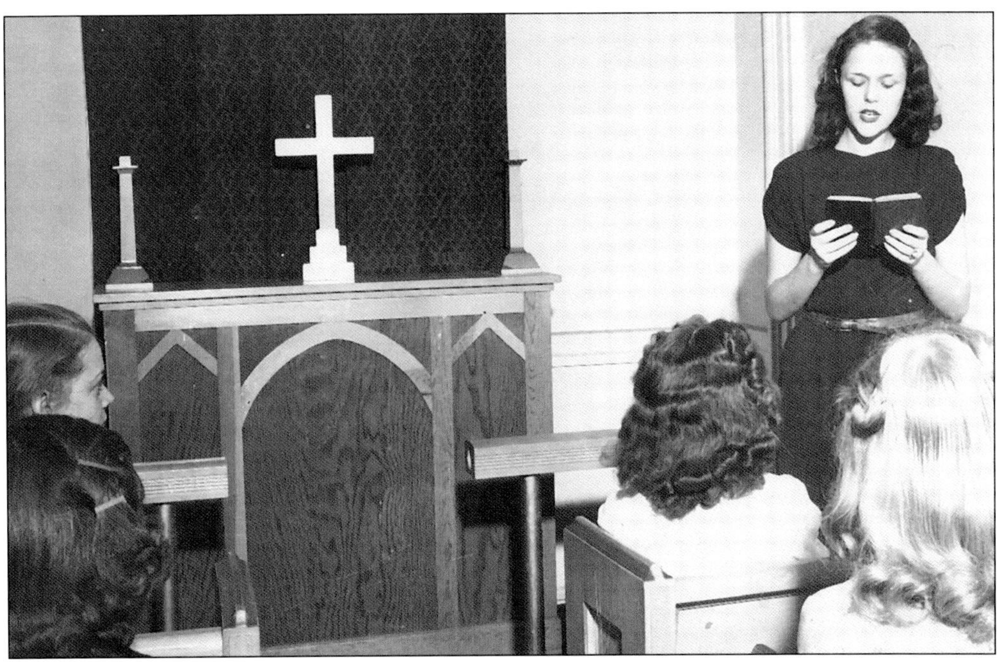

As can be seen in this photograph, religion was an important part of campus life in the late 1940s.

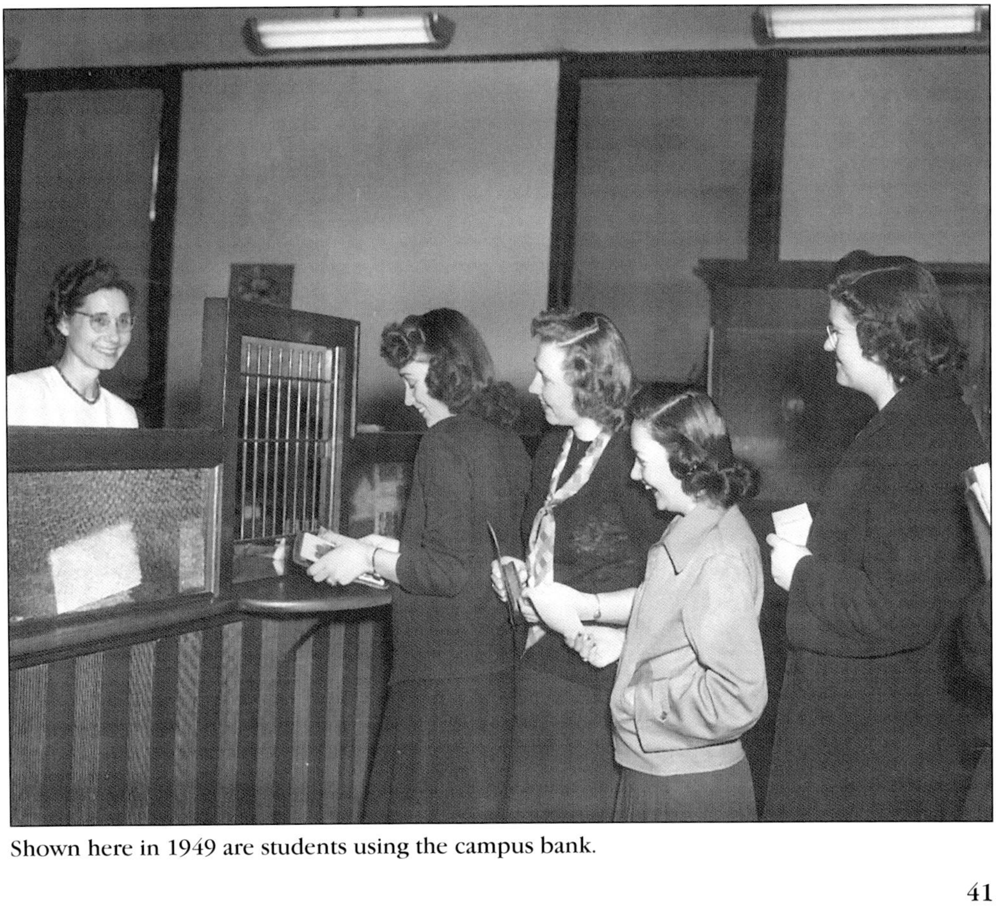

Shown here in 1949 are students using the campus bank.

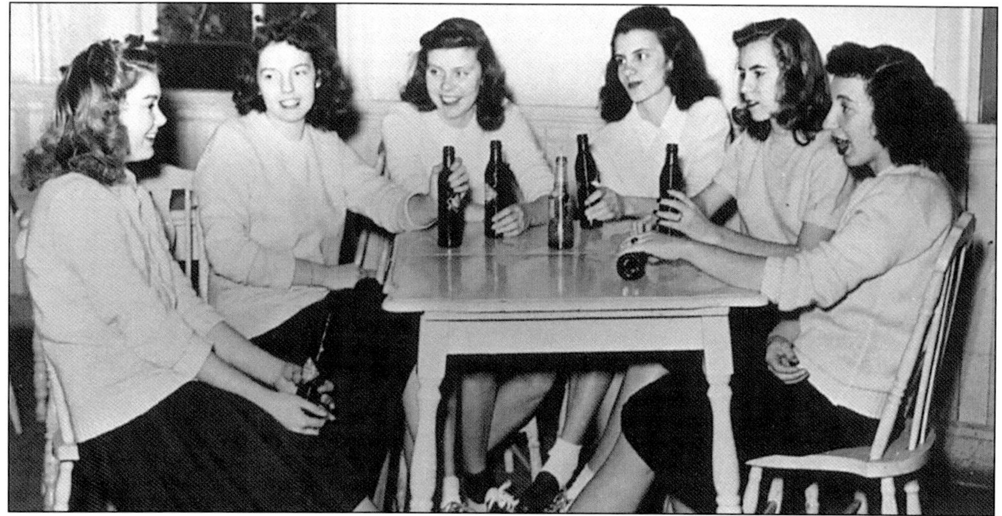

These students are enjoying a refreshment at the Canteen in 1948. The Canteen was in use as the snack bar until 1949. It was very small and could handle only about 30 students at a time. Bottled drinks, cookies, and sandwiches were the only items available.

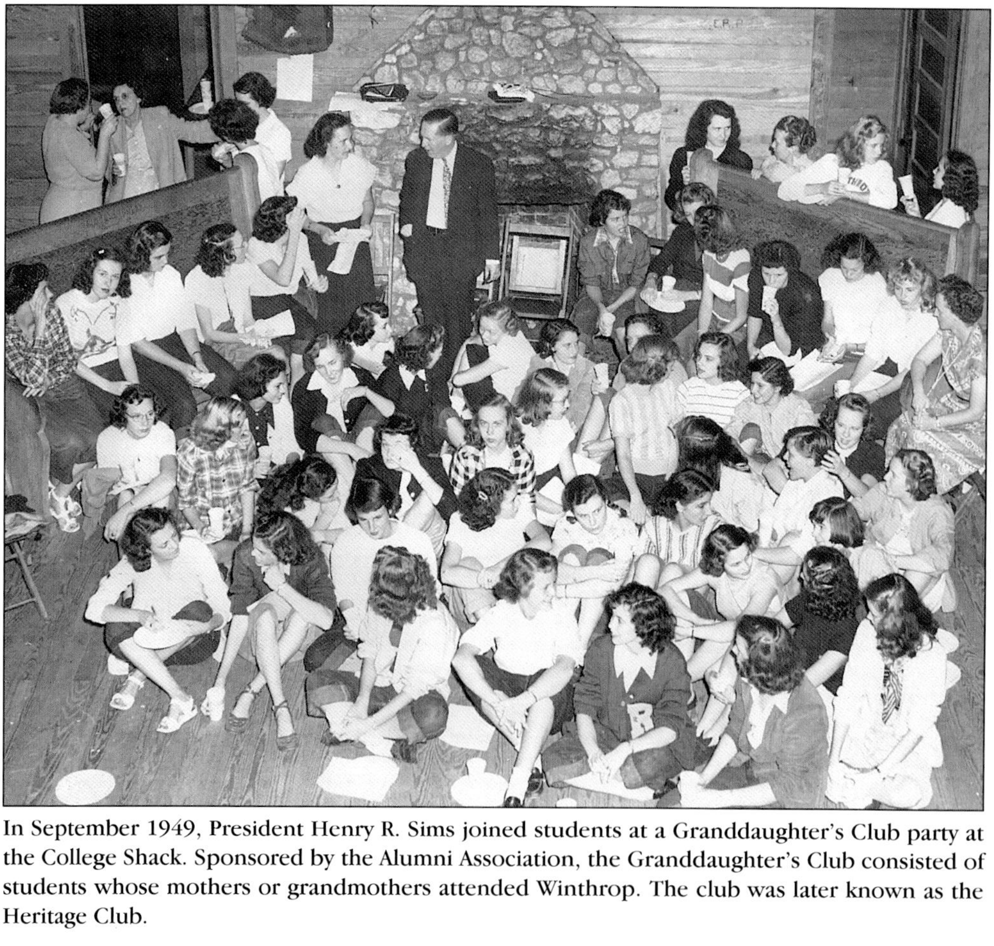

In September 1949, President Henry R. Sims joined students at a Granddaughter's Club party at the College Shack. Sponsored by the Alumni Association, the Granddaughter's Club consisted of students whose mothers or grandmothers attended Winthrop. The club was later known as the Heritage Club.

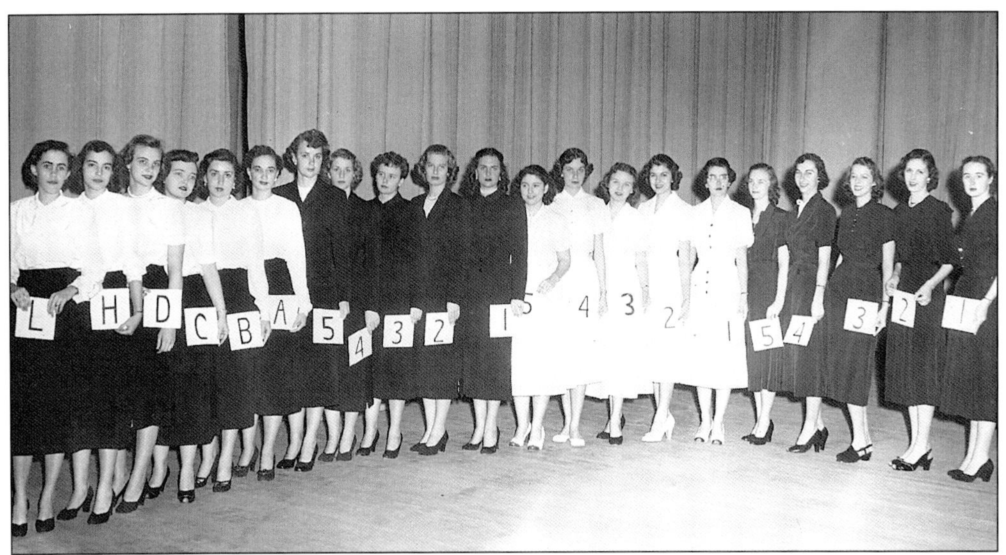

This photograph shows uniform selection in 1951. Worried about declining enrollment, the Winthrop faculty discussed for the first time at a 1951 faculty conference meeting the feasibility of abolishing the uniform requirement. During the next few years, students began to criticize openly the uniform requirement, claiming that uniforms were uneconomical, inconvenient, and impractical. The Winthrop administration took note of the changing attitude, reviewed its dress policy, and in December 1954 recommended to the Board of Trustees that the college abolish the uniform requirement. The board unanimously agreed, expressing the hope that the change would increase the college's enrollment. In January 1955, President Sims made a formal announcement that the winter semester of 1955 would be the last year for which Winthrop would require uniform dress.

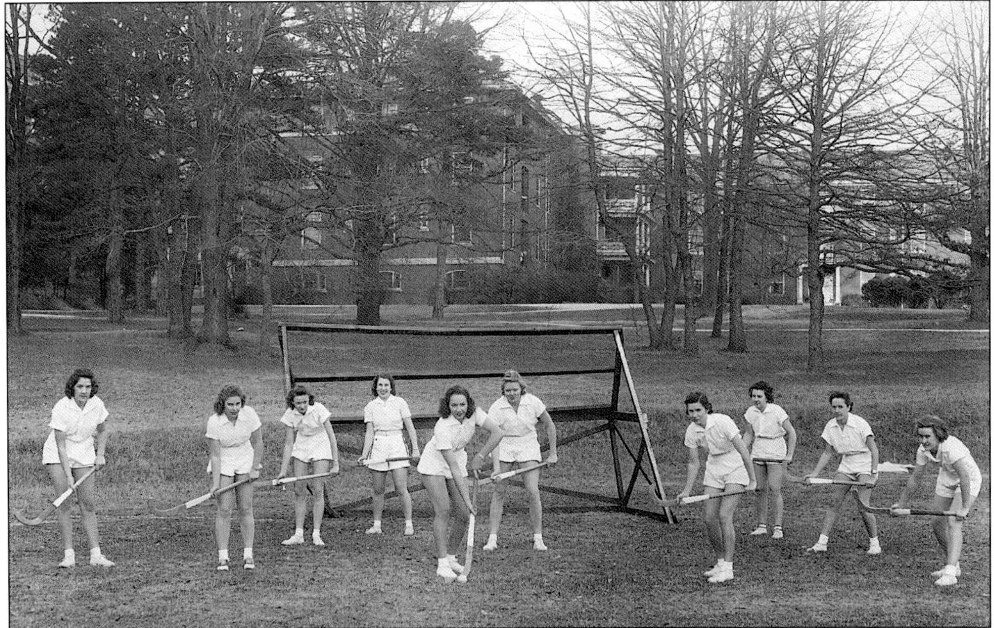

In 1953, students from a physical education class enjoyed a game of field hockey, which was one of the most popular campus sports at the time.

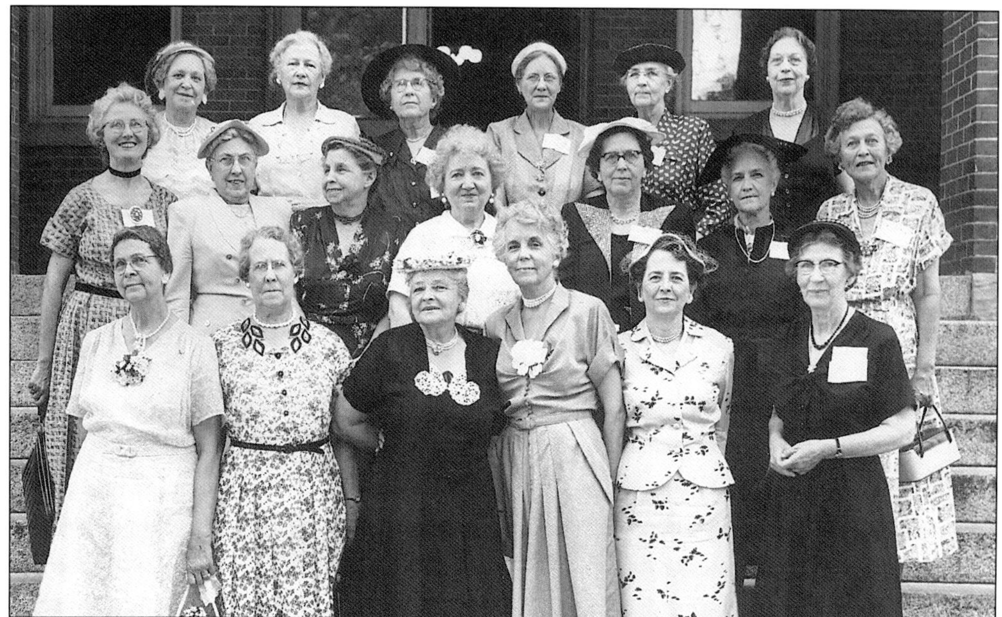

The Class of 1909 pose for a photo on the steps of Main Building on May 29, 1954. They are, from left to right, as follows: (bottom row) Jimmye Britton Watson, Berta Bush Pate, Mary Hough Swearingen, Kate Lenoir, Margaret Ross Hudnall Willis and Miss Olivia Adams; (middle row) Mildred Cunningham Hall, Elizabeth Satterwhite Napier, Annette Stover Jaeckel, Lucile Randle, Mary Lathan Craig, Kathleen Minus Stille, and Jennie Sanders; (top row) Jenks Johnston Anderson, Nellie Watkins Lee, Colin Phillips, Abbie Bryan, Kate Hunter Westrope, and Annie Davis Epting.

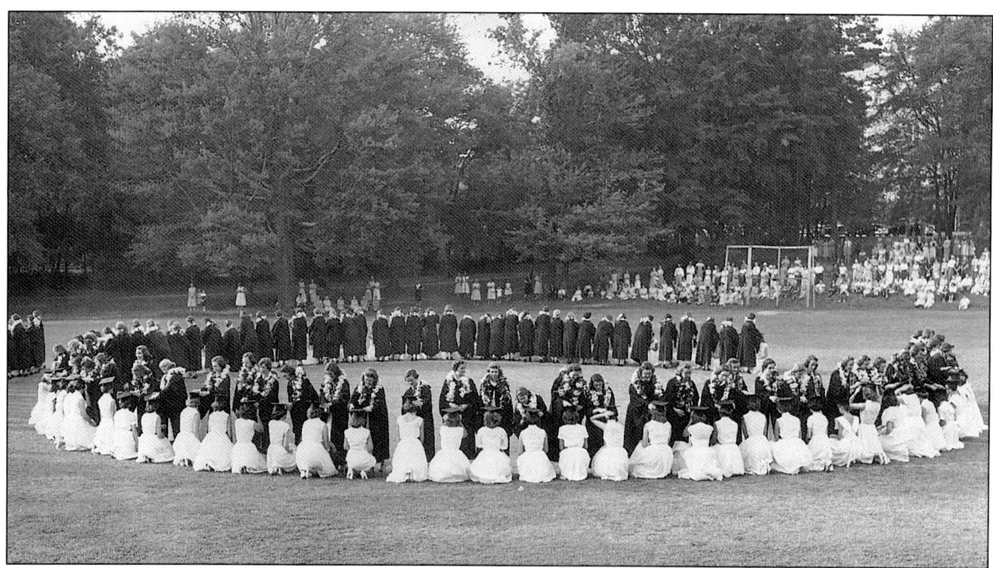

This is the Daisy Chain procession for 1953. The tradition began in 1903. First staged at Winthrop, the ceremony consisted of members of the graduating class and their junior sisters. Following commencement, the young women joined a procession across the front campus, halting at the fountain to sing. The seniors placed their mortar boards on the heads of the juniors, thus symbolizing succession to senior status.

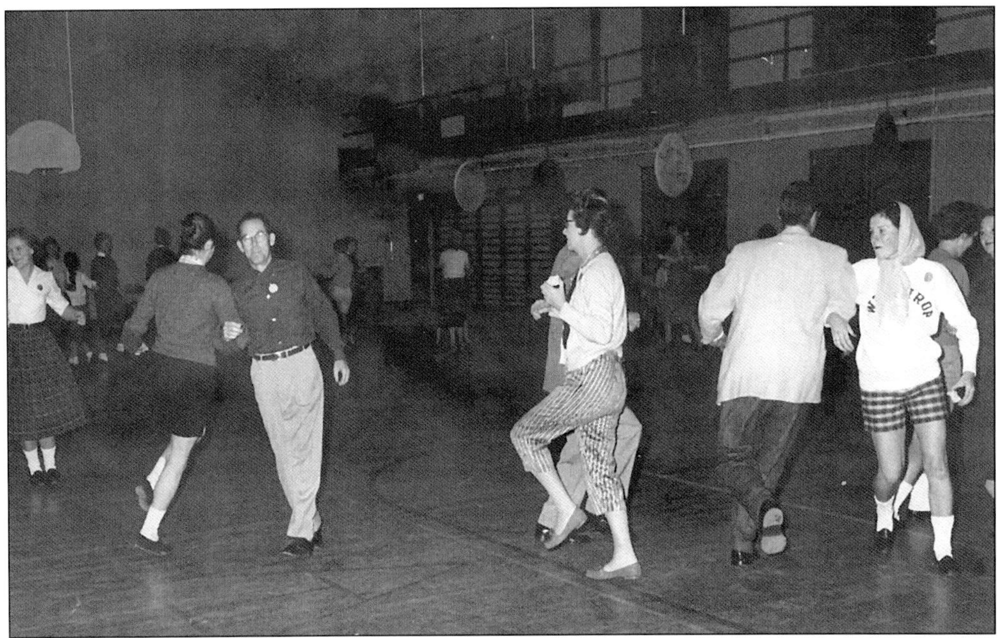

In 1958, the Winthrop Recreation Association sponsored an "Apple Polishing" party.

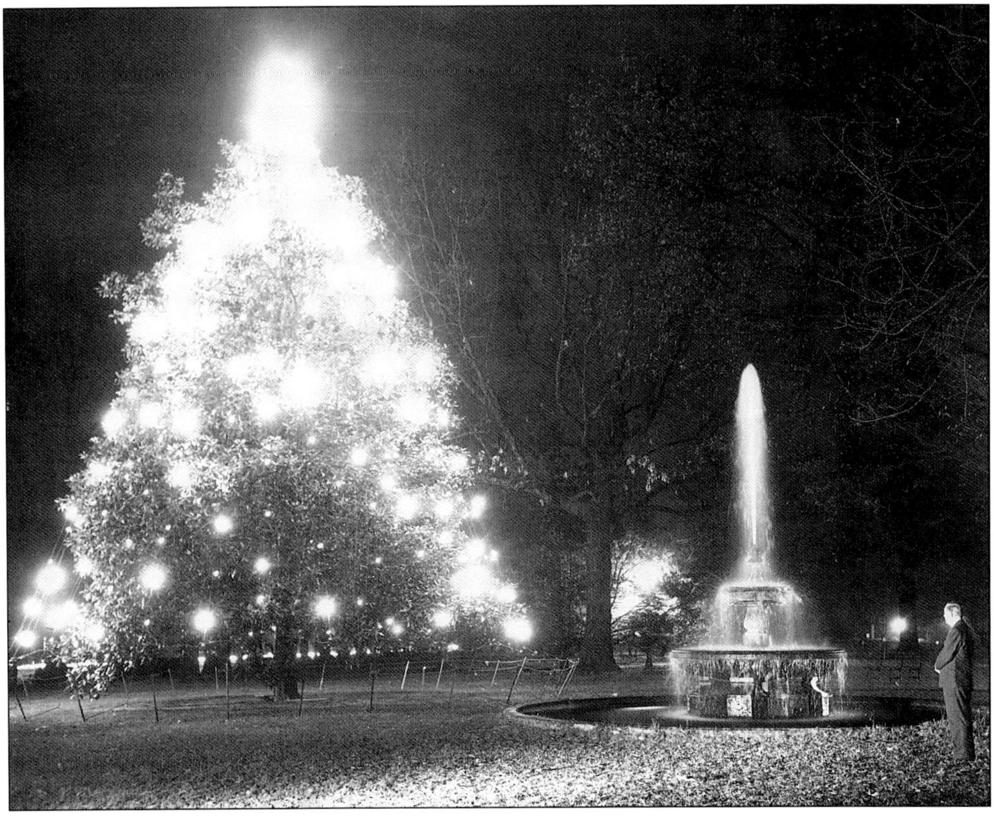

President Sims is pictured here observing the college's Christmas tree in 1955. Christmas has always been central to campus life during the school's long history.

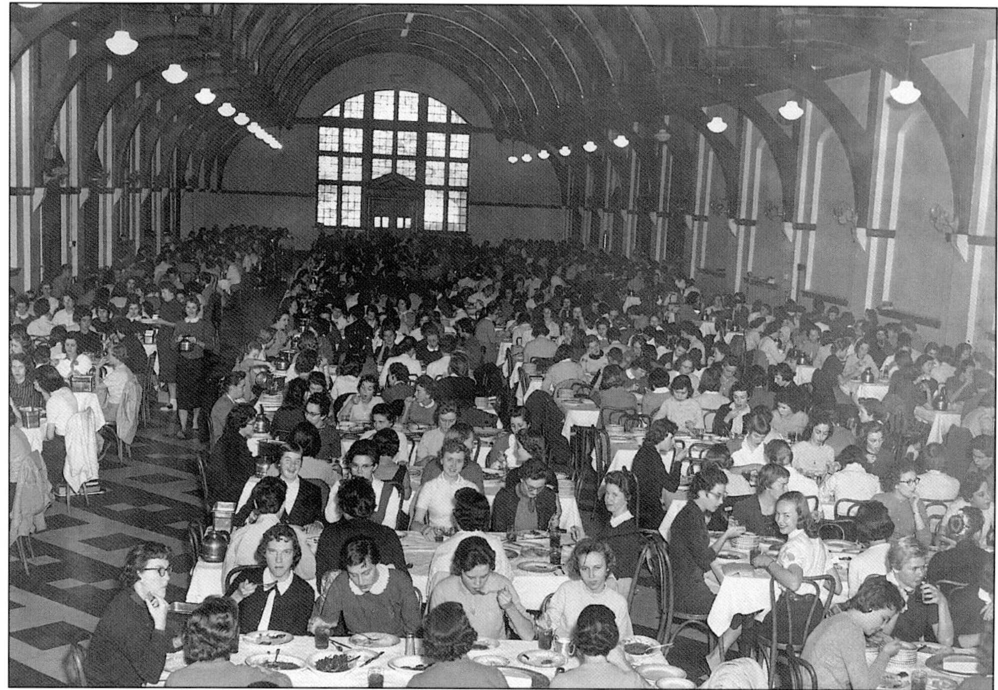

This is McBryde Cafeteria as it looked in 1958. The back part of Main Building contained Winthrop's first dining hall. Built at a cost of $32,000 in 1909, it was renamed in 1967 for Sarah Crosby Chappell McBryde, who worked as a Winthrop dietician from 1919 to 1945.

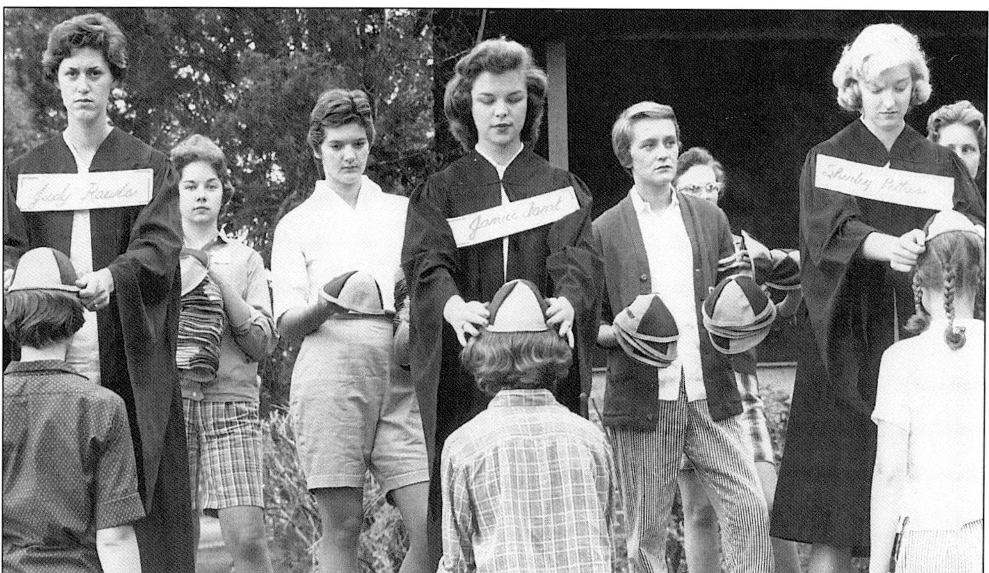

This photograph shows Rat Week in 1959, a tradition that has its roots in the late 1940s. Freshmen were kept busy during the week with such duties as cleaning rooms, carrying books, writing letters, being agreeable to uppeclassmen, and serving upperclassmen as upperclassmen saw fit. Rat Week required all new students to wear the rat cap all the time for the entire week. Rat Week was discontinued in the Fall of 1979 to comply with the new hazing policy adopted by the Winthrop Board of Trustees in the November 4, 1978 meeting.

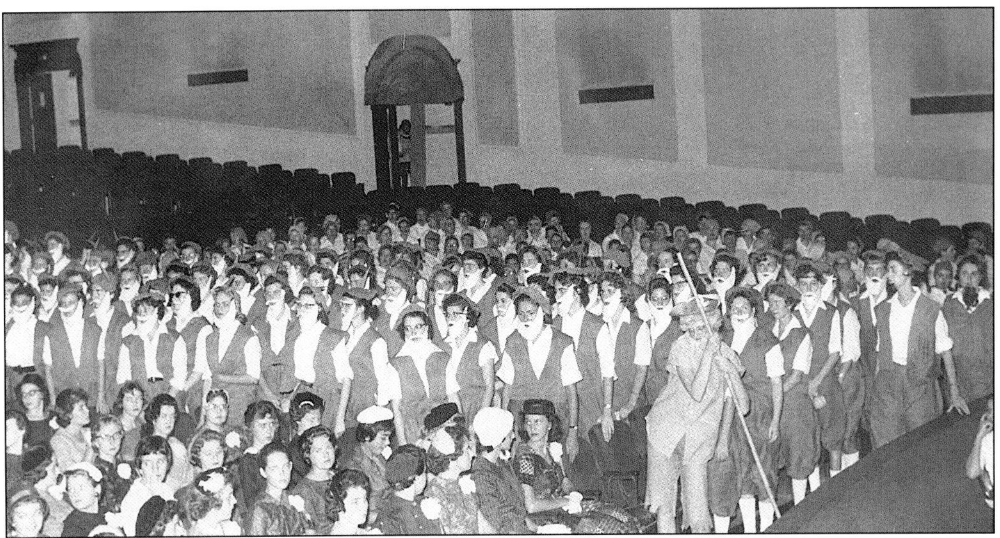

This photograph captures Classes Night in 1959. At this annual event, each of the four Winthrop classes presented a skit. The night had a theme, and the class that built the best program around the theme was the winner, proudly earning the reputation as having the best school spirit.

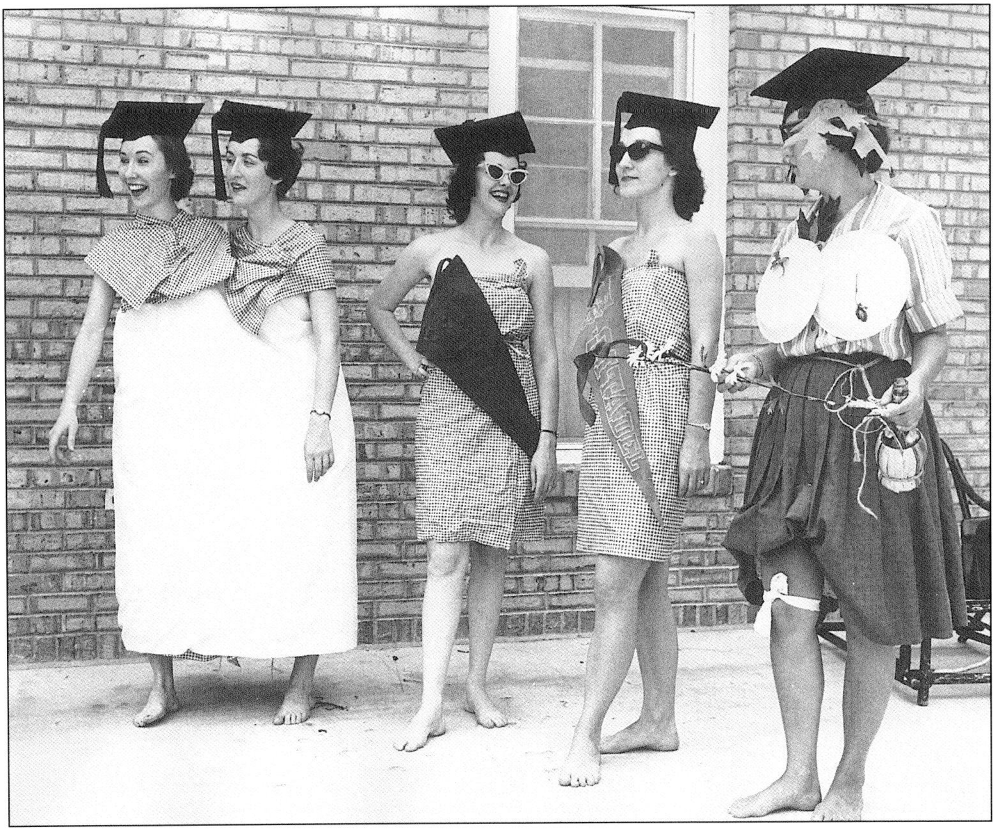

The Senior Order clown around in this photo taken during the 1962–63 term. The prestigious Senior Order consisted of seniors who are recognized as the most outstanding seniors in all phases of college life. To lead and improve student activities is the organization's purpose.

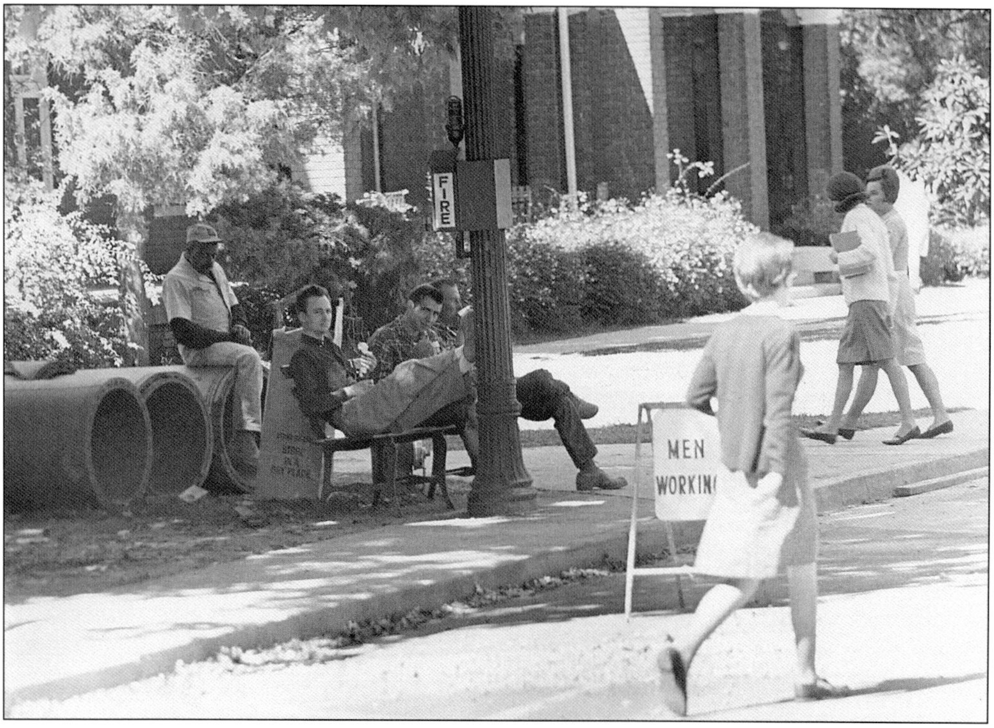

In 1966, as this photograph shows, workmen on the Winthrop campus enjoy "watching all the girls go by."

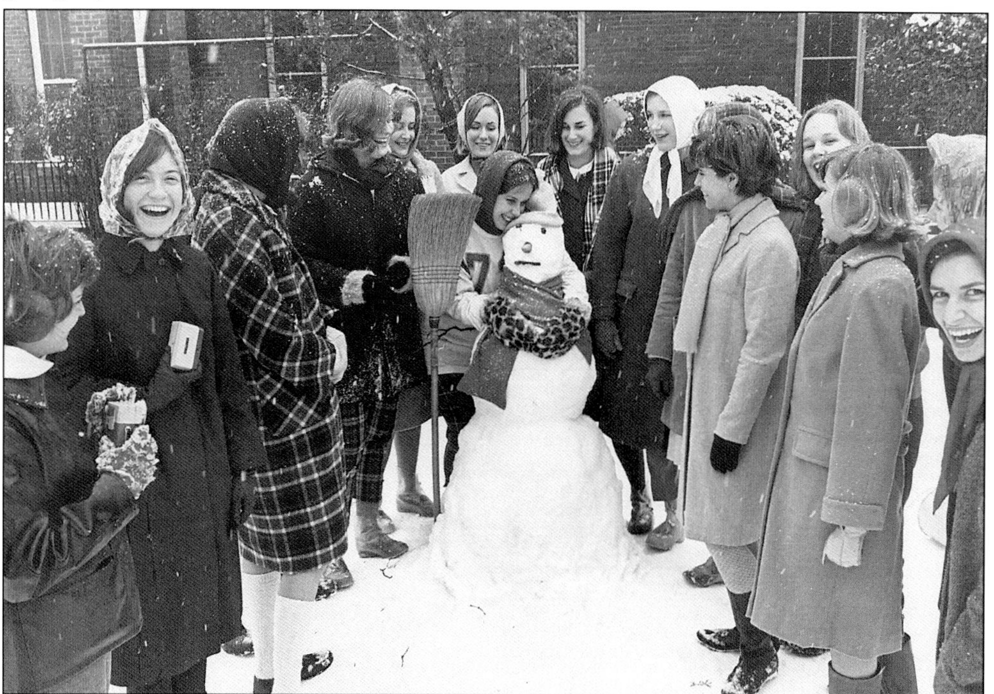

This photograph captures a truly rare scene– snow on the Winthrop campus. Students bundle up and enjoy the occasion.

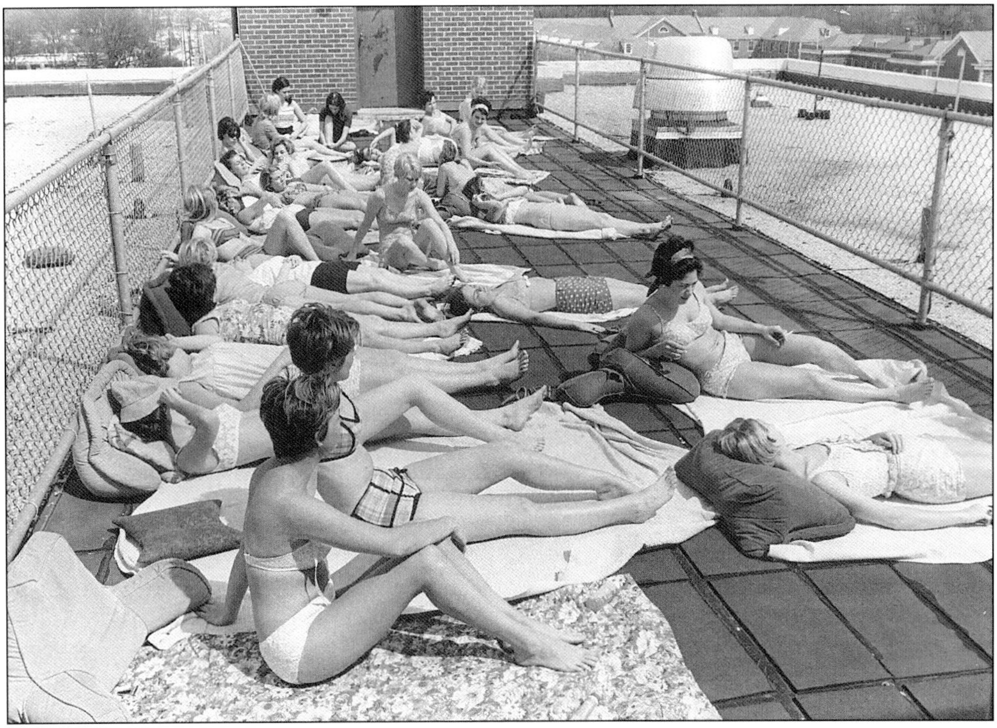

As can be seen here in 1969, catching some rays is a favorite student pastime.

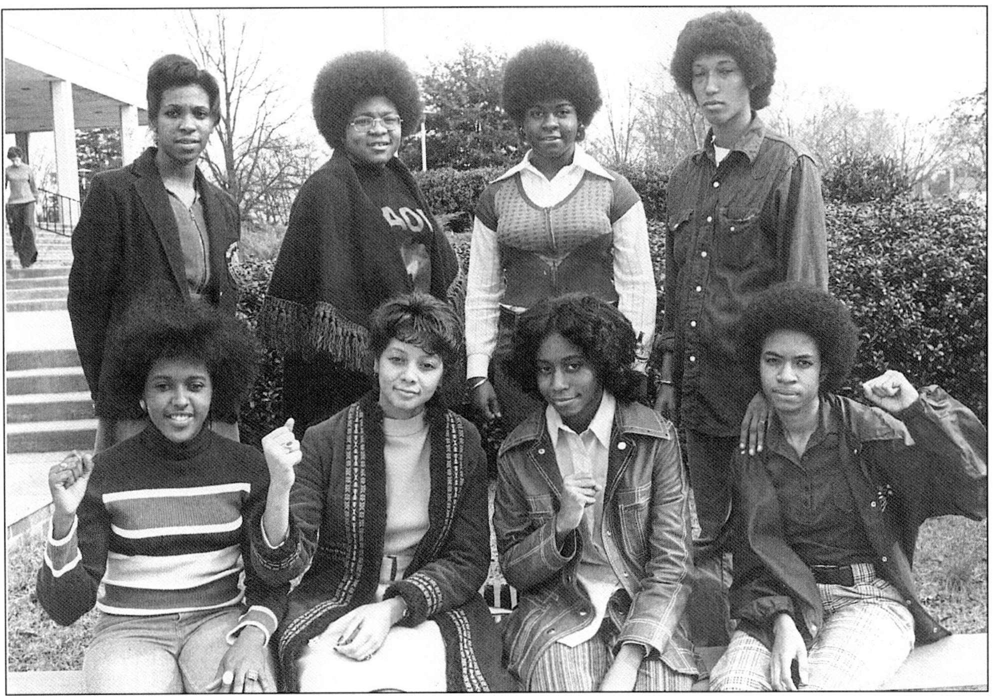

Ebonites pose for a photo during Black Week in January 1974. During the past 25 years, the Ebonites, as their records in the Winthrop Archives verify, have become one of the most dynamic student organizations on the Winthrop campus.

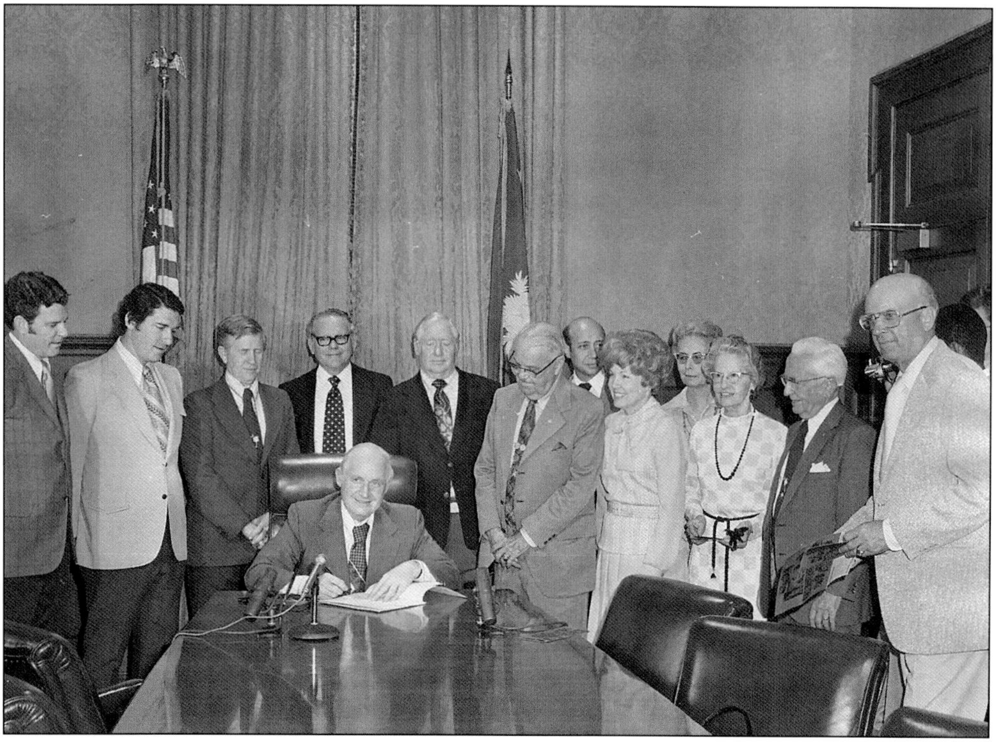

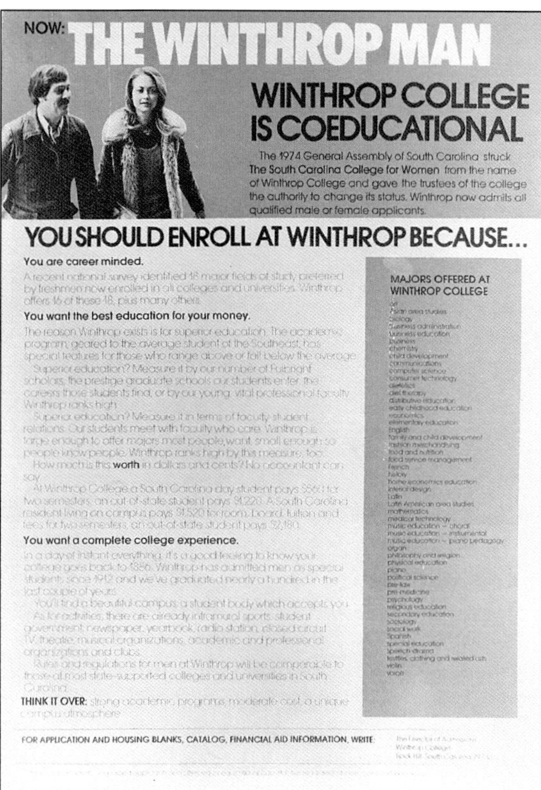

Coeducation comes to Winthrop. At its first meeting in October 1973 with incoming president Charles B. Vail, the Winthrop Board of Trustees gave its support for an all-out push for co-education. On March 18, 1974, Governor John Carl West, husband of Winthrop alumna Lois Rhame West, signed into law a bill giving the Winthrop Board of Trustees the authority to decide the co-education issue. The board immediately moved to amend the college's charter. A new era at Winthrop had begun. Men could attend the college without restrictions.

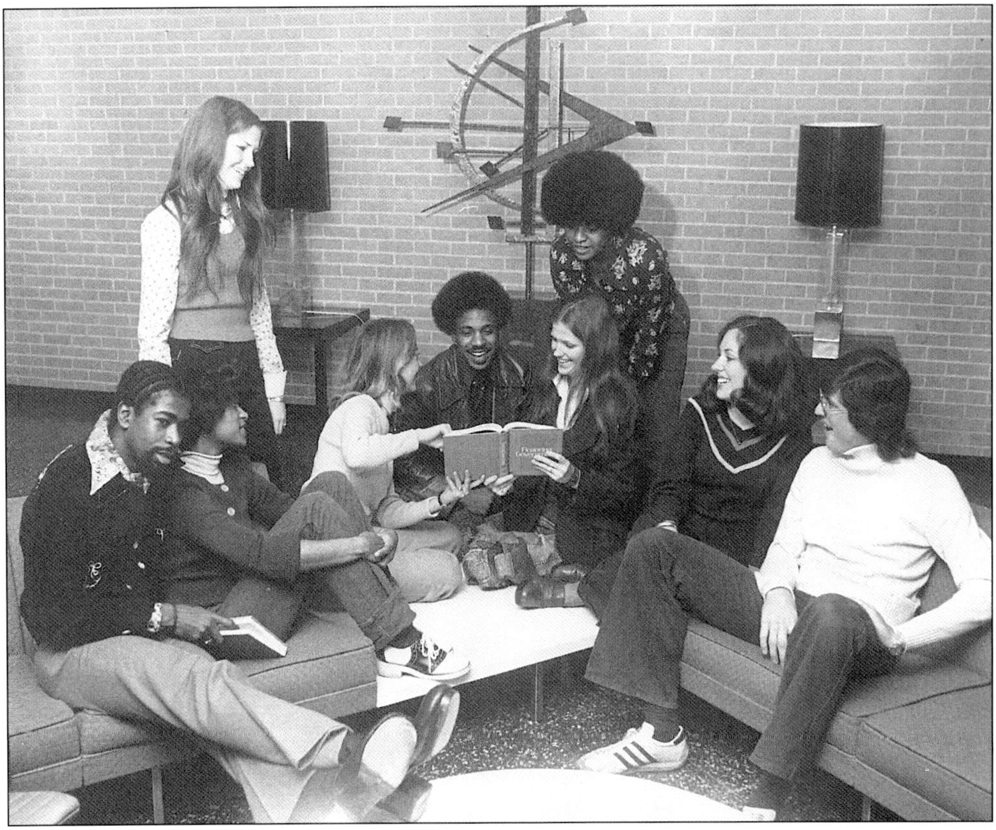

As this photo shows, by the mid-1970s, Winthrop was a rapidly changing campus.

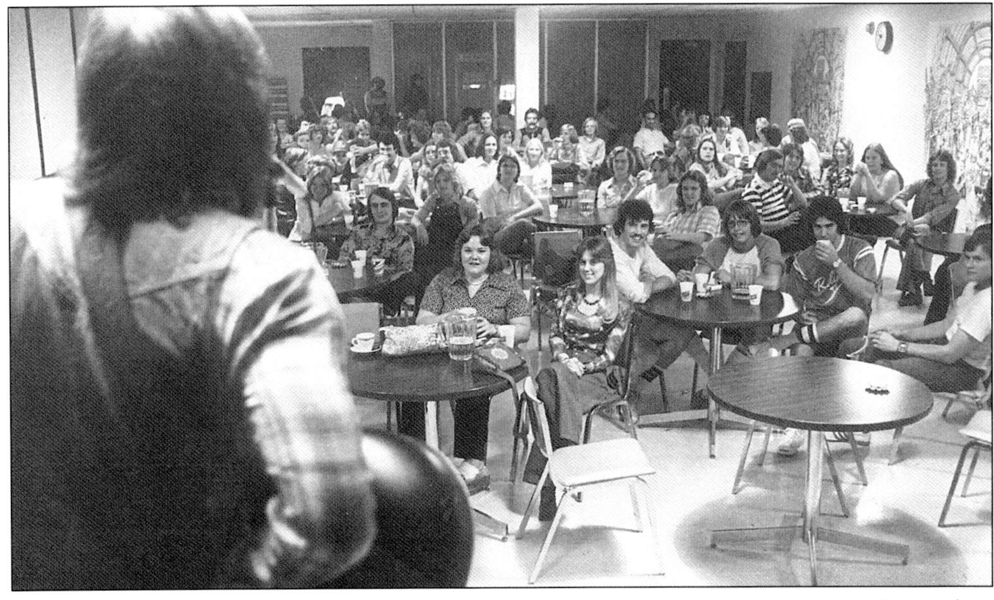

Across the Street, located in the basement of Dinkins Student Center, was a popular student hangout in the late 1970s.

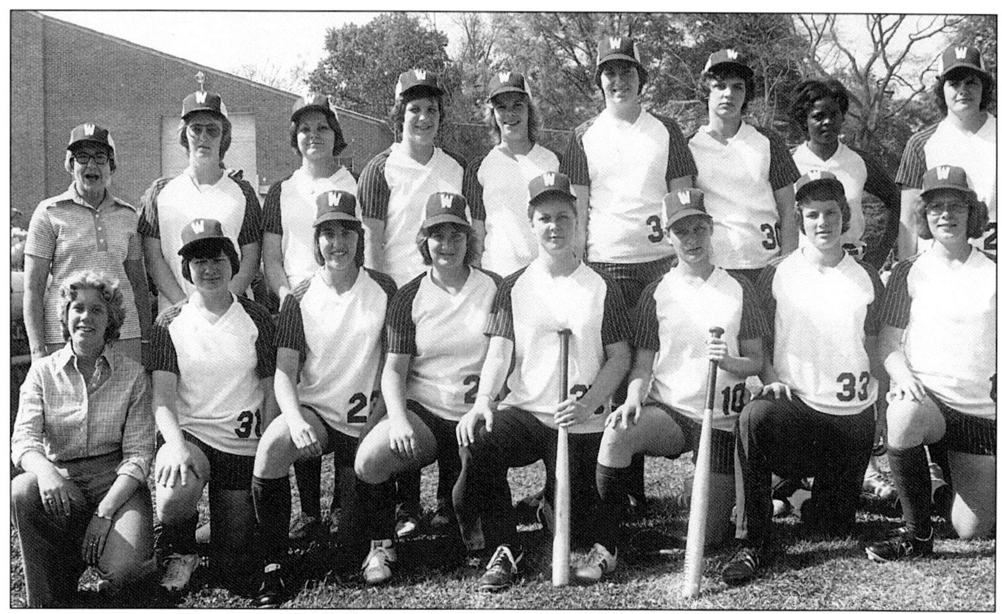

Members of the Winthrop women's softball team pose for a photo in April 1976.

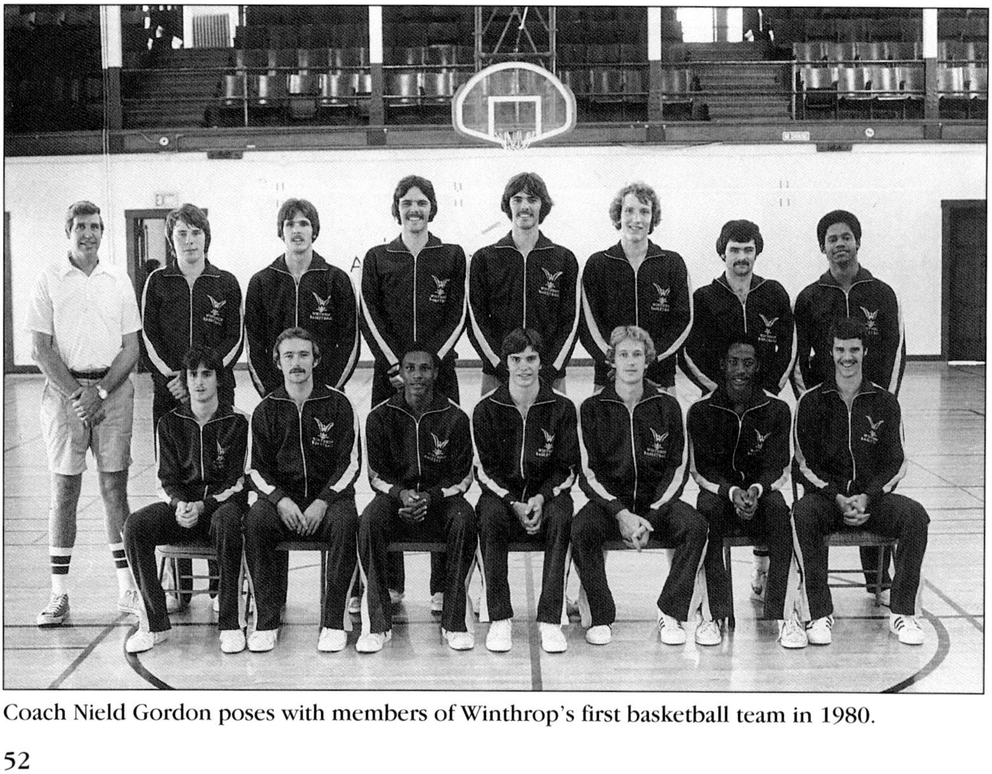

Coach Nield Gordon poses with members of Winthrop's first basketball team in 1980.

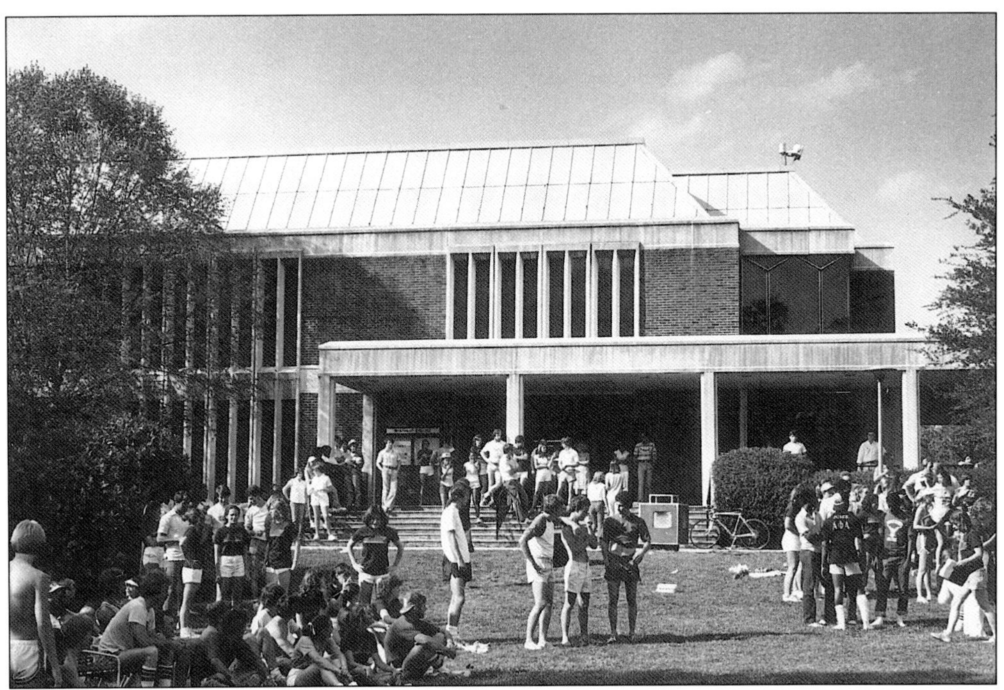

Greek Day is celebrated in April 1980. With men on campus came fraternities.

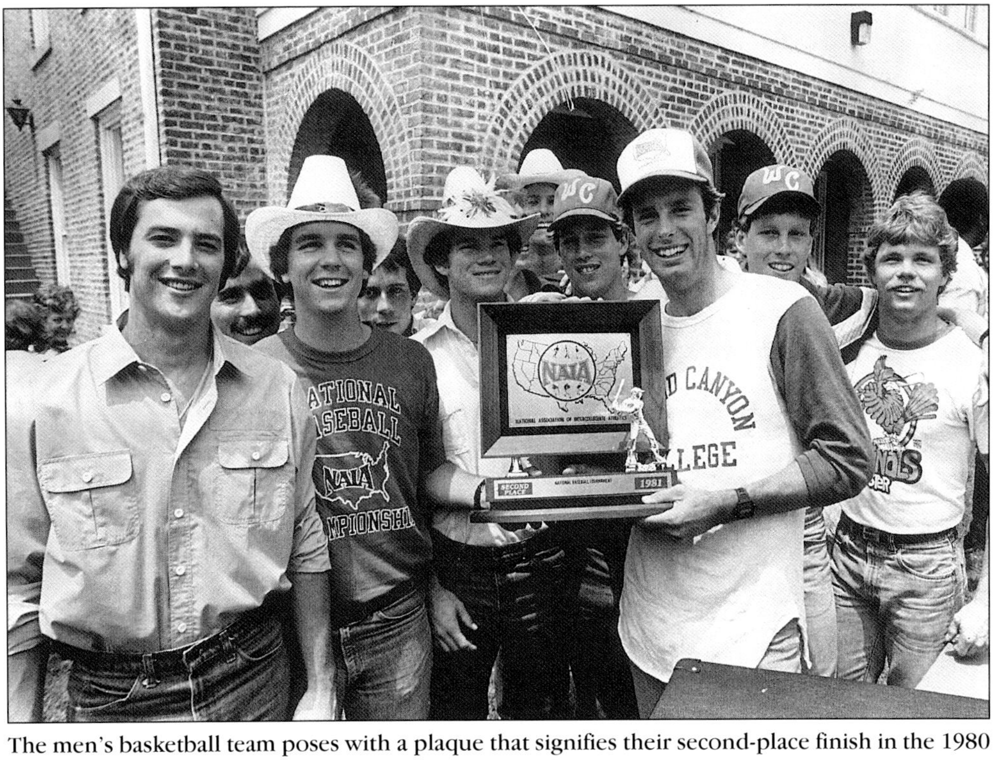

The men's basketball team poses with a plaque that signifies their second-place finish in the 1980 NAIA College Basketball Tournament.

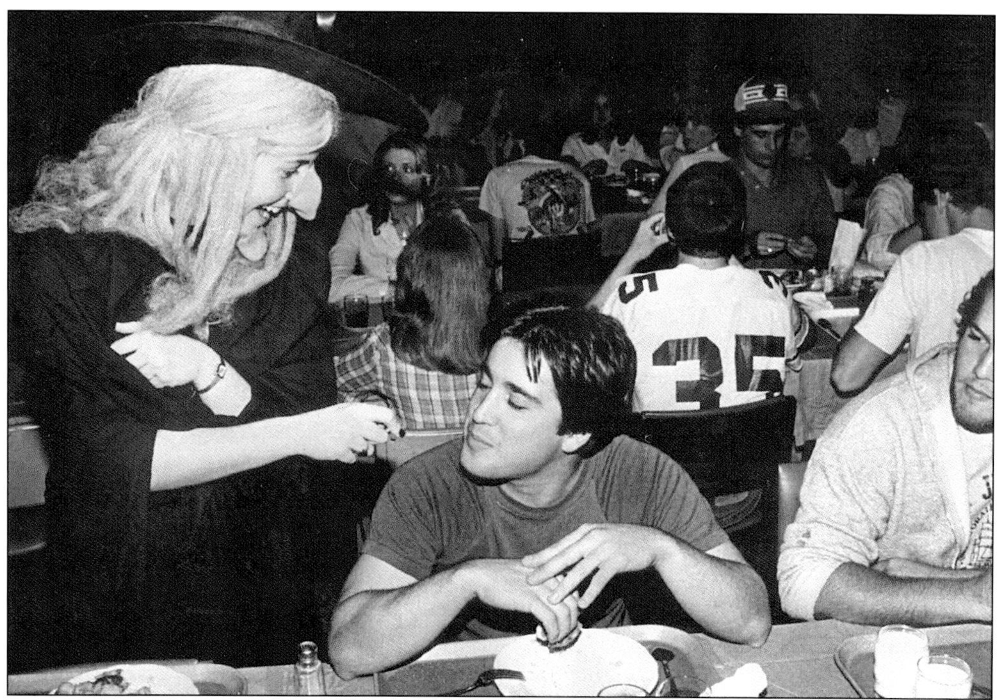

This is a 1981 scene from Halloween Happening, another strong Winthrop tradition.

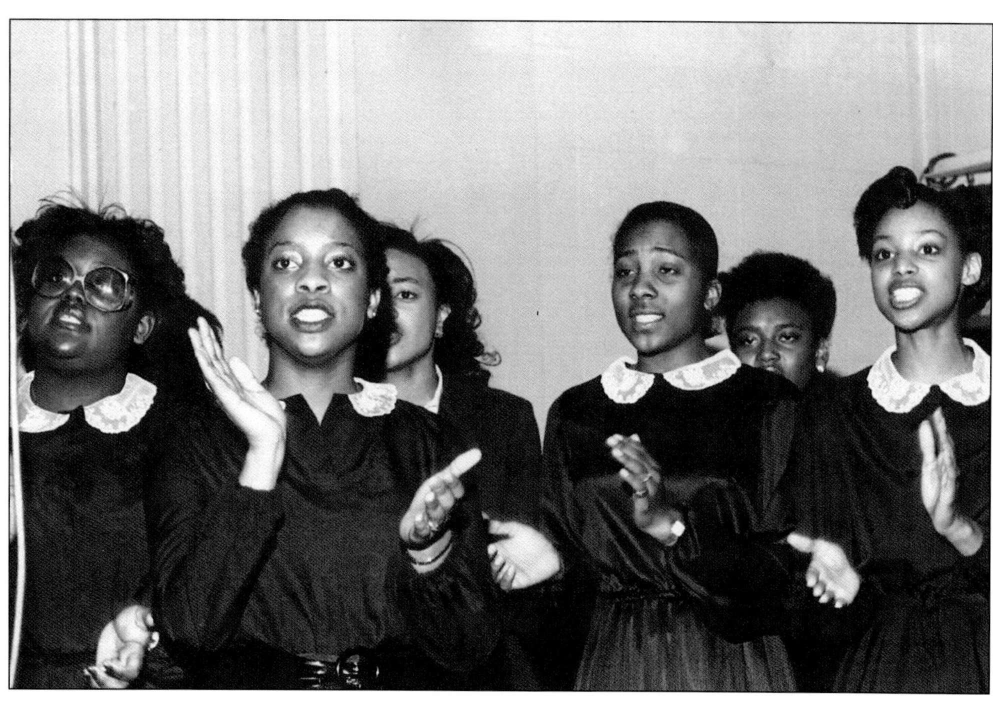

The Ebonite Gospel Choir is seen here performing in January 1982.

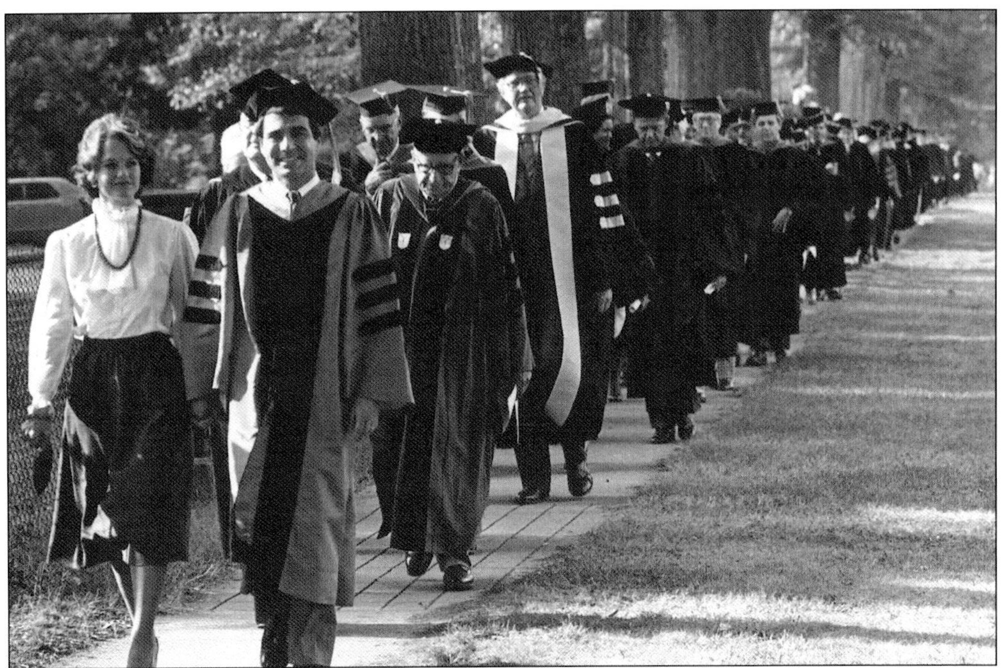

President Phil Lader and wife, Linda, lead the Blue Line at the 1983 convocation. The Blue Line was one of the traditions President Lader revived during his brief tenure at Winthrop. As traditionally celebrated, students would dress in their blue uniforms, and, led by the president, they would walk down Oakland Avenue to Sunday church services

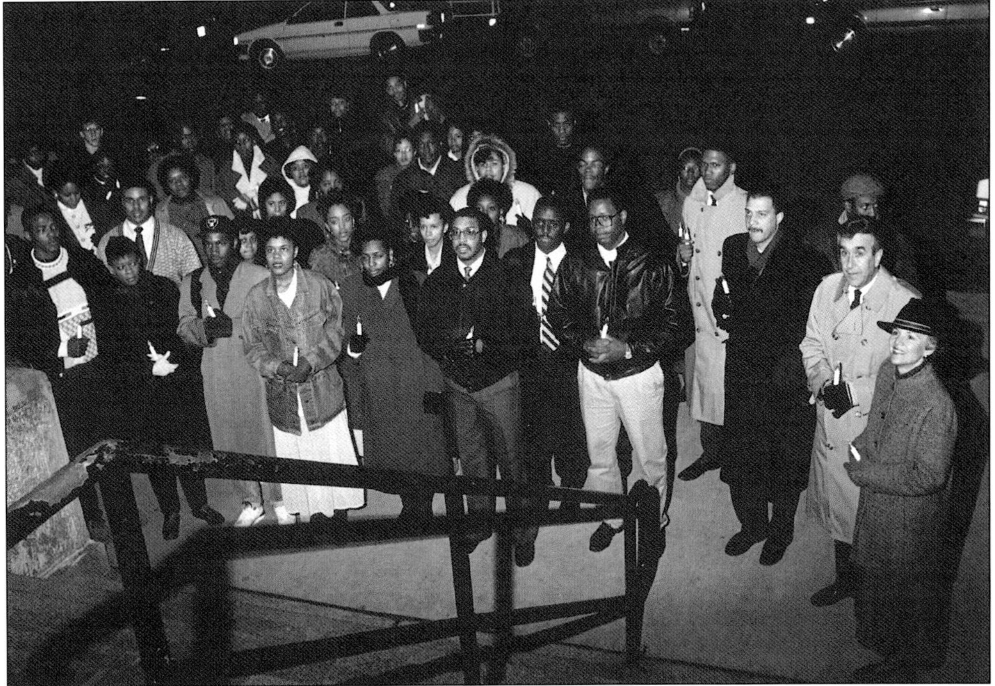

Members of the college's administration, faculty, staff, and student body gather for a Martin Luther King Jr. vigil in 1991.

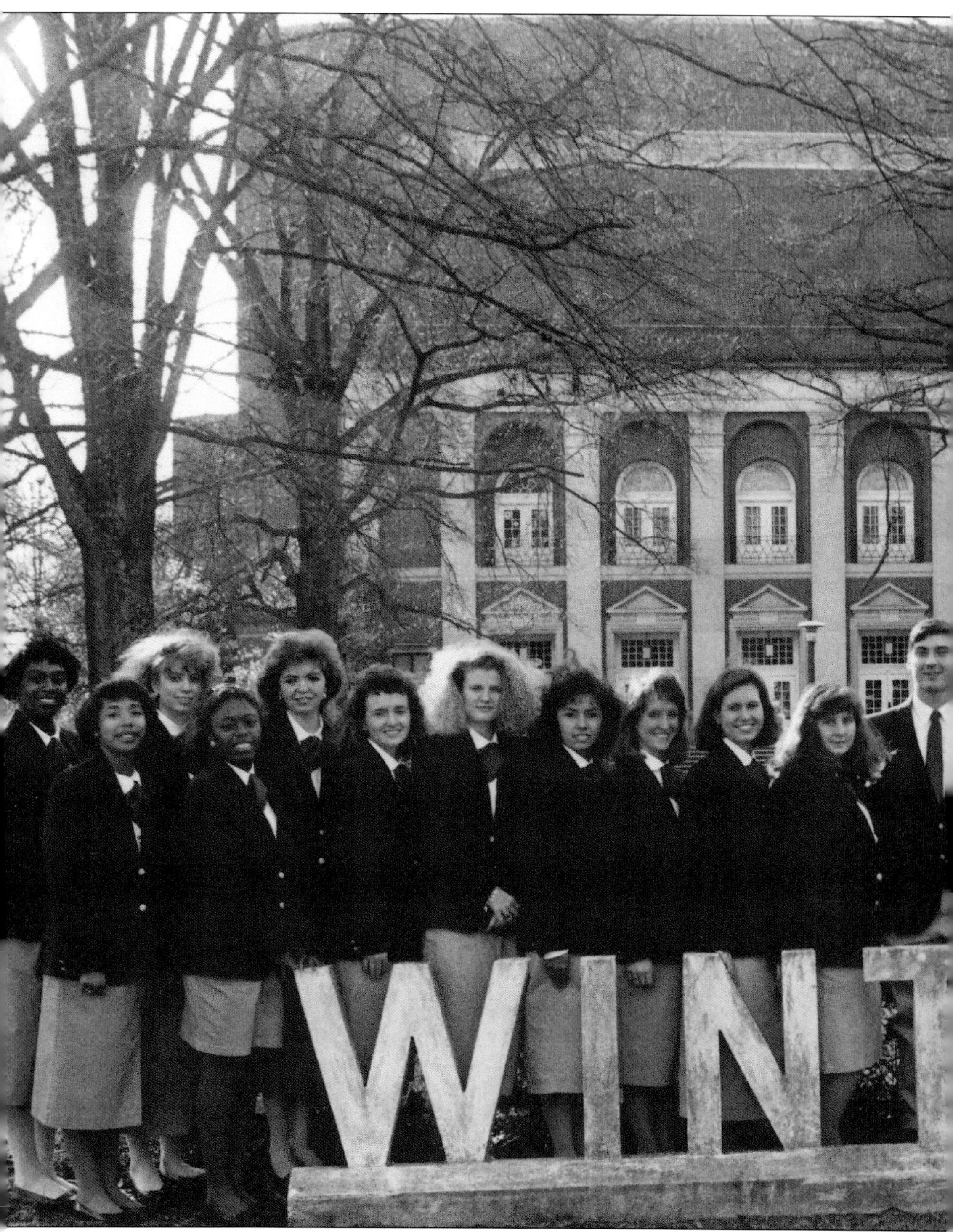

The Winthrop Ambassadors pose for a photo in January 1992.

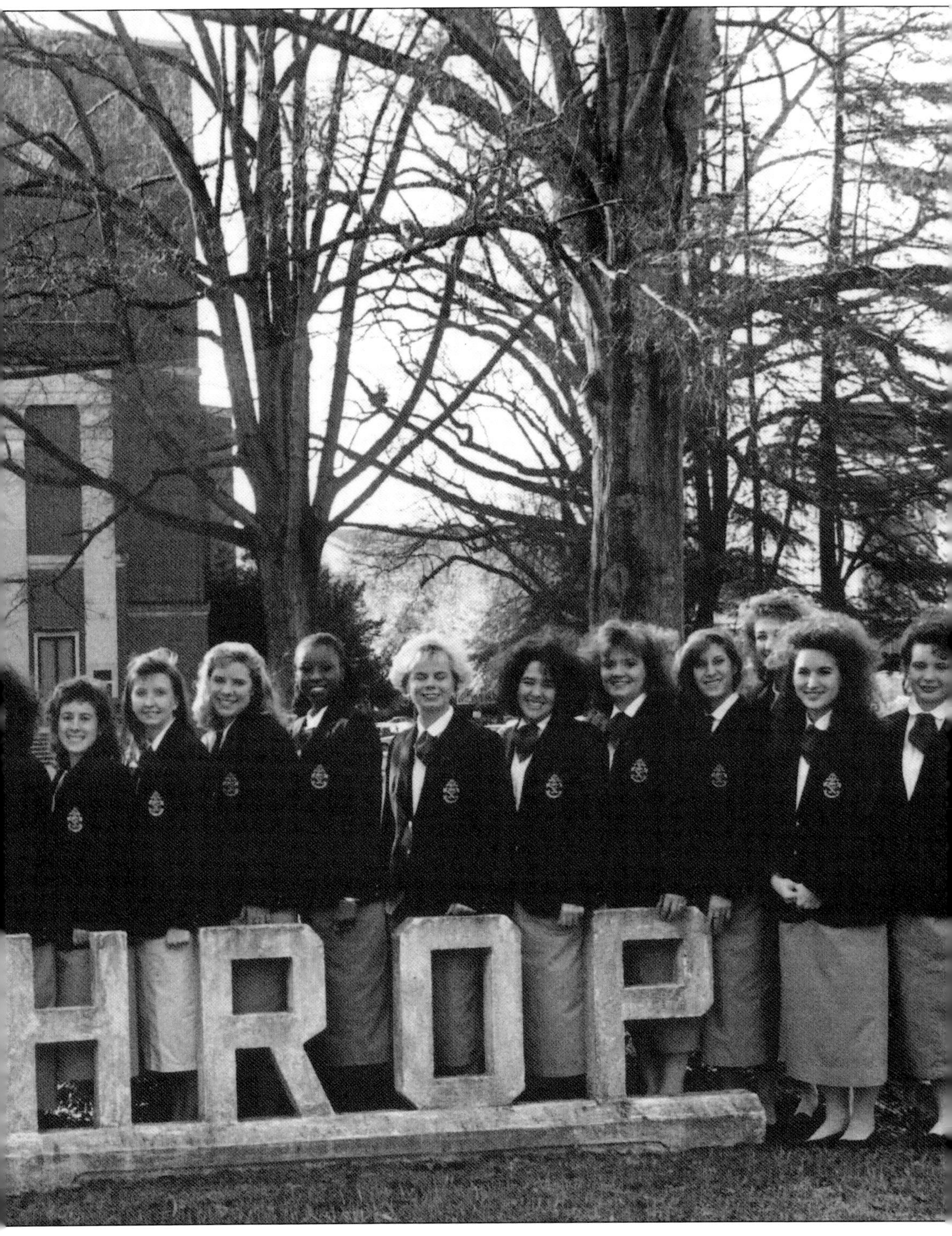
HROP

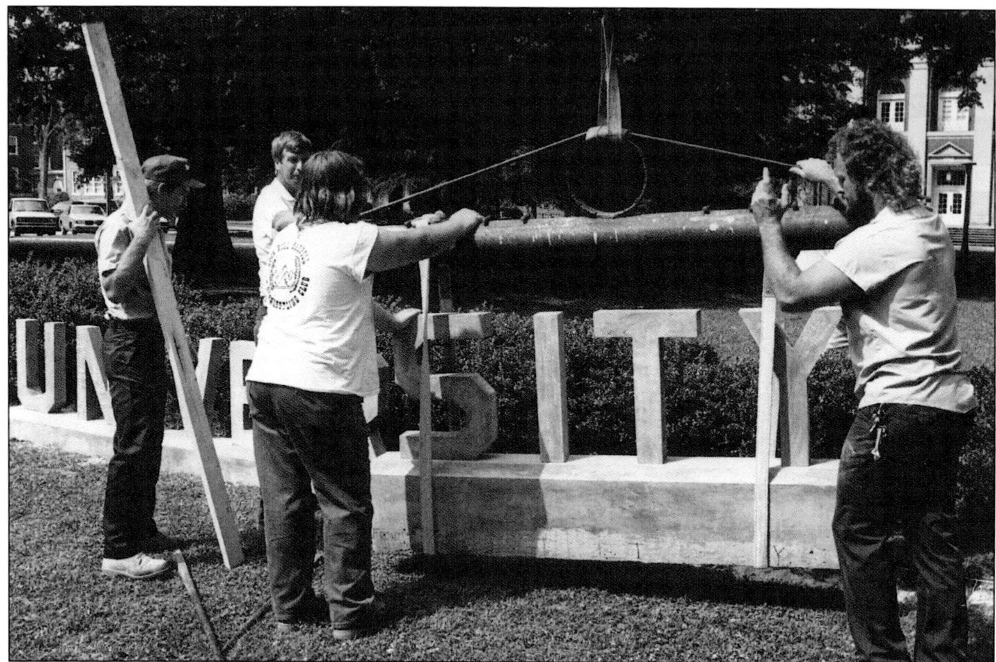

In 1992, Winthrop changed its name from Winthrop College to Winthrop University, marking the beginning of a new era in the institution's history.

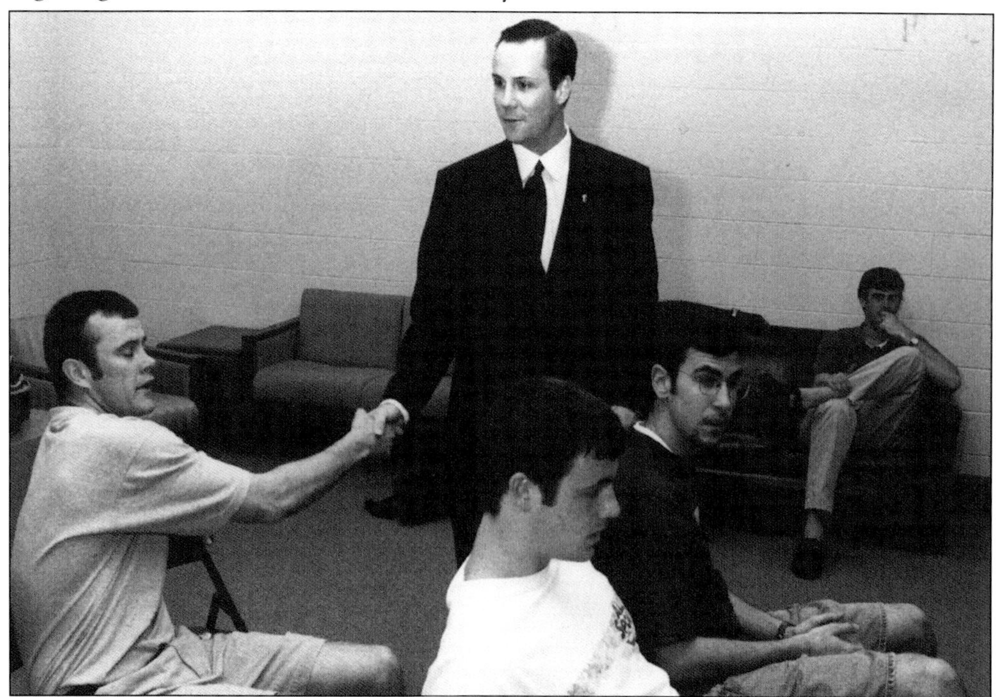

Greg Marshall, Winthrop's men's basketball coach, greets Winthrop students in March 1998. The following year, Marshall would lead the Winthrop Eagles for the first time into the NCAA basketball tournament. For the first time in its history, but certainly not the last, the Winthrop family would experience "March Madness."

Three

Buildings and Grounds

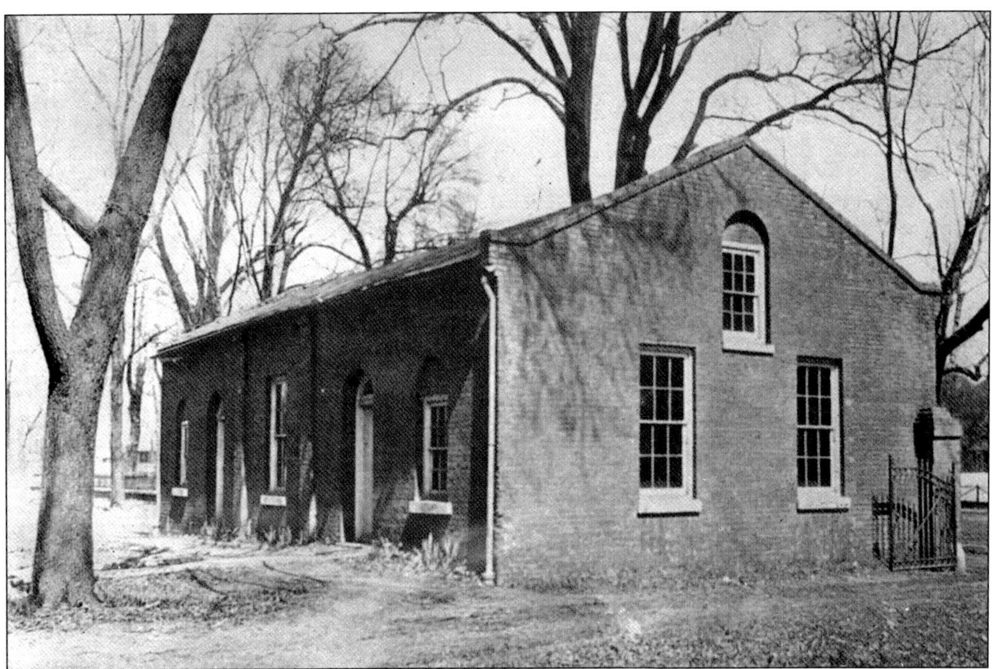

Officially named the Columbia Seminary Chapel, Winthrop's beloved "Little Chapel" was built as the stable and carriage house on the grounds of the Ainsley Hall mansion in Columbia about 1823. In 1830 it was converted into a chapel for the Columbia Theological Seminary. The Little Chapel became Winthrop's first facility in 1886.

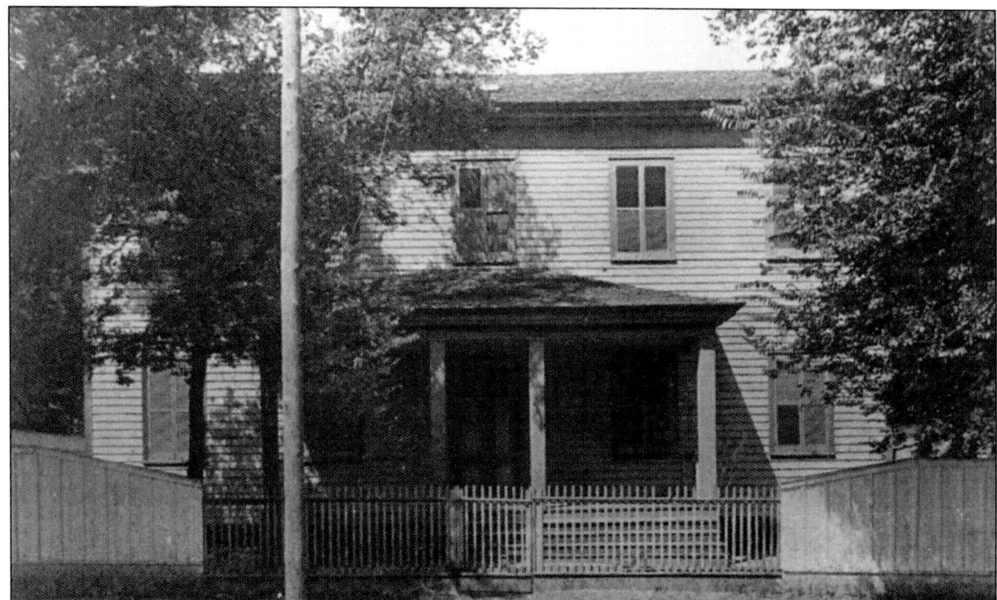

After its first year of operation in Columbia, Winthrop Training School, as the institution was then known, moved to a house on Marion Street. The school remained there until it moved to Rock Hill in 1895.

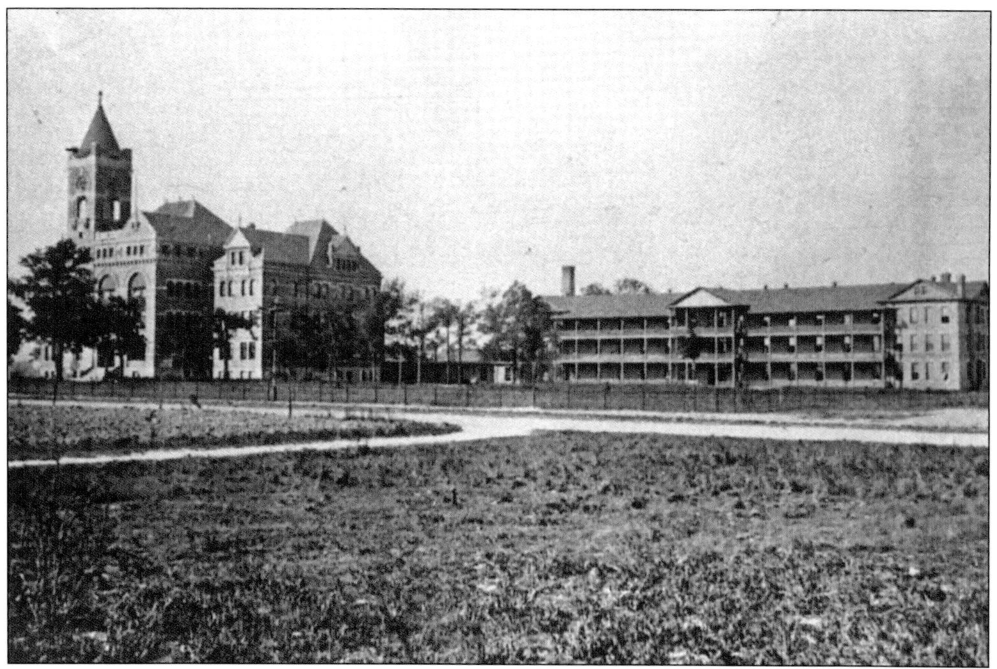

This is Main Building (later Tillman Hall) and North Dormitory as they—and the campus—looked in 1896. Main Building was completed in 1894 and has served as the focus of Winthrop's campus ever since. North Dormitory, named because it was located on the north side of the campus, was renamed Margaret Nance in honor of Winthrop founder D.B. Johnson's mother. When completed, it was three stories high, contained 157 rooms, and could accommodate 282 persons.

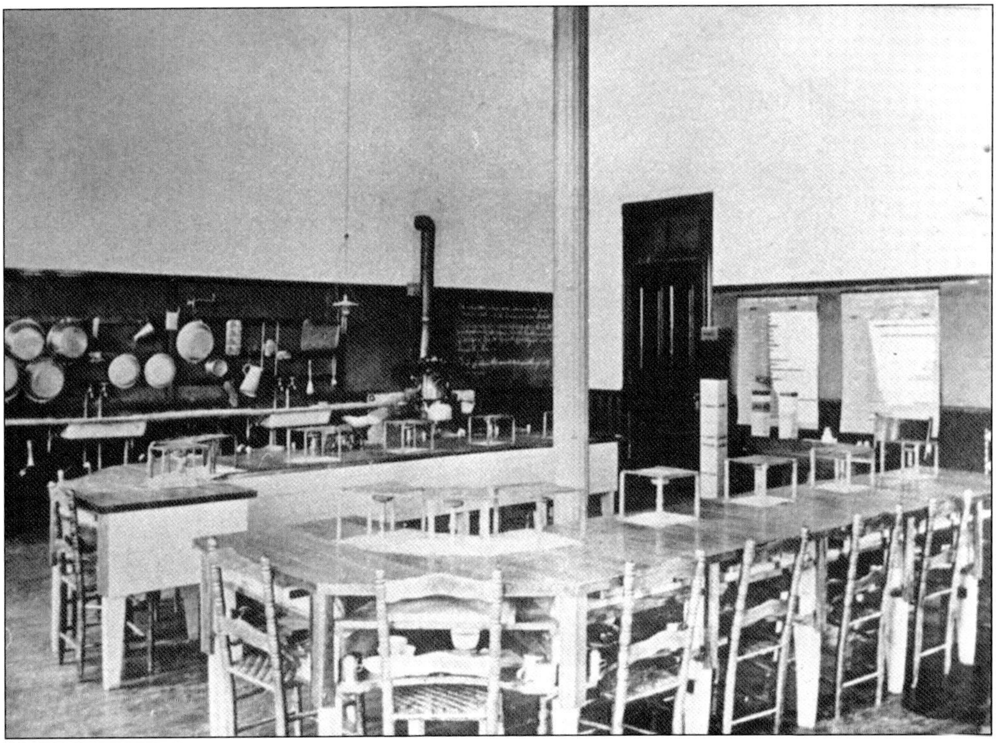

This is a view inside Main Building in 1895. When Rock Hill's Winthrop opened its doors in the fall of 1895, Main Building housed administrative offices, classrooms, laboratories, library, museum, an auditorium, art room, two social halls, and a gymnasium with swimming pool.

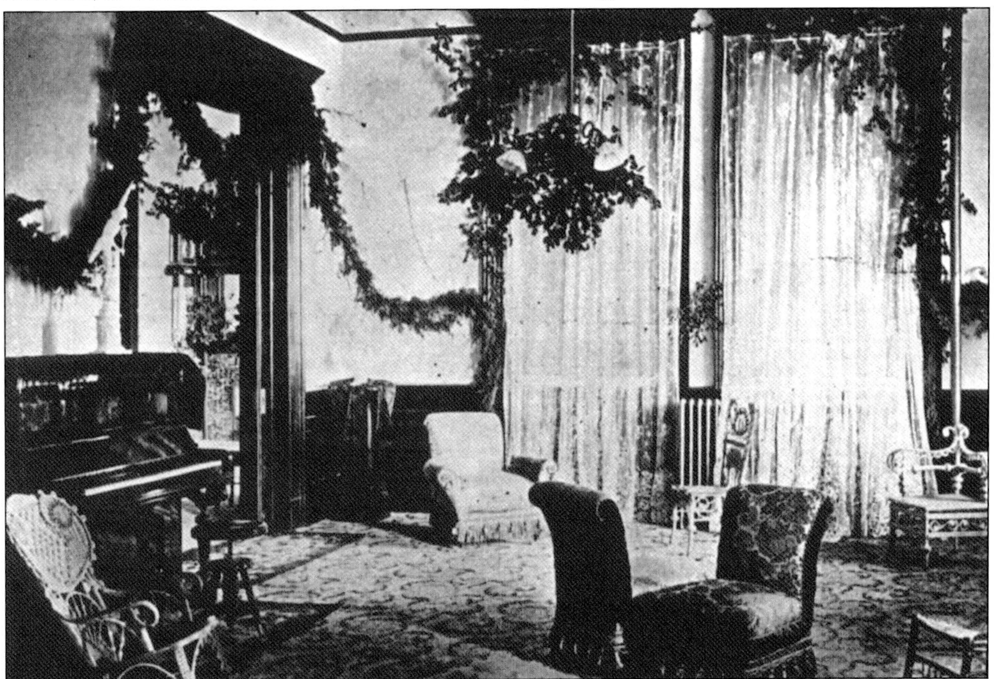

This is the reception parlor in Main Building as it looked in 1895 at Christmas.

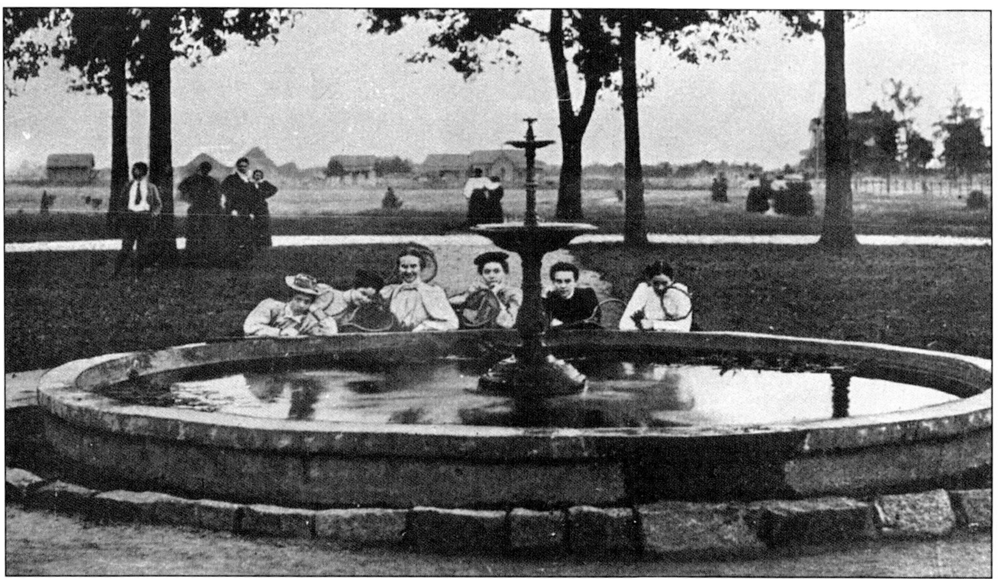

Students relax at the College Fountain after a game of tennis in 1897. Note the pristine background that the Dinkins Student Center now occupies.

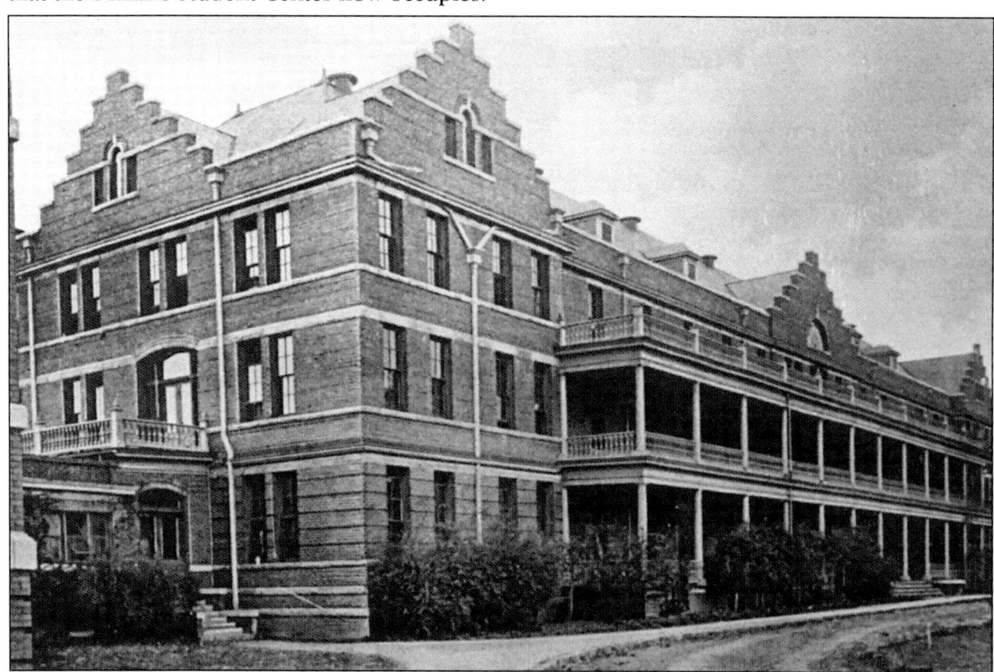

This is South Dormitory as it looked soon after its construction in 1901. This building was Winthrop's second dormitory. In 1925, it was renamed McLaurin for Daniel W McLaurin, a Dillon, South Carolina native, Confederate war veteran, and a charter member of Winthrop's Board of Trustees from 1891 to 1899 and 1903 to 1928. McLaurin was also used for art instruction, and the basement of the extension was used for indoor recreation and music practice. From 1975 to 1983, McLaurin housed the Human Development Center, which coordinated interdisciplinary services for the developmentally disabled. In 1983, McLaurin was renovated and now serves as office space for the School of Visual and Performing Arts.

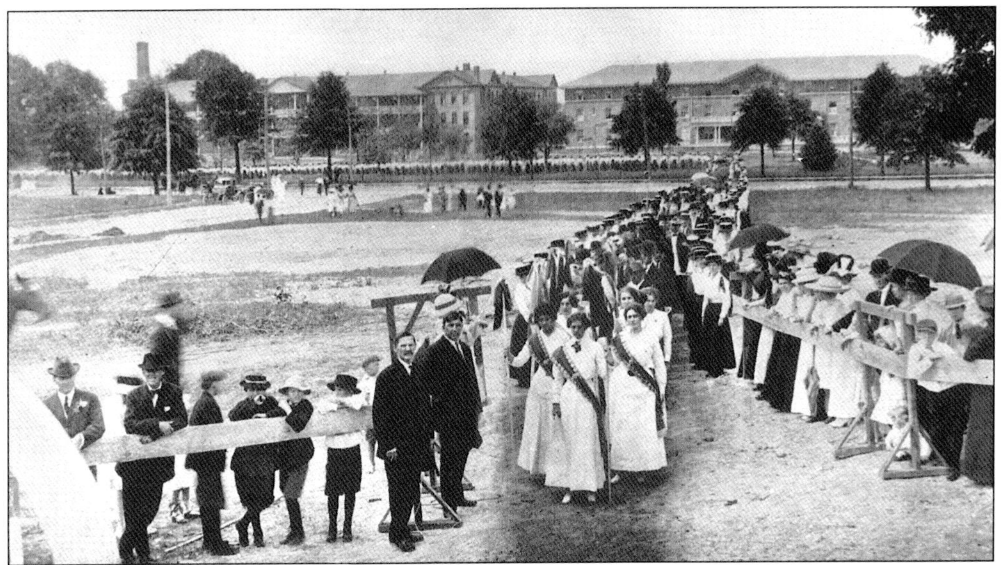

This photograph shows the ceremonies for the laying of the Winthrop Training School cornerstone in 1912. Believed to have been inspired by the famous Tudor-Gothic Hampton Court Palace in England, the building cost $125,000. In 1969, it was renamed in honor of Sarah Withers, the first principal of the Training School. In 1981, the building was placed on the National Register of Historic Places. Withers now houses the College of Education.

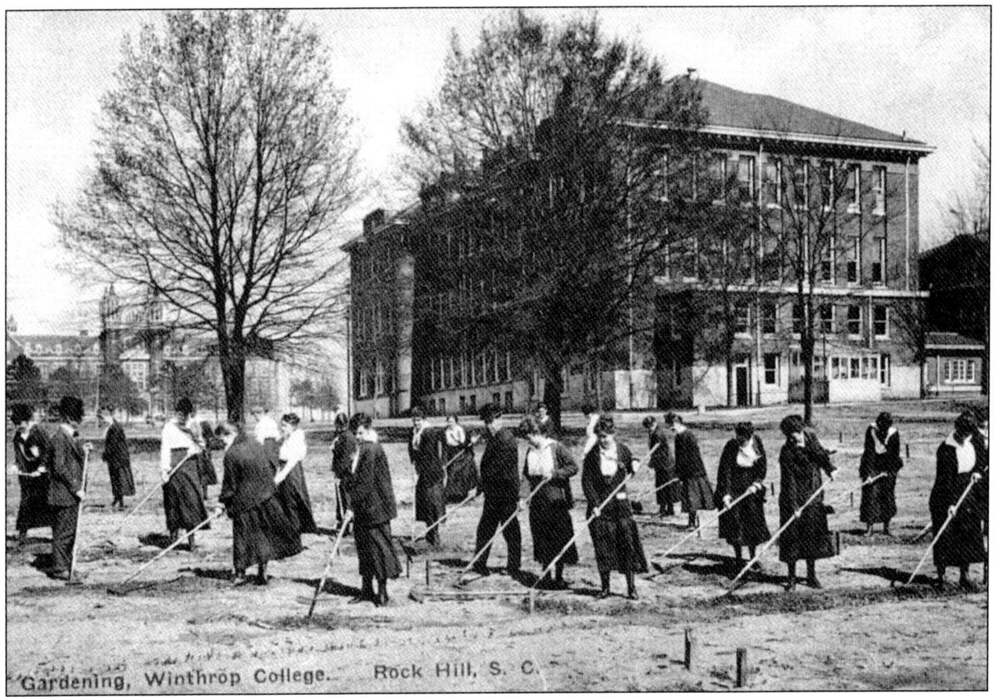

Vegetables and poultry were raised not just on the College Farm, but at other places on campus, including D.B. Johnson's private garden and, as this 1916 photo shows, in practice plots for students on the north side of the campus.

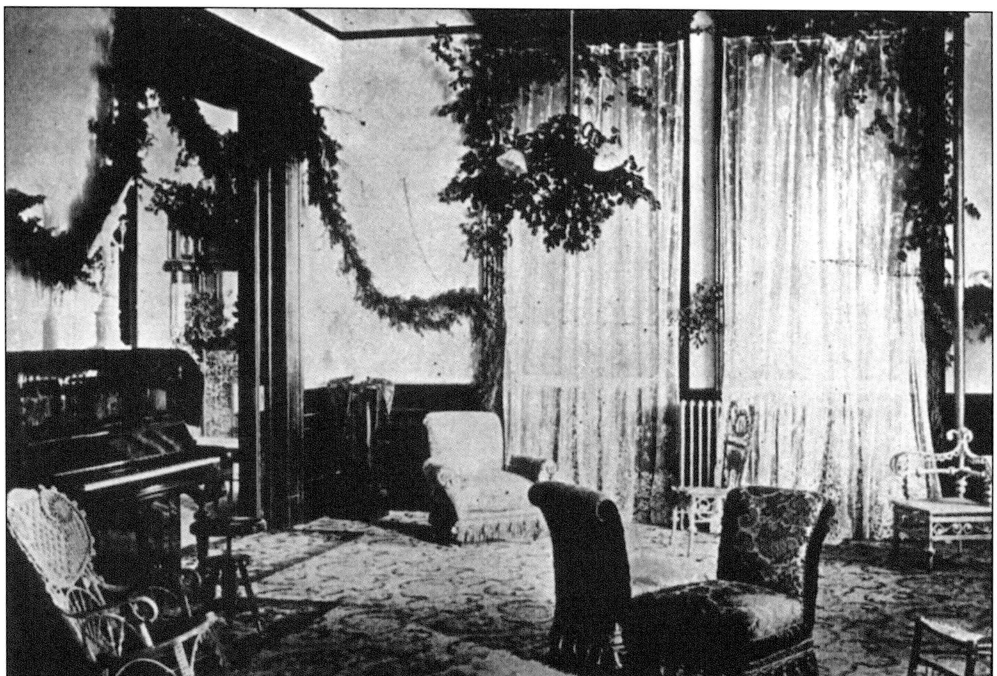

A brightly decorated reception parlor in Main Building reflects the Christmas spirit at the turn of the 19th century.

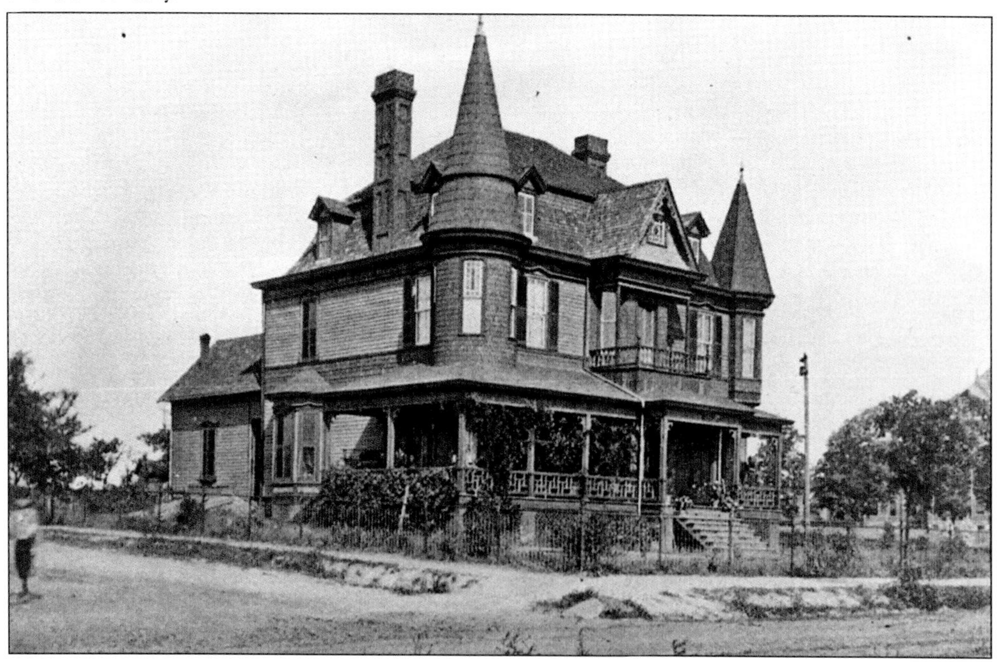

The President's House is seen here as it looked before renovation radically changed the exterior; the balconies, turrets, and bay windows were removed. Built by W.H. Stewart of the Rock Hill Land and Town Site Company as his private residence, the President's House was included in Rock Hill's 1893 bid to move Winthrop from Columbia to the city. The residence was fashioned in the Queen Anne Victorian style.

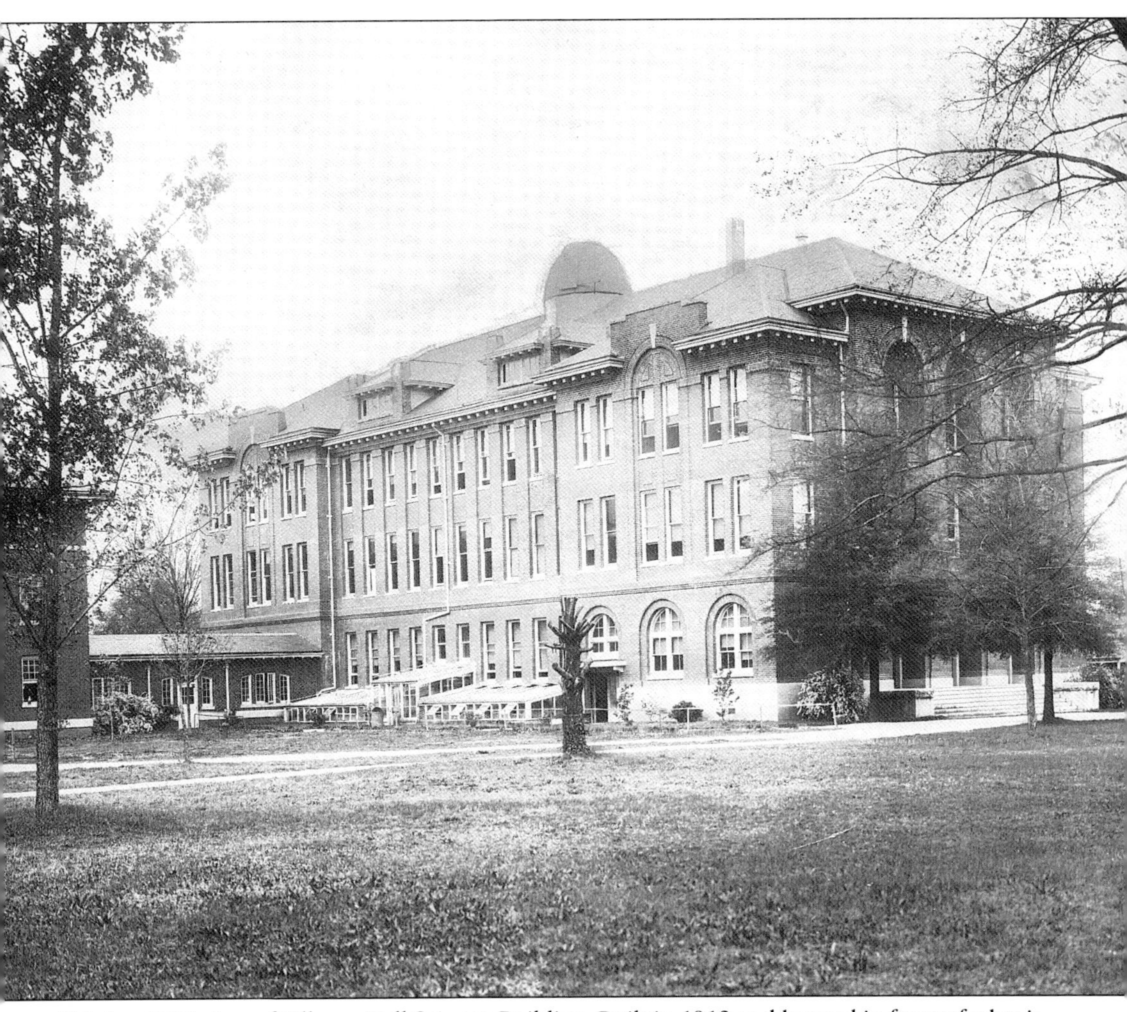

This is a 1920 view of Tillman Hall Science Building. Built in 1912 and located in front of what is today the Kinard building, Tillman Hall was razed in 1962.

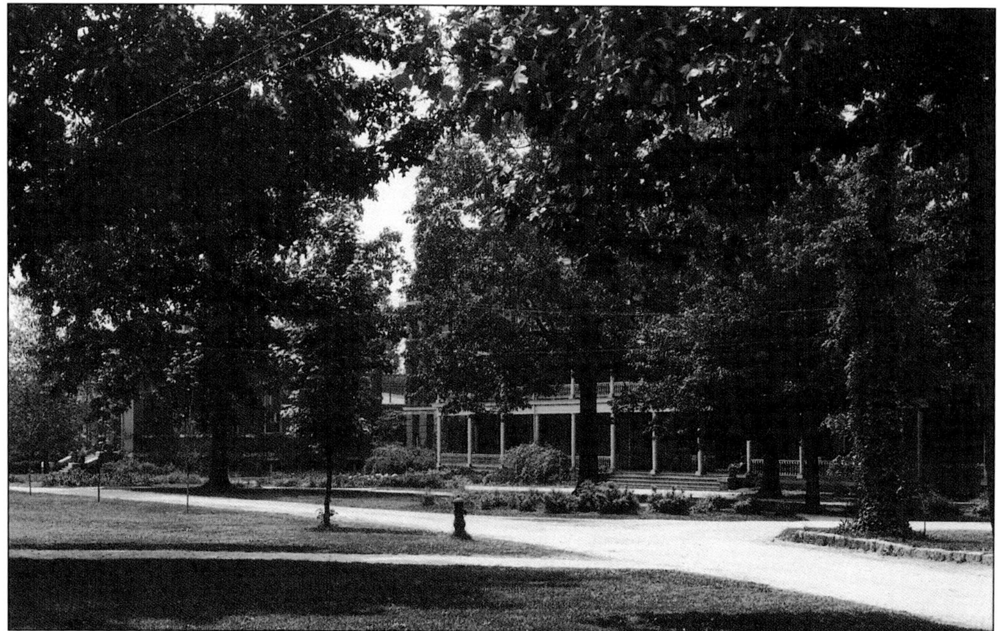

This is a rustic 1920s view of McLaurin Hall (left) and the Carnegie Library (right). Built by money donated by Andrew Carnegie, the famed industrialist and philanthropist, the building served as the library until 1969, when Dacus Library opened. Renamed "Rutledge," in honor of the middle name of Mrs. D.B. Johnson, the building today serves the Art Department.

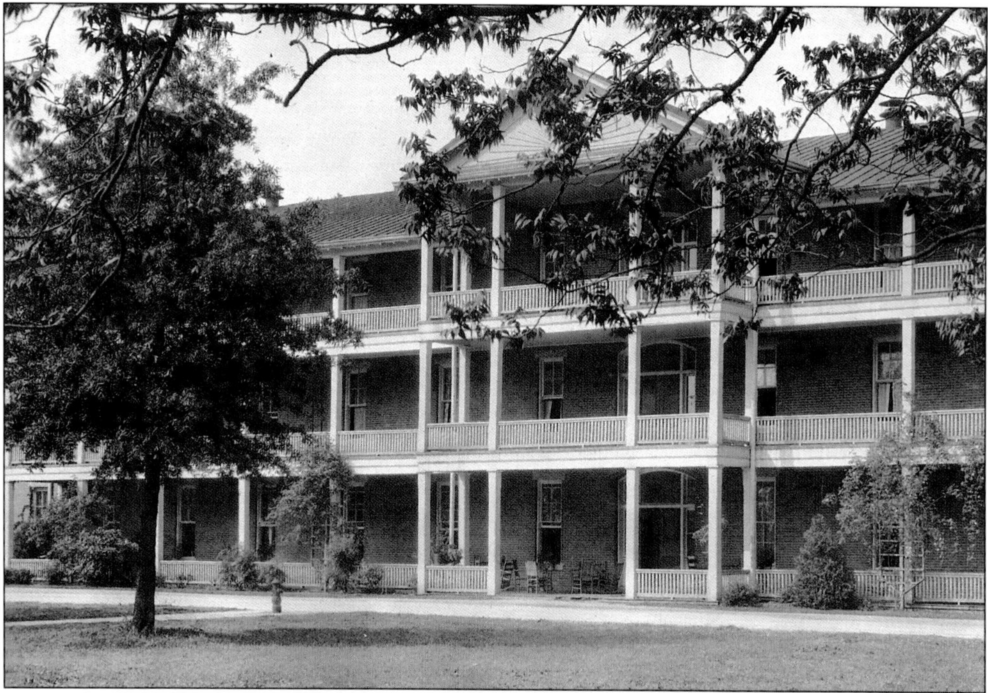

Margaret Nance is seen here as it looked in the 1920s. The building was closed in 1973 and then one floor was reopened in 1978 to house fraternity and sorority offices. Today, Margaret Nance is a residence hall for female students.

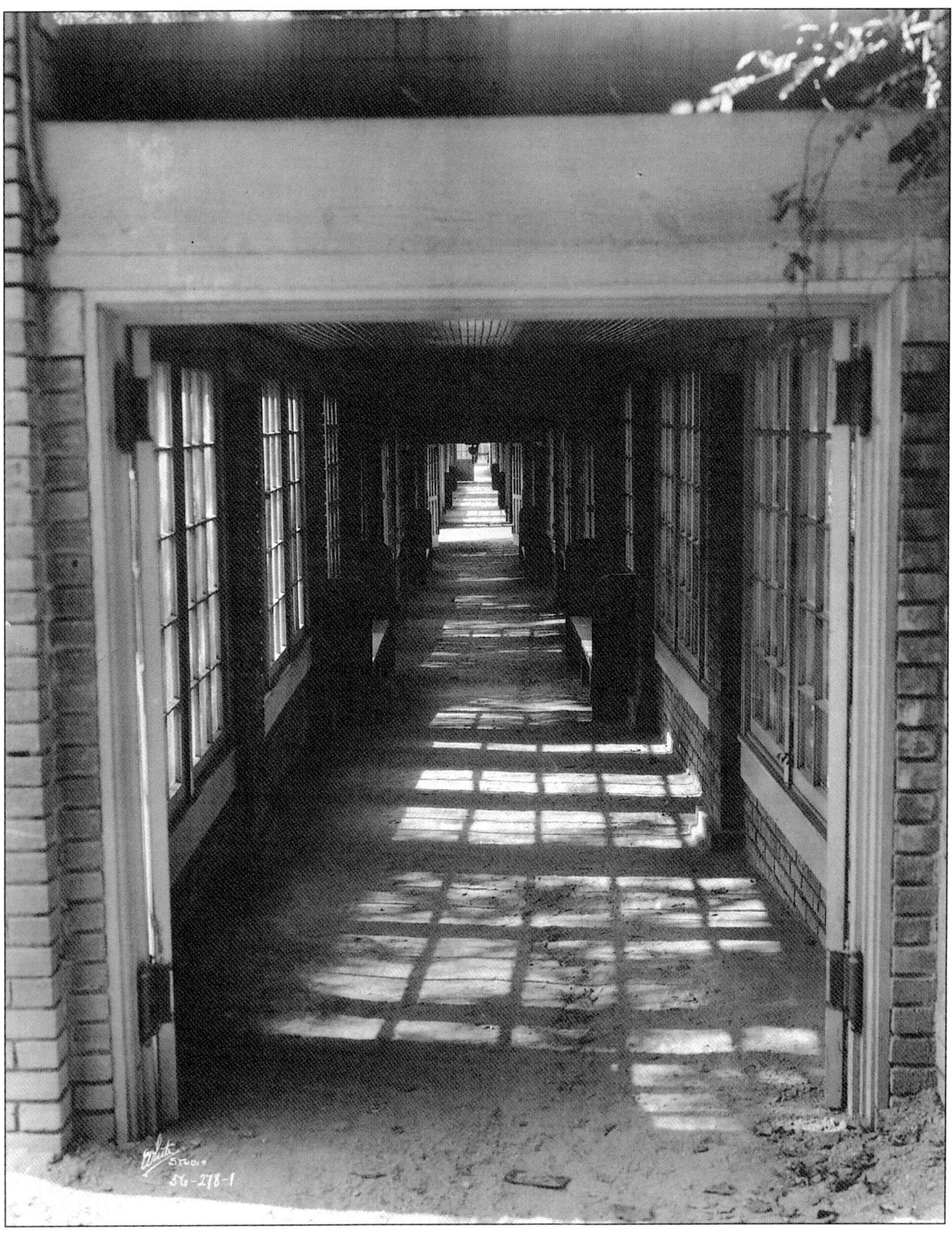

This photograph reveals the interior of the covered way leading from Main Building to Margaret Nance. Later a brick floor was added.

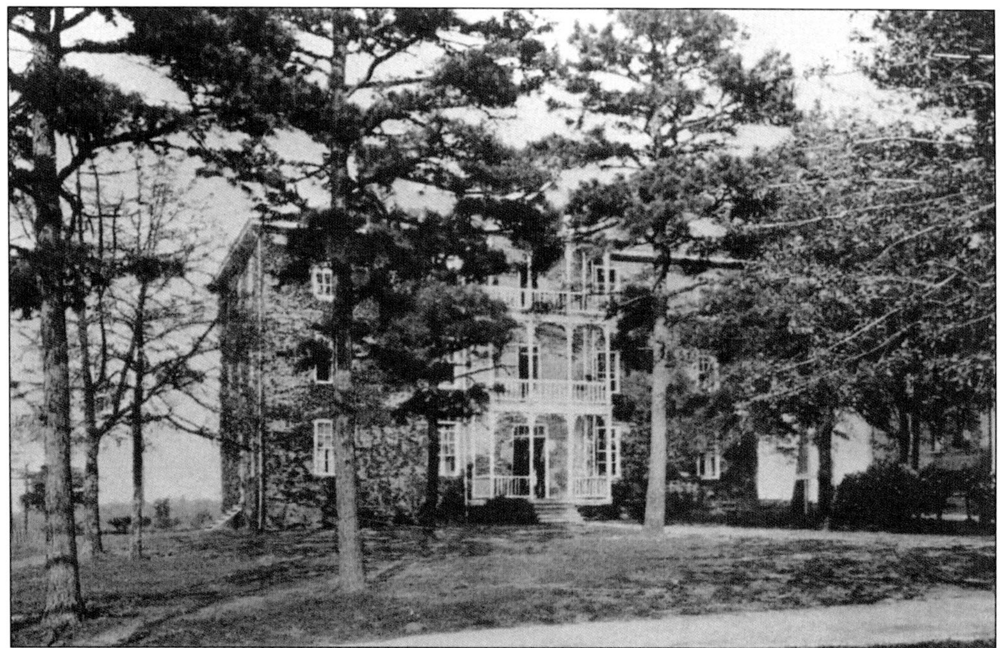

Catawba Hall was completed in 1891 north of what is now Withers Building. It was originally the dormitory of the Rock Hill Presbyterian High School and was later used as a faculty resident and then a storage house. The building was razed in 1968.

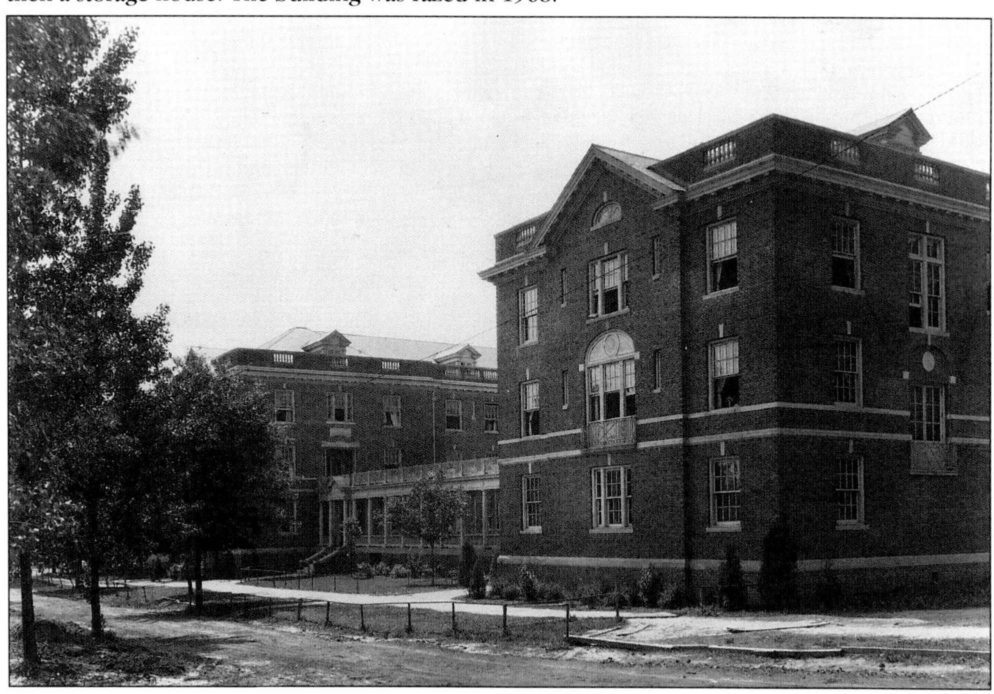

Roddey Hall, seen here in the 1920s, was formerly known as West Dormitory. In 1973, the building was renamed in honor of William Joseph Roddey, an original member of the Winthrop Board of Trustees (1893–1945) from Rock Hill, and was converted into efficiency apartments for students.

This is Byrnes Auditorium as it looked soon after its construction in 1939. Byrnes Auditorium and Conservatory of Music is named in honor of James F. Byrnes, former governor of South Carolina and secretary of state (1945–1947), who helped get funds from the Public Works Administration to match state funds and construct the auditorium as well as Thurmond Building.

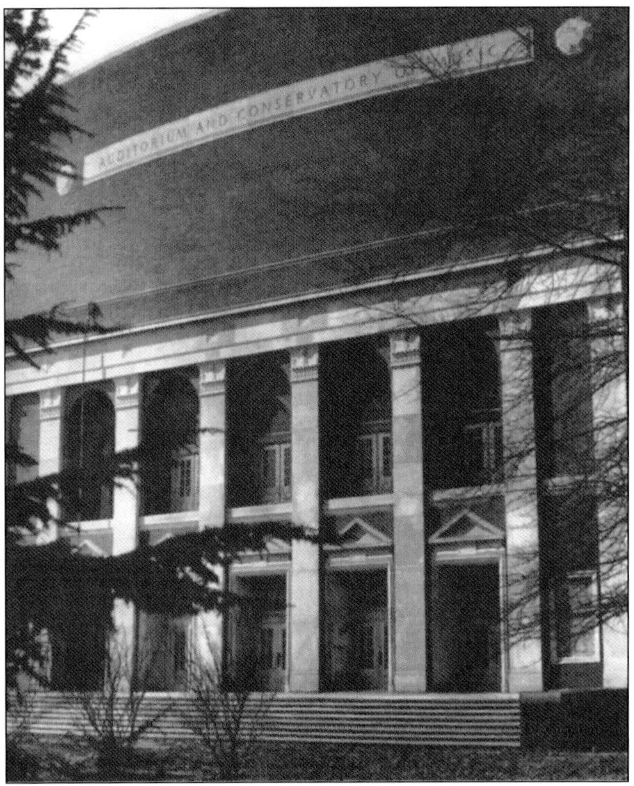

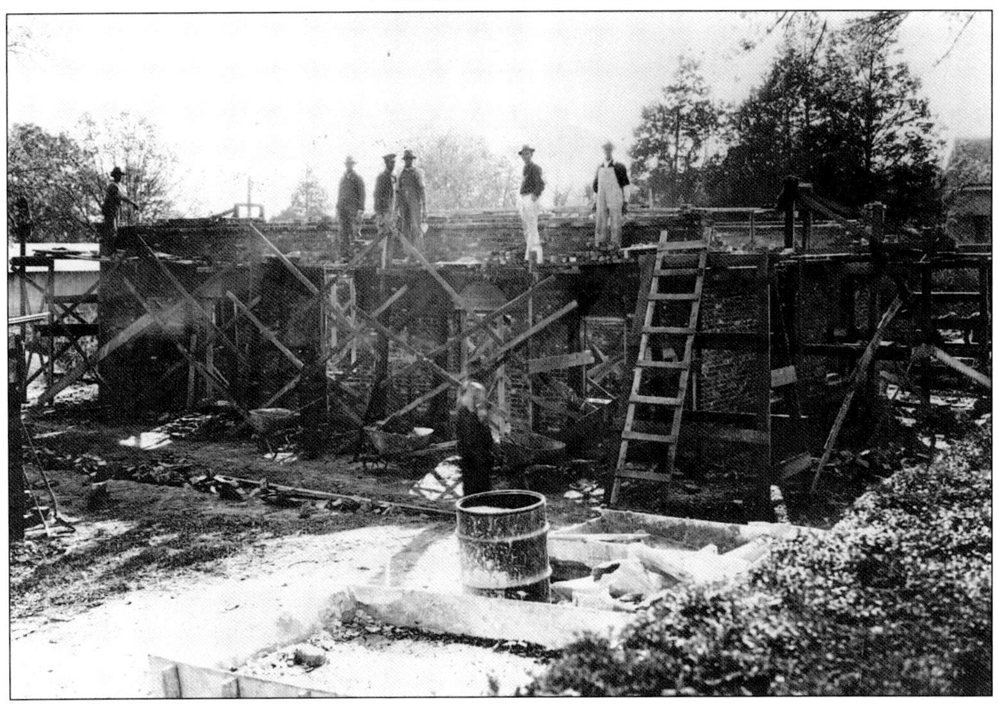

In 1936, the Little Chapel was transferred brick by brick from Columbia to Rock Hill. Here are some of the workers who reconstructed the building exactly as it stood in the state capitol.

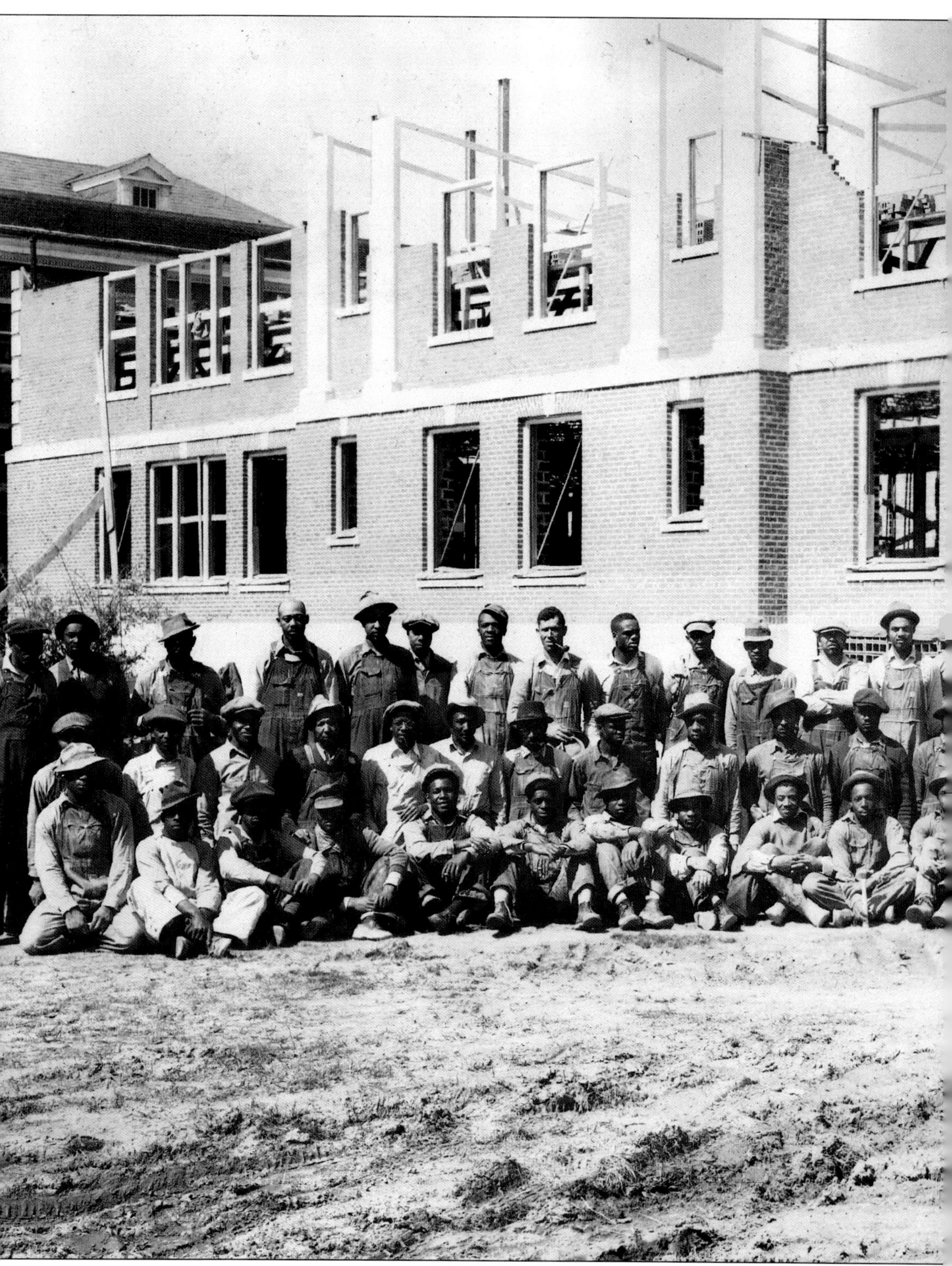

This photograph captures the workers who built Phelps Hall in 1942. Completed the following year, the building is named in honor of Dr. Shelton Phelps, Winthrop's third president (1934–

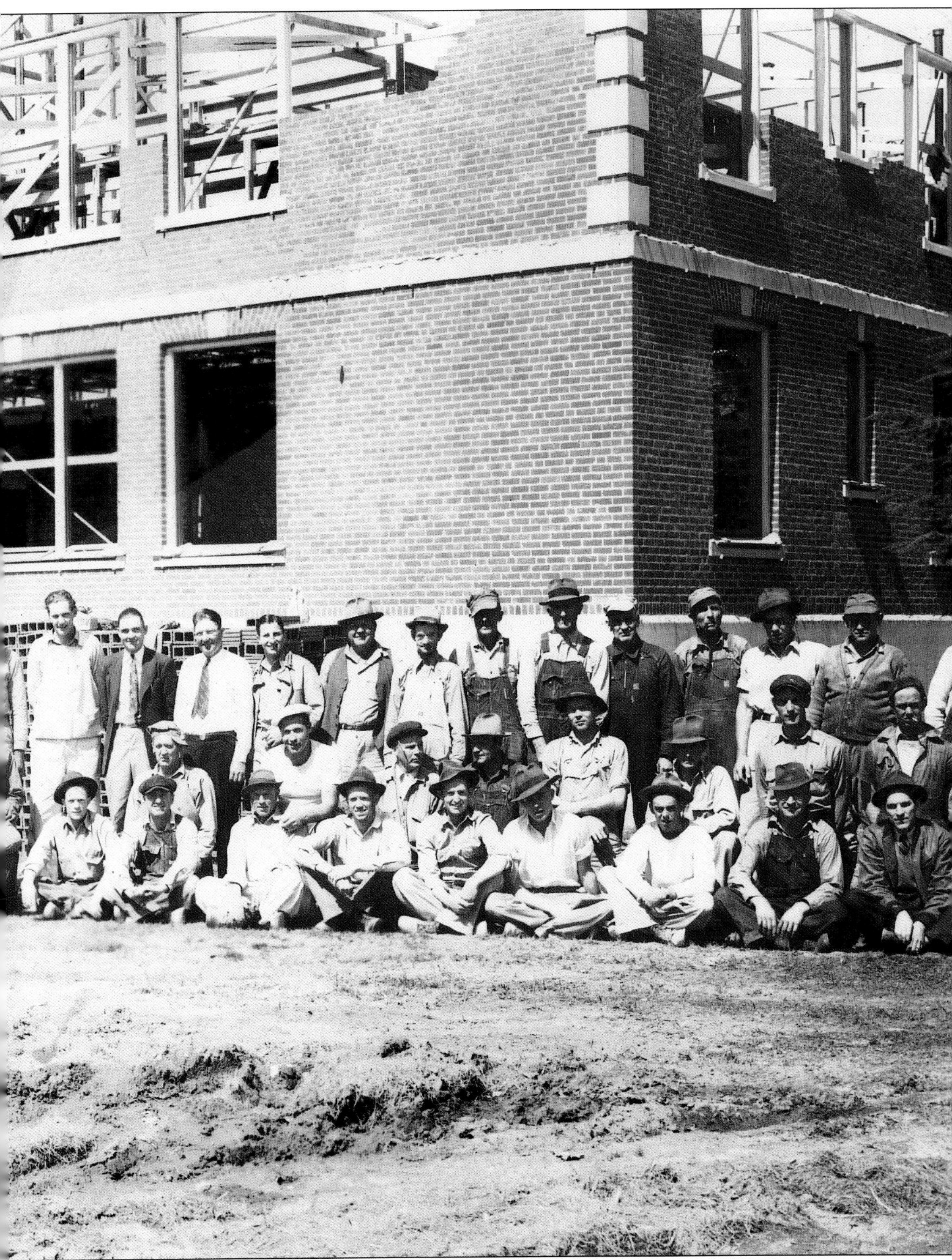

1943). At one time called Senior Hall, Phelps was initially used as a Senior Residence Hall. A new wing was added in 1962. Today, Phelps is a residence hall for female students.

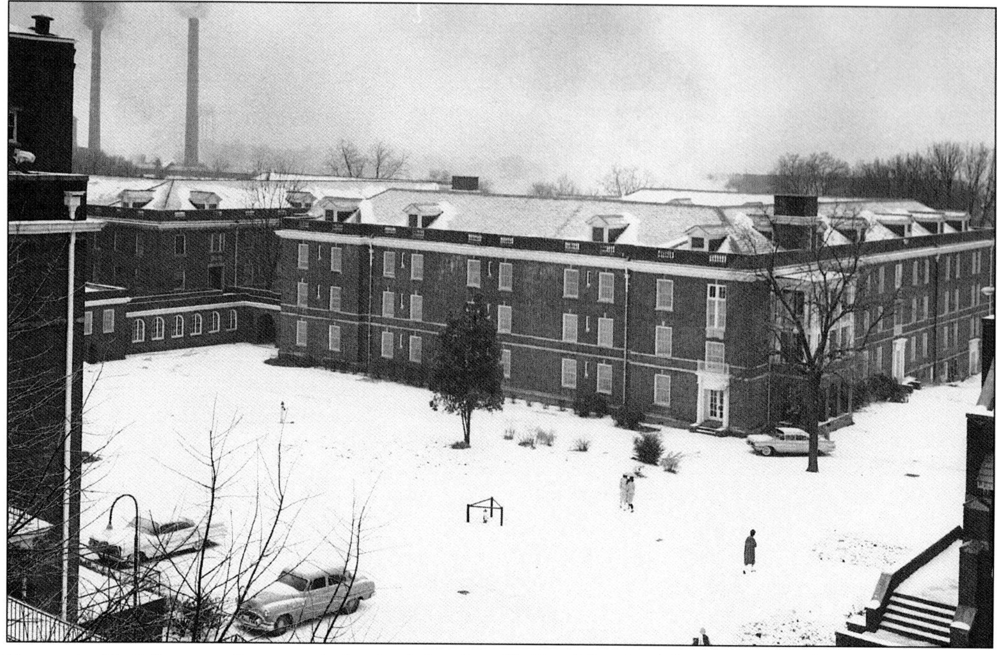

Brazeale Hall is seen here as it looked in the 1940s. The building is named in honor of J.E. Brazeale of the Winthrop Board of Trustees (1919–1926). The building was closed in 1972 and reopened as student apartments in 1977.

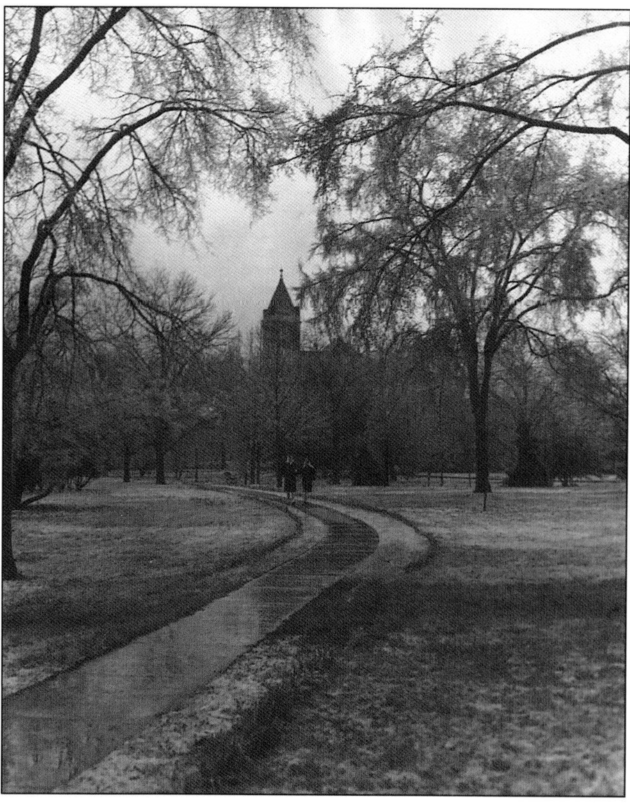

This is a picturesque view of the campus in 1948.

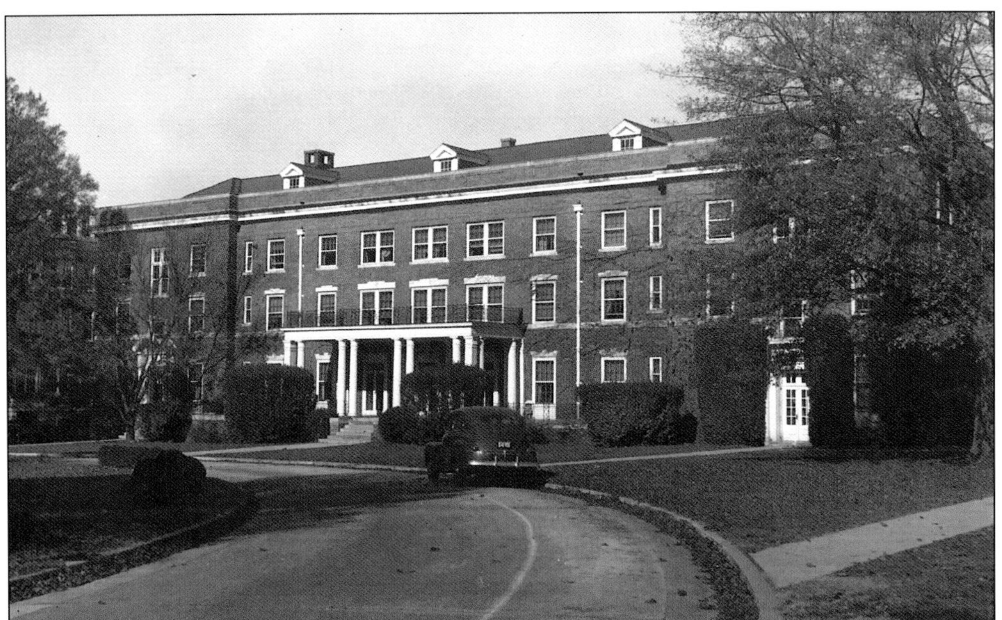

This photograph shows Joynes Hall about 1949. Built in 1926, Joynes was originally named Winthrop's Teachers Dormitory and used as a residence hall for single faculty members. In 1969, it was converted to a residence hall for foreign students but closed in 1973 because the administration felt foreign students would benefit more from closer contact with American students. In 1973, the inside was remodeled and it became the Joynes Center for Continuing Education, so named in honor of Edward Southey Joynes, a former member of the Board of Trustees (1886–1917).

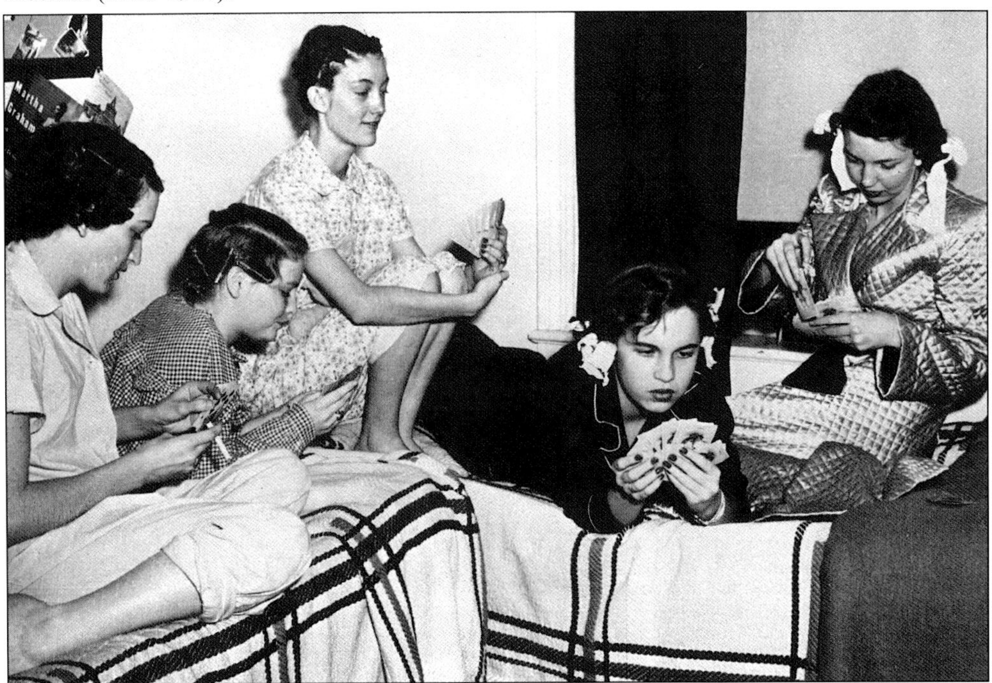

These students are relaxing and playing cards about 1950.

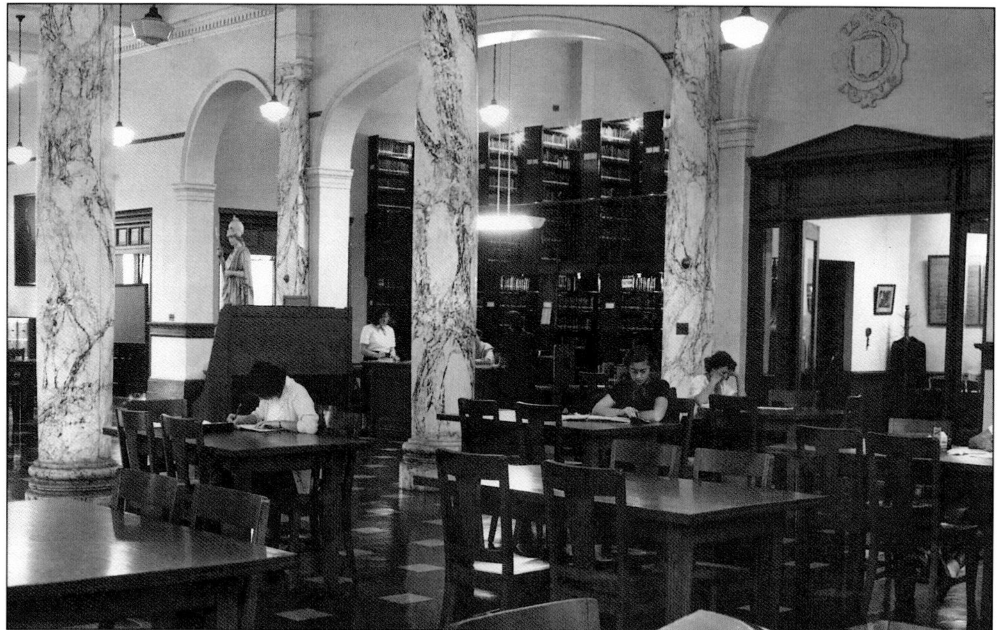

The Carnegie Library, seen here about 1955, is an example of the Classical Revival architectural style, which incorporates features of the French Imperial design popularized under the reigns of Louis XIV and Napoleon III.

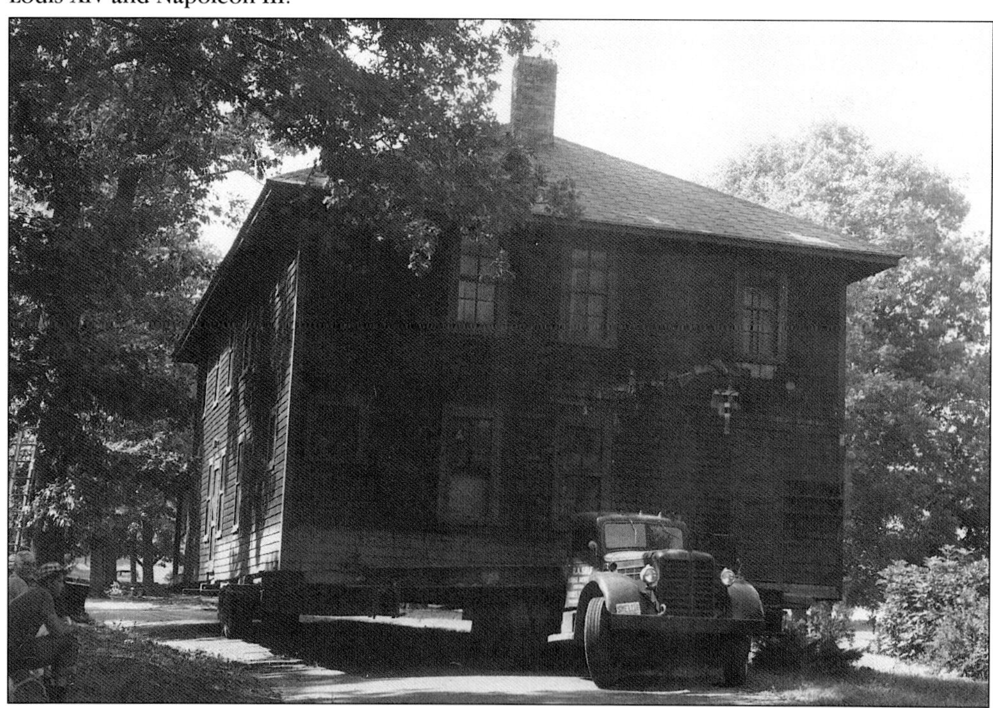

About 1960, the College Shack was moved a number of feet east to be brick veneered and enlarged. The students referred to the shack at the time as "Charlie's Chateau," for Winthrop president Dr. Charles S. Davis, who served from 1959 to 1973. The Shack was originally built in 1932.

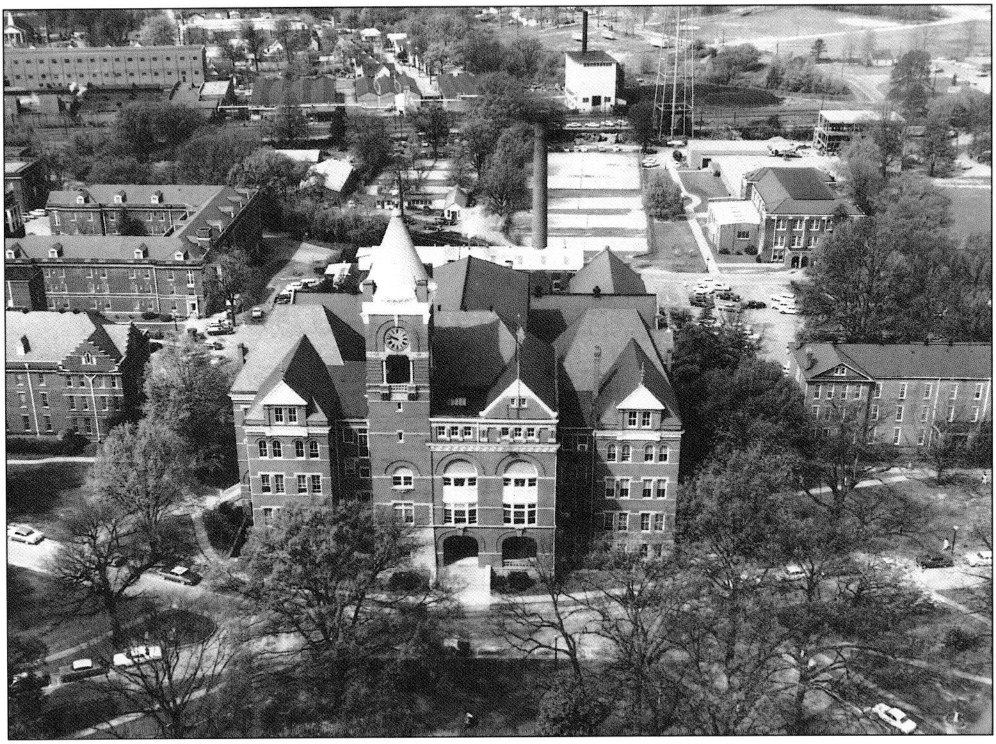

This photograph provides an aerial view of Tillman and part of the Winthrop campus in April 1964.

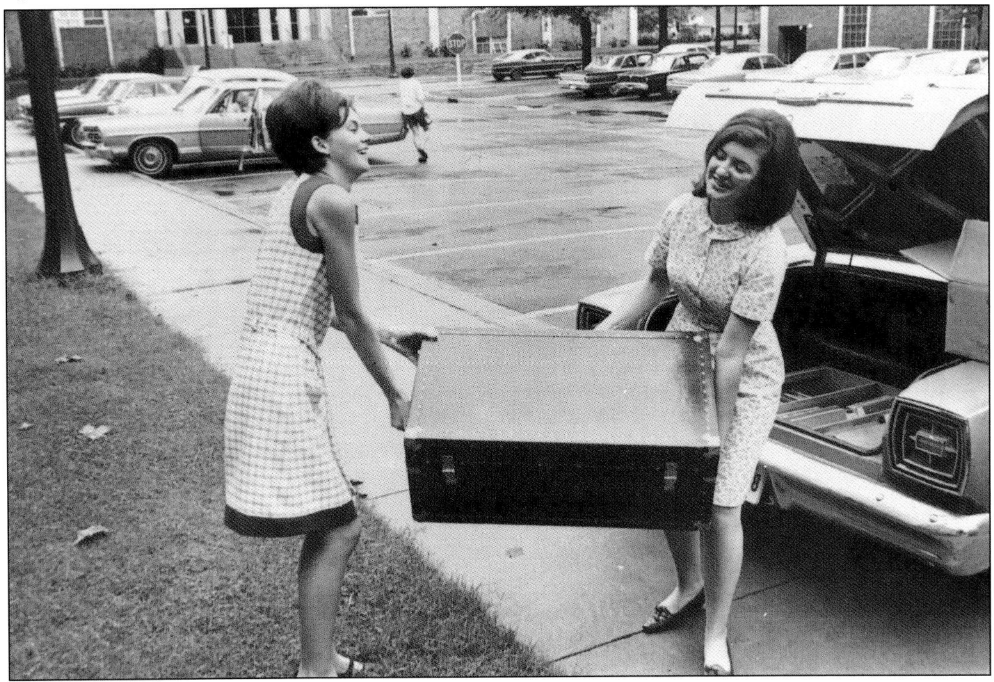

This is a familiar scene at Winthrop played out each year. Students Brenda Johnson (left) and Beverly Hall are moving back on campus in 1967 for another school year.

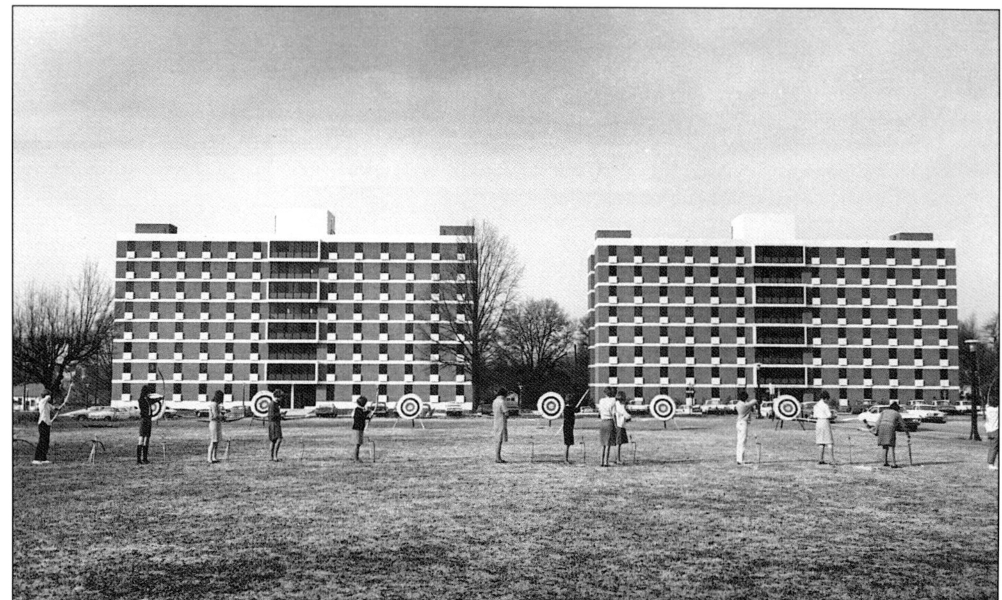

The archery range, seen in April 1968, stands before the dramatic backdrop of Richardson Hall and Wofford Hall. Richardson is named for former South Carolina governor John Peter Richardson Jr., who recommended the establishment of a state college for women in 1894. Wofford Hall is named for Kate V. Wofford, a 1916 Winthrop graduate who became a professor of education at the University of Florida and was the first woman president of the South Carolina Education Association.

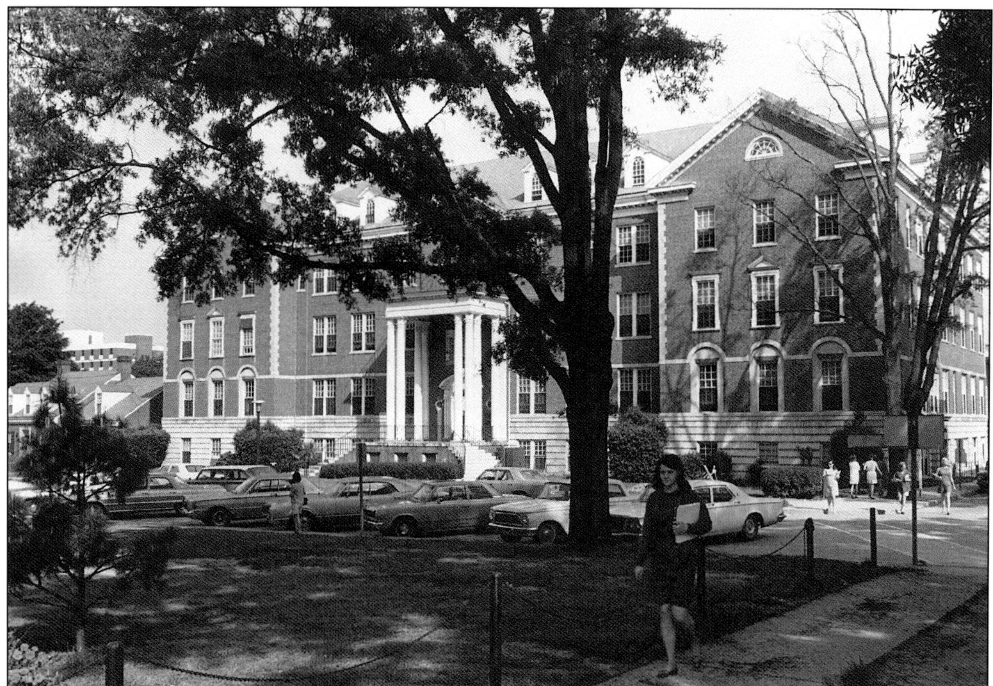

This is Thurmond Hall as it looked in 1969. The building was constructed to house the School of Home Economics program. Today, it is the center for the College of Business.

The Lee Wicker building, photographed in 1969, was named for Mrs. Lee Wicker Kinard. She was the wife of Winthrop's second president, Dr. James P. Kinard, who served from 1928 to 1934. The building was originally a residence hall for seniors but today houses female residents of all class ranks.

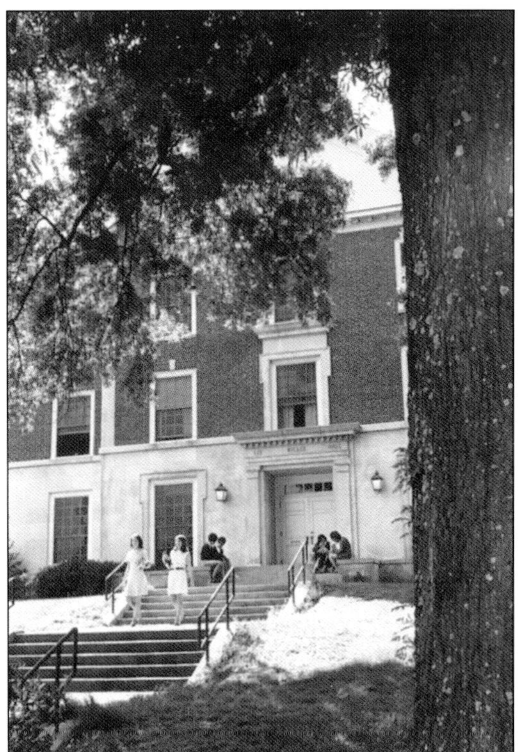

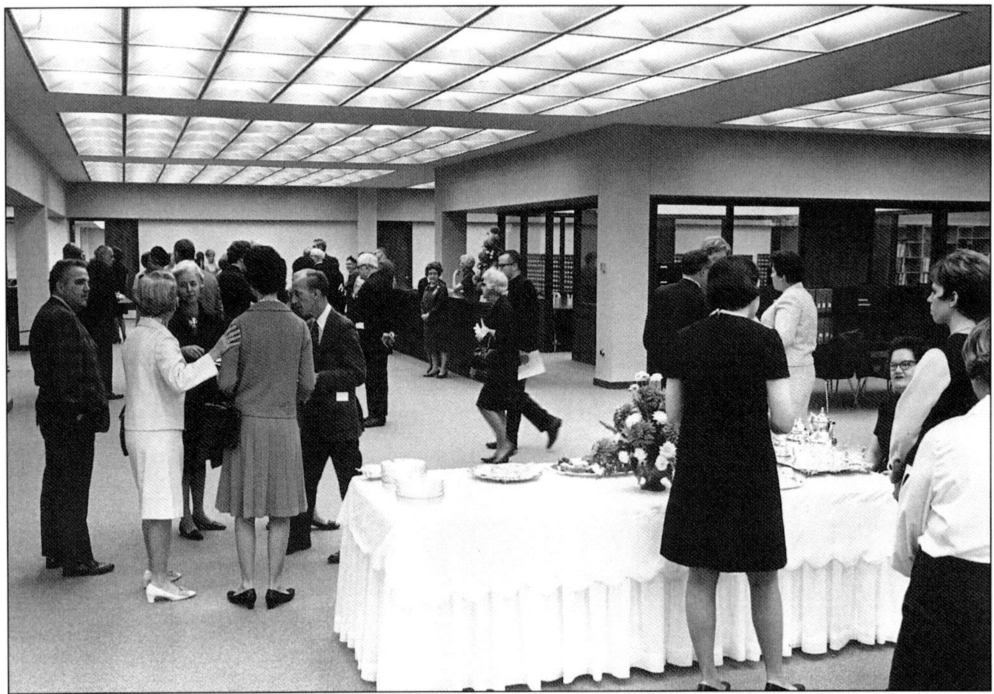

This photograph captures the dedication of the new Dacus Library in 1969. The building is named for Ida Jane Dacus, Winthrop's first librarian, who was also the first South Carolina person to receive professional training in librarianship.

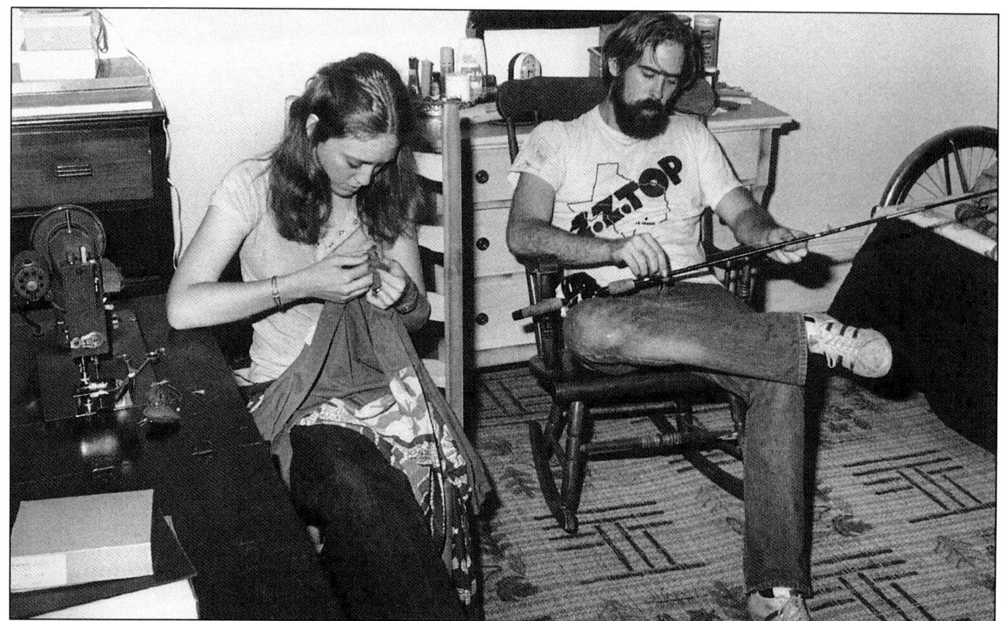

Students Judy and Jim Clayton relax in their Roddey Hall apartment in April 1975.

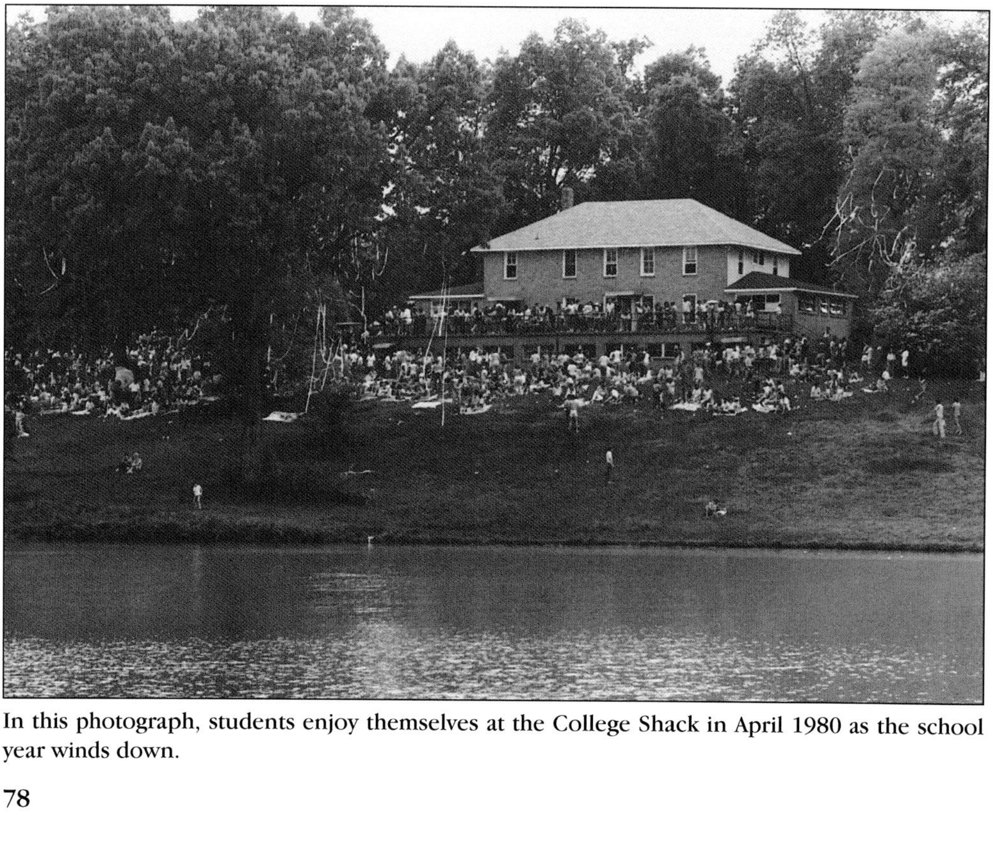

In this photograph, students enjoy themselves at the College Shack in April 1980 as the school year winds down.

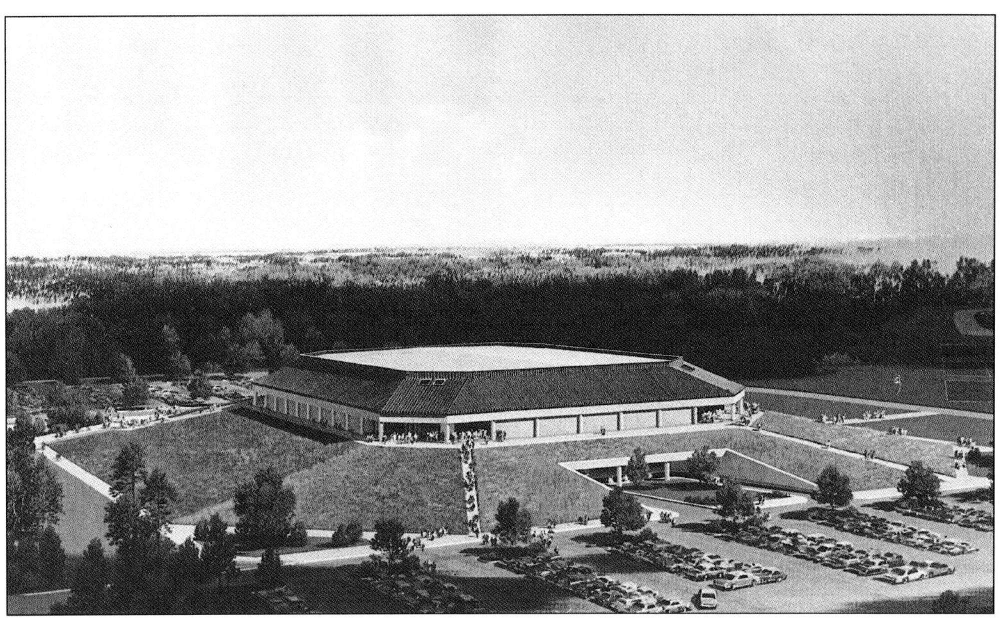

Built in 1982, Winthrop's Coliseum can seat 6,000 people and is designed to accommodate athletic events, musical concerts, and trade shows.

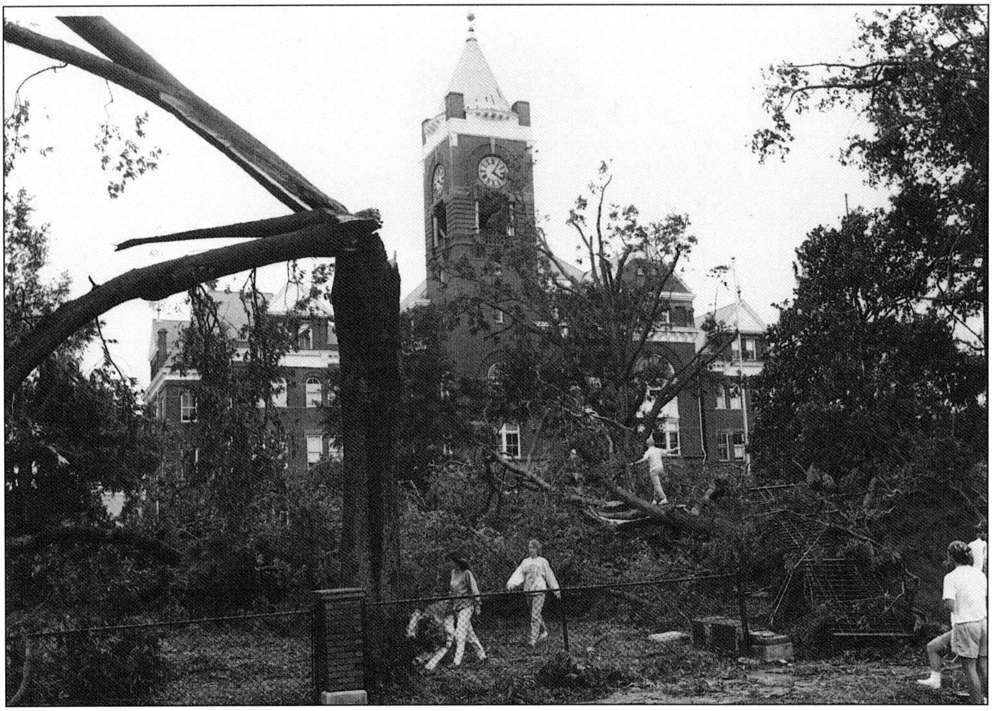

Winthrop managed to survive the wrath and devastation of Hurricane Hugo in September 1989, but it did have an impact on Winthrop's beautiful campus.

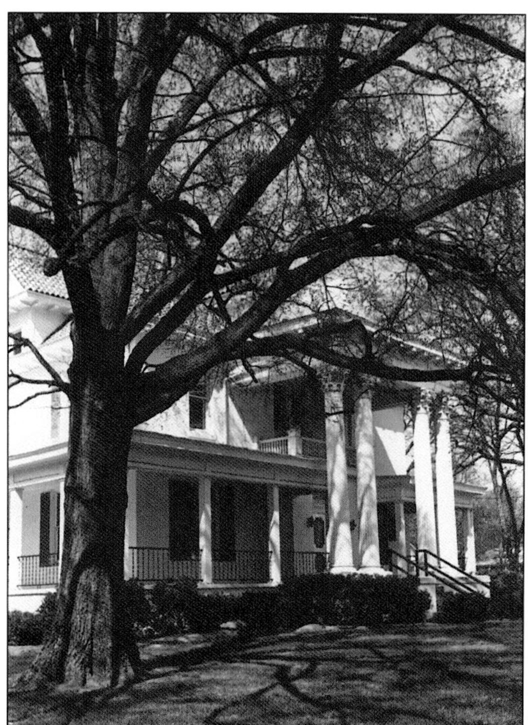

The Stewart House, seen about 1982, housed the Alumni Association. The building was purchased from Mr. W.H. Stewart in 1912 for $10,000. Initially, it was the Home Management House, the place where all Winthrop seniors practiced the details of housekeeping. The building has also housed the International Center, and today, the Admissions Office.

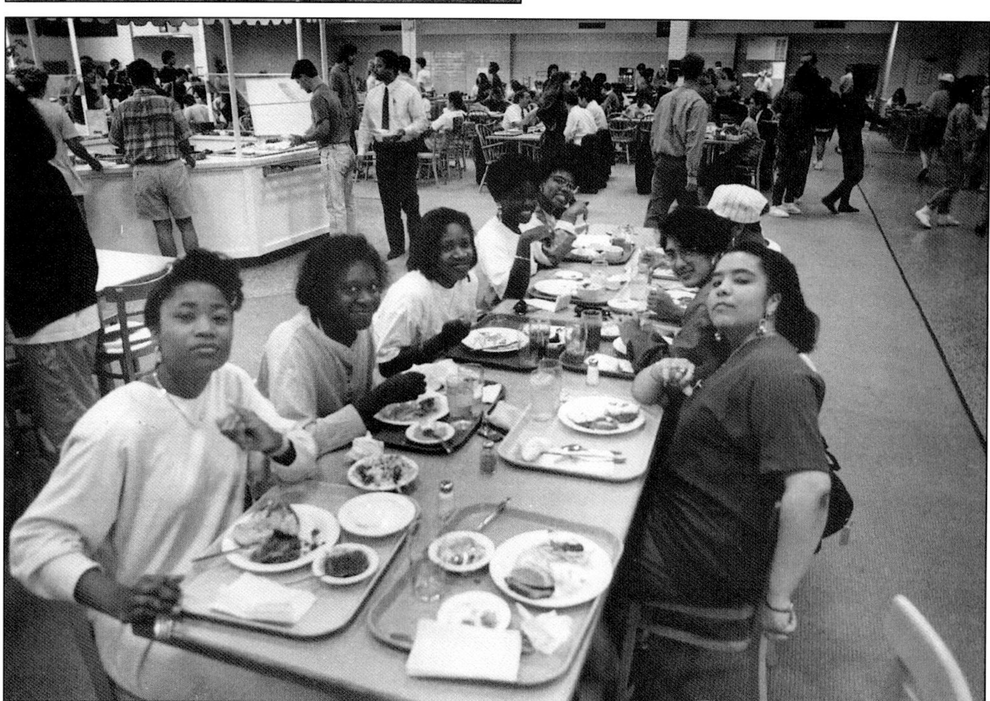

Students enjoy a meal in the Thomson Cafeteria in April 1992. Constructed in 1962, the building is named for Dr. James William Thomson, a Winthrop faculty member from 1898 to 1930, who also served as Dean of the College during this time. Today, Thomson is a co-ed residence hall for sophomores, juniors, and seniors.

Four

Faculty and Staff: A Tradition of Professionalism

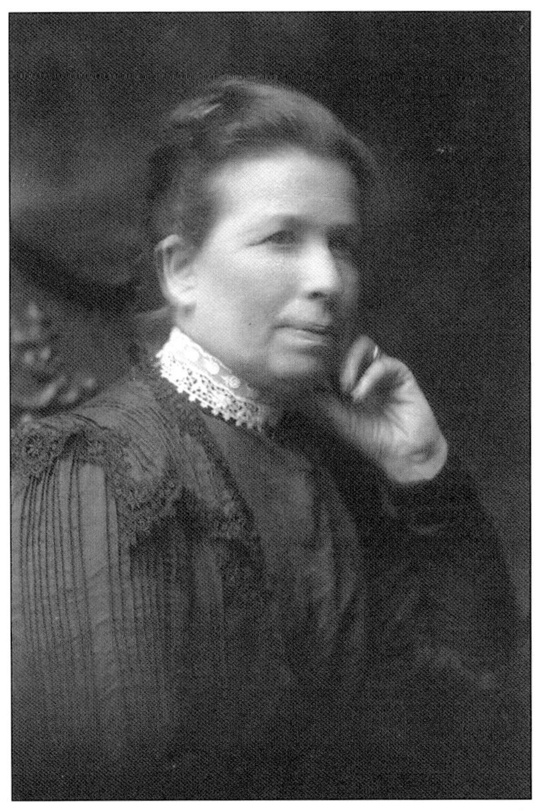

Mary Hall Leonard, Winthrop's first teacher, was handpicked by President D.B. Johnson. Miss Leonard was working at the Bridgewater Normal School in Massachusetts when Johnson went to see her and talked her into coming south to help him start his first school.

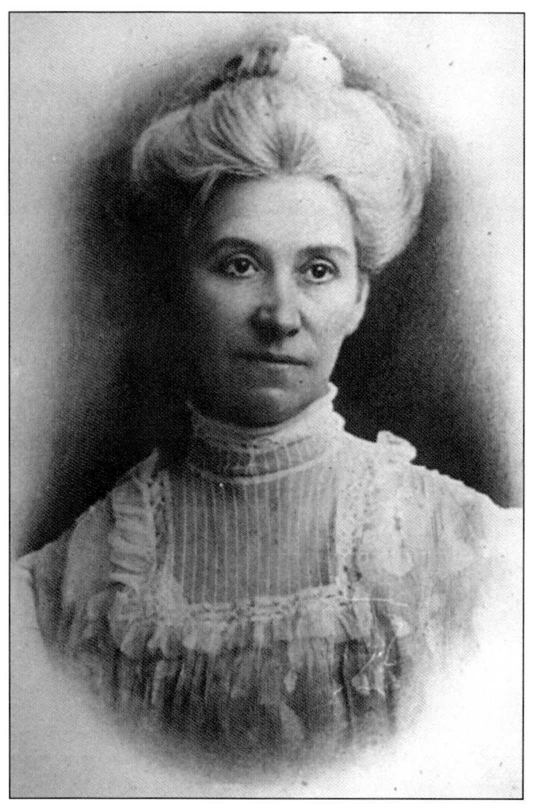

When President Johnson organized the Winthrop Training School in Columbia, he chose Annie Bonham to train students wanting to become elementary schoolteachers. She did such a superb job that most of her students went on to find careers as teachers in colleges and state departments of education across the country. Dr. Johnson was extremely disappointed when Miss Bonham did not follow him to Rock Hill in 1895. Instead, she opened her own private school in Columbia, an open-air school, which was based on the philosophy that physical education was the basis for good health. It may have been the first open-air school in the South.

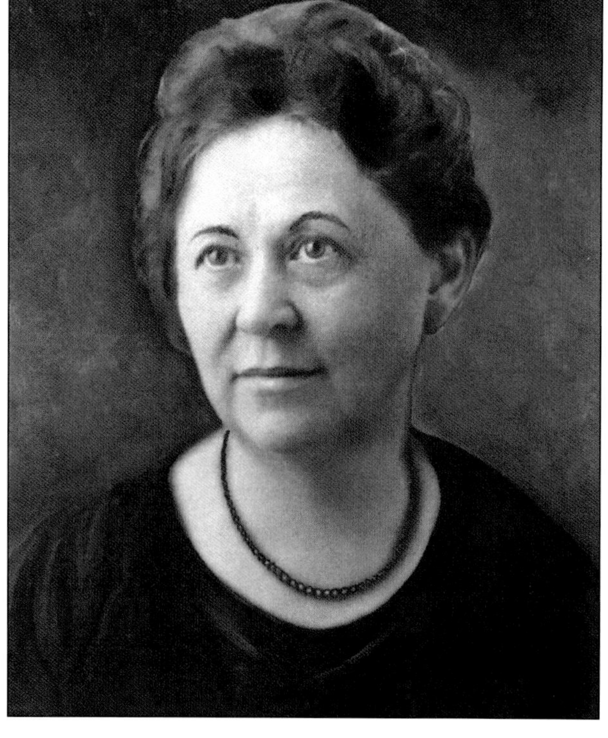

Miss Minnie Macfeat, an 1888 alumna of Winthrop, was instrumental in establishing the preschool education at Winthrop. The first Winthrop preschool course was offered in 1900, the year Winthrop's laboratory kindergarten opened under the direction of Minnie Macfeat. The Macfeat Nursery was later named in her honor.

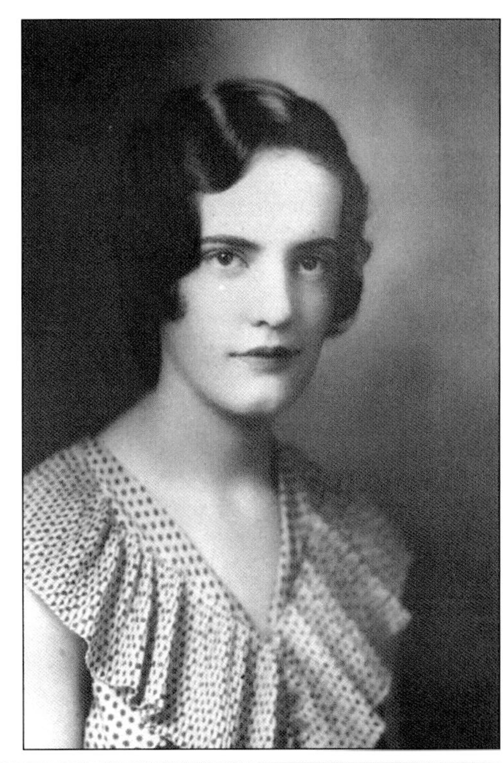

Mary Elizabeth Frayser (1868–1968) came to Winthrop from Richmond, Virginia, in 1912 as the state agent for rural and mill village community extension work. She became one of the South's outstanding women leaders in twentieth-century South Carolina. Later, she started one of the first night schools for mill employees in the state and was involved in the South Carolina Interracial Institute, the South Carolina Congress of Parents and Teachers, the South Carolina League of Women Voters, the South Carolina Federation of Women's Clubs, and the South Carolina Federation of Business and Professional Women' Clubs, among other organizations. Miss Frayser was also instrumental in helping to create the South Carolina public library system.

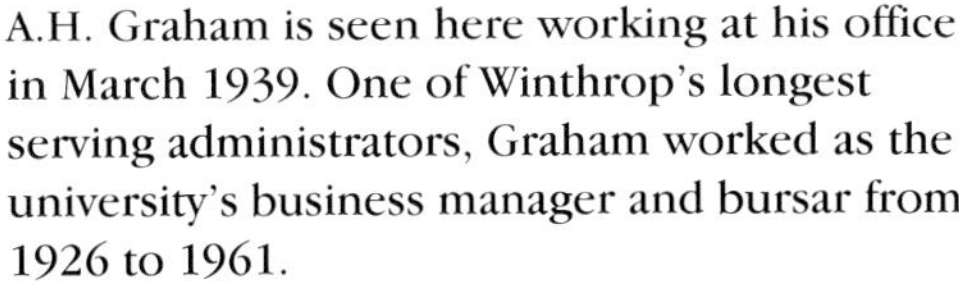

A.H. Graham is seen here working at his office in March 1939. One of Winthrop's longest serving administrators, Graham worked as the university's business manager and bursar from 1926 to 1961.

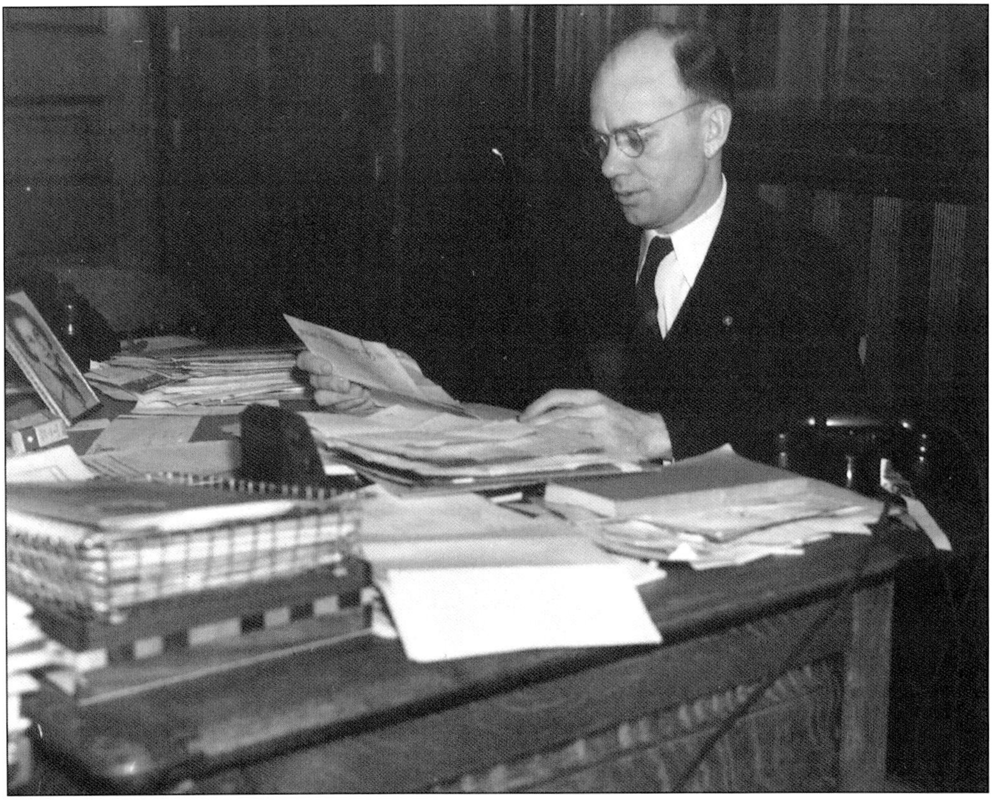

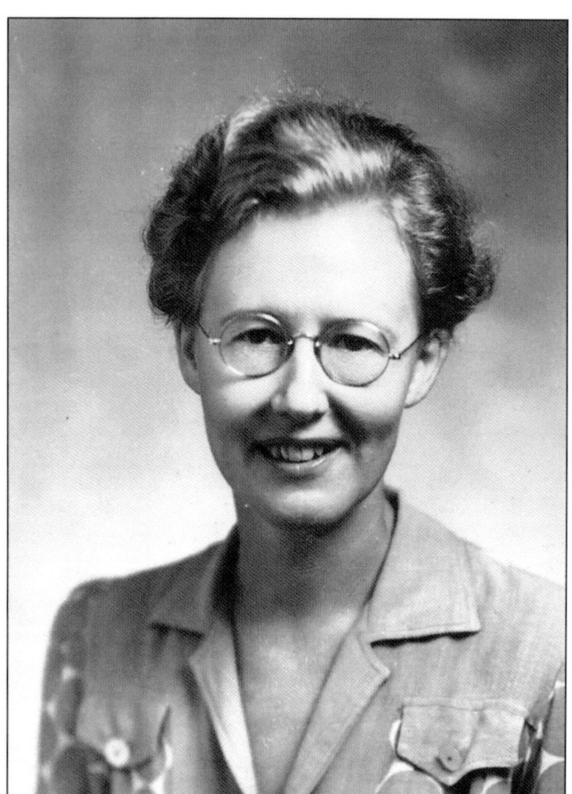

A Winthrop professor of government from 1927 to 1931 and from 1937 to 1952, Dr. Ruth Roettinger was a frequent speaker on political subjects and women's issues. Dr. Roettinger died in 1956.

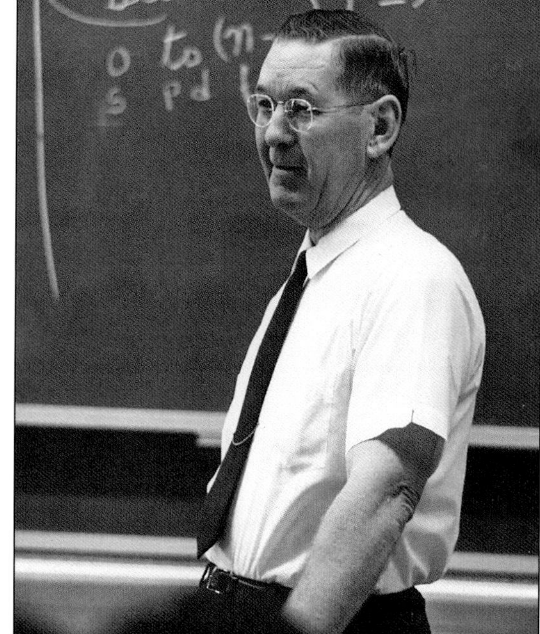

Known to his students as "Fessor," Ralph E. Blakeley taught chemistry and physics at Winthrop from 1922 to 1929 and from 1943 to 1965. Blakeley received his B.A. degree from Erskine College and his Master's from Vanderbilt University. He died in 1993 at age 92.

Dr. Hampton Jarrell served Winthrop as a professor of English from 1932 to 1969 and as the English Department's chair from 1954 to 1969. Dr. Jarrell was a scholar and frequent speaker at the Catawba Region's civic, literary, and women's clubs. Dr. Jarrell authored *Wade Hampton and the Negro: The Road Not Taken*, which he published in 1949.

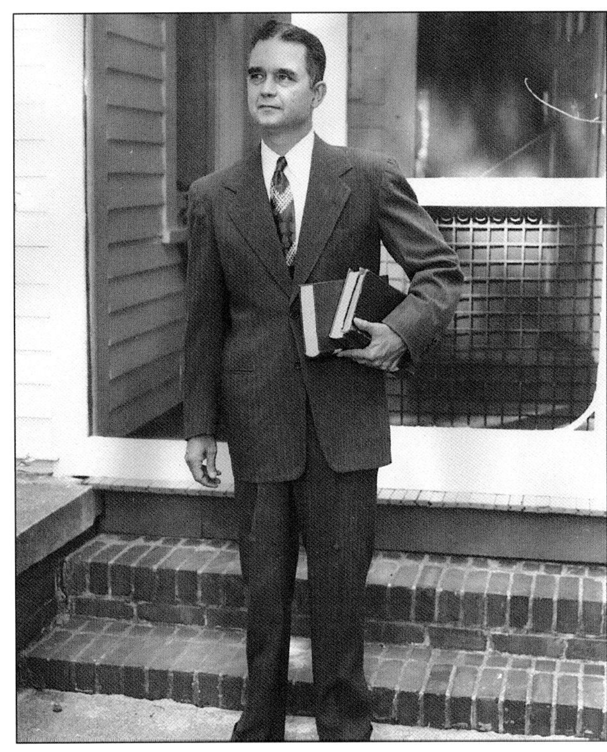

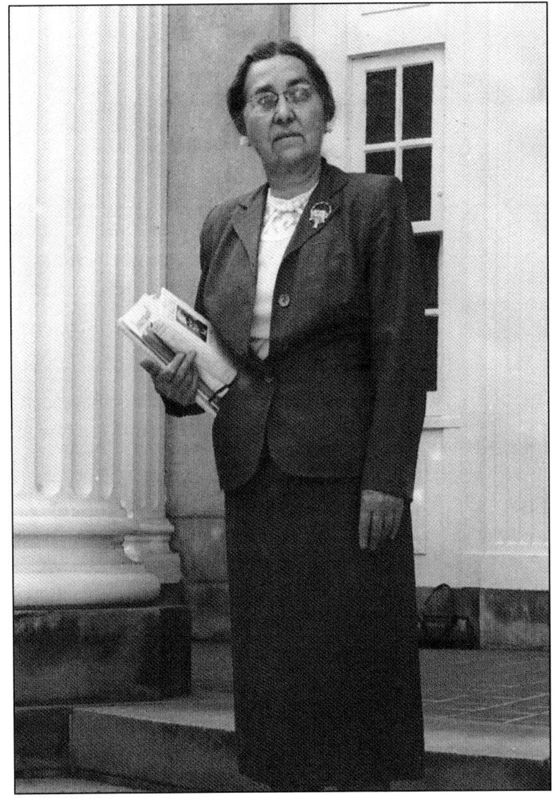

Dr. Elizabeth Johnson was head of the Modern Languages Department from 1952 to 1953 and poet laureate of the South Carolina Federation of Women's Clubs from 1937 to 1941. Dr. Johnson died in 1979 at the age of 88.

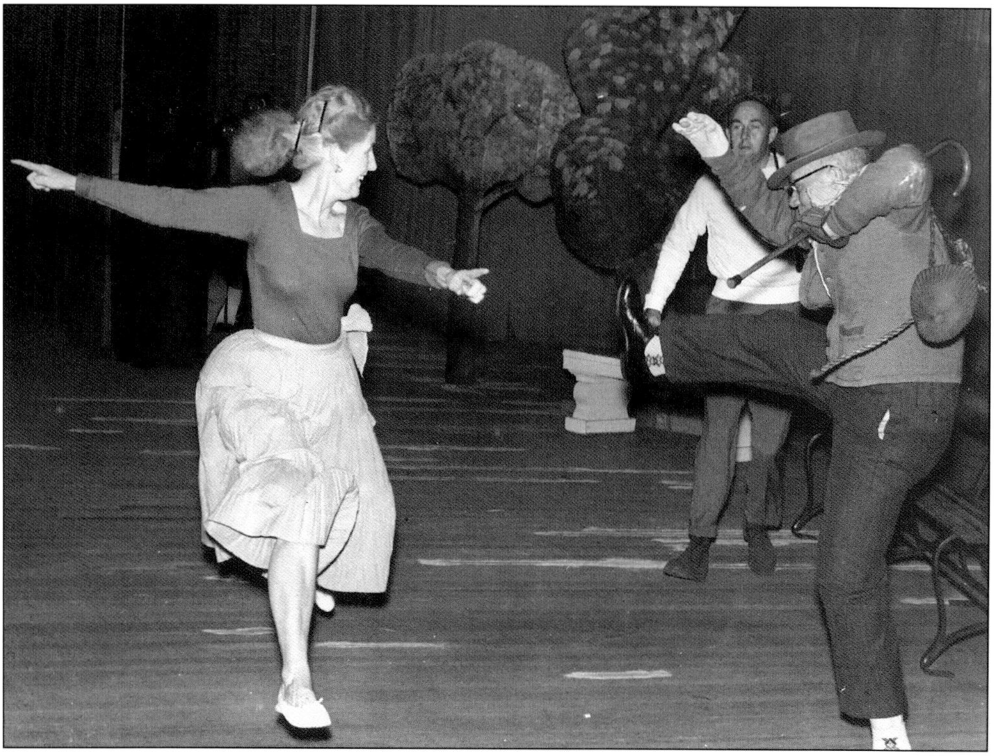

Mrs. Alice Hayden Salo (left) leads Winthrop employees in a merry dance at a Faculty-Staff Night festivity held during the 1956–57 school year. She was a Winthrop professor of physical education and dance theater at Winthrop for 32 years, a volunteer with Hope House for 15 years, and a member of the Daughters of the American Revolution and United Daughters of the Confederacy. Mrs. Salo died in 1996.

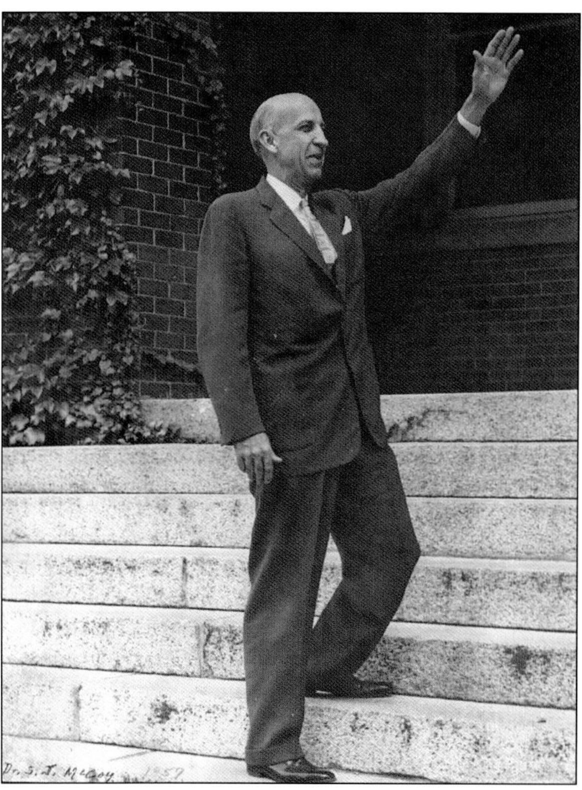

Dr. S.J. McCoy, photographed here in 1957, served as Dean of the College from 1949 to 1959. Under his leadership, Winthrop added the Geography Department, the Philosophy and Religion Department, and the Dramatic Arts Department.

Staff member Willie Graham, pictured in 1958, is representative of the many staff members who have served Winthrop faithfully during the past 100-plus years. He worked at Winthrop from 1929 to 1971.

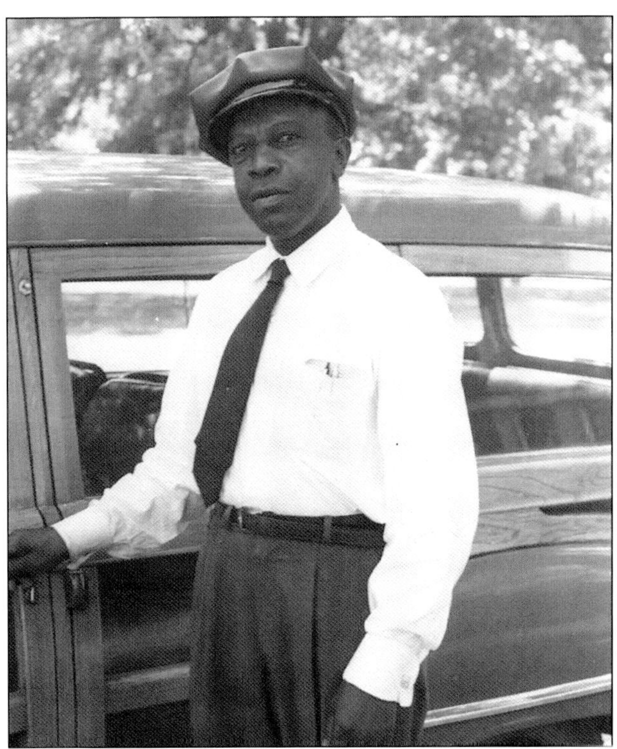

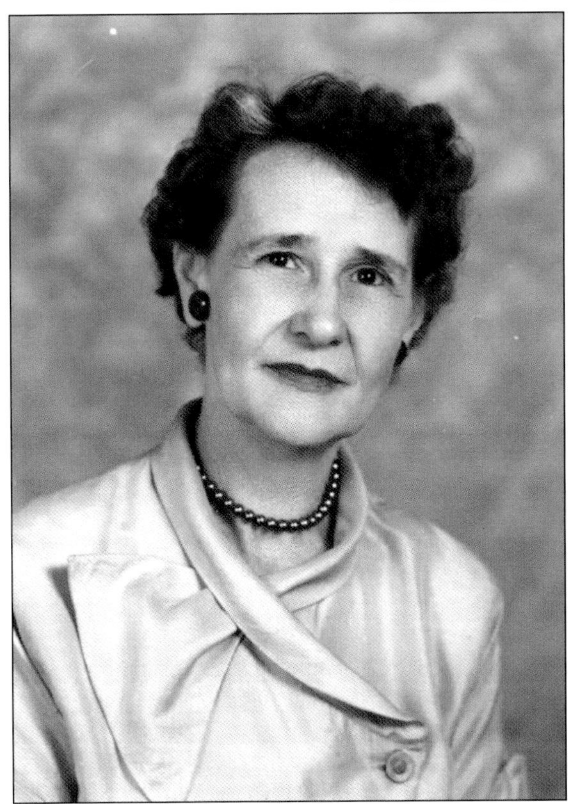

As a hostess at Winthrop University from 1953 to 1983, Maude Barnette cared for and influenced multitudes of young people. Mrs. Barnette died in 1998 a few months after her 100th birthday.

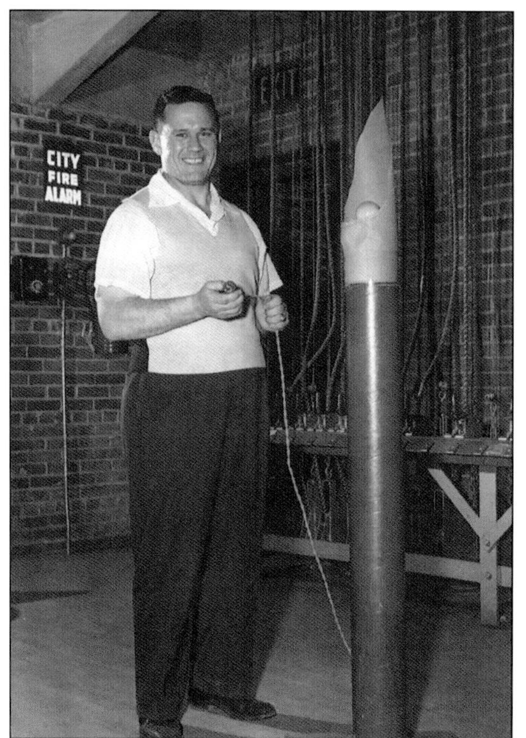

During his long association with Winthrop (1951 to the present), Bill Culp has been a campus institution. Following his father, Leonard Parks Culp, who served as the university's physical plant director for 39 years, Bill joined Winthrop as a maintenance engineer in 1951. He was later promoted to physical plant director and then to assistant vice president for renovations. In 1997 Bill Culp's place in Winthrop's history was immortalized when the school's air-conditioning plant was named the William L. Culp Chiller Plant.

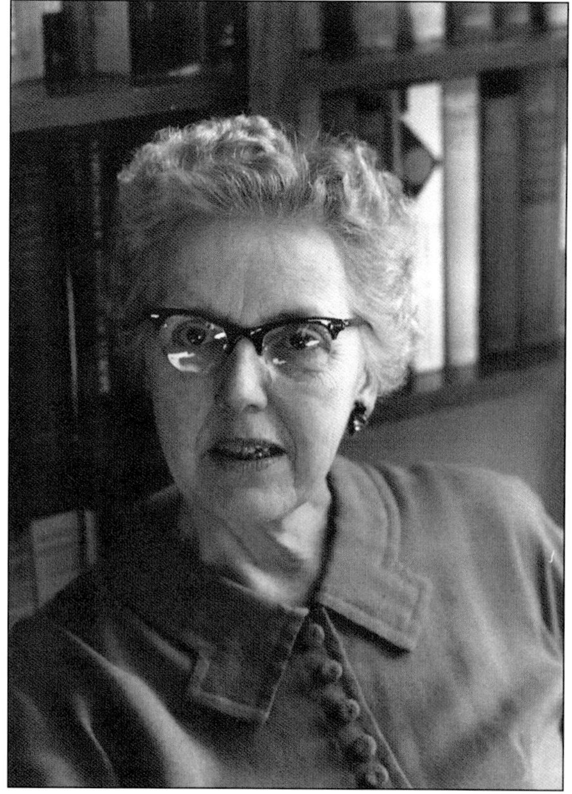

Dr. Mildred C. Beckwith, photographed here in 1963, served Winthrop ably as a professor of history from 1944 to 1972. She received her B.S. degree from Northeast Missouri State Teacher's College and her Ph.D. from Ohio State University.

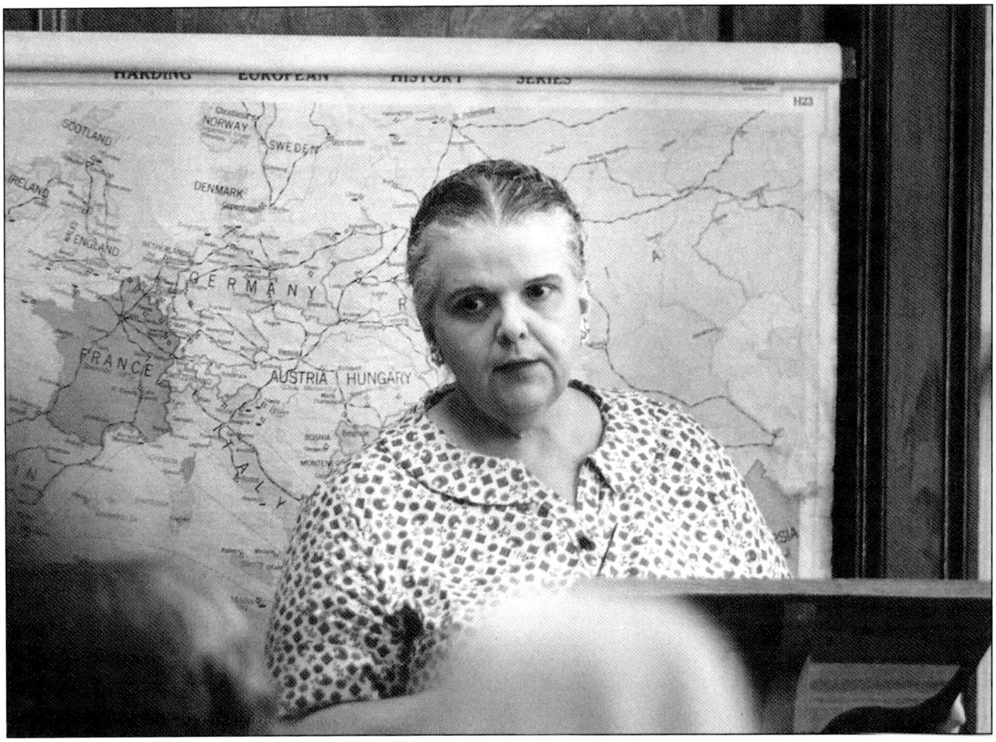

Dr. Mary Elizabeth Massey, one of Winthrop's distinguished scholars, taught at Winthrop for 24 years and served as Winthrop's History Department chairman from 1960 to 1964. She also served as president of the Southern Historical Association in 1972 and received Winthrop's Distinguished Professor Award in 1965. As a noted historian of the Civil War, she published several books on the subject. She died in December 1972.

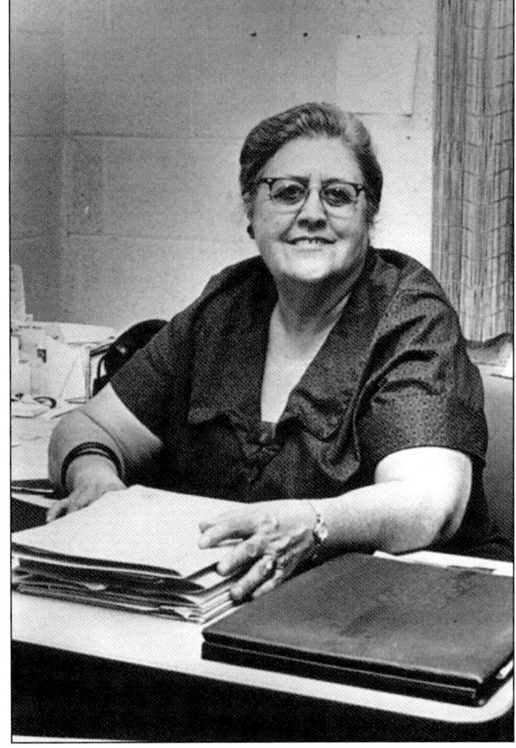

Dr. Julia Post served Winthrop for 30 years as the director of physical education until her retirement in 1962. To many physical education majors of "the Post Era," Julia Post and physical education at Winthrop were synonymous. Miss Post died in 1988.

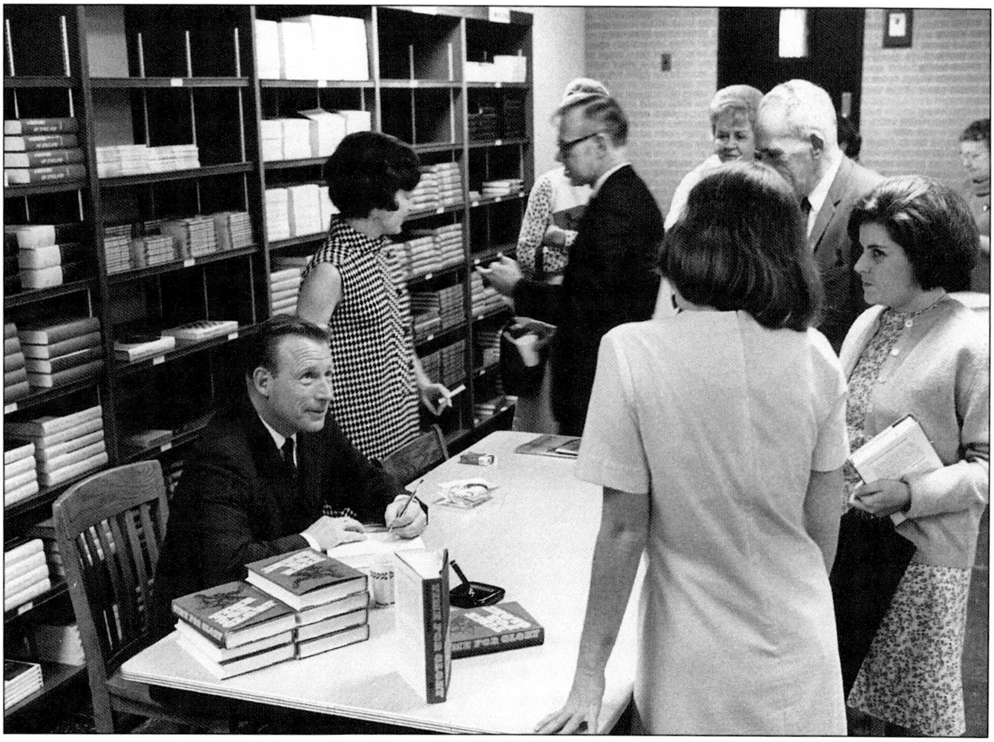

Bob Bristow is pictured at an autograph party for his first novel *Time for Glory* in October 1968. Bristow served as a professor in the English Department from 1961 to 1987. He is also author of *Night Season* (1970), *A Faraway Drummer* (1973), and *Laughter in Darkness* (1974).

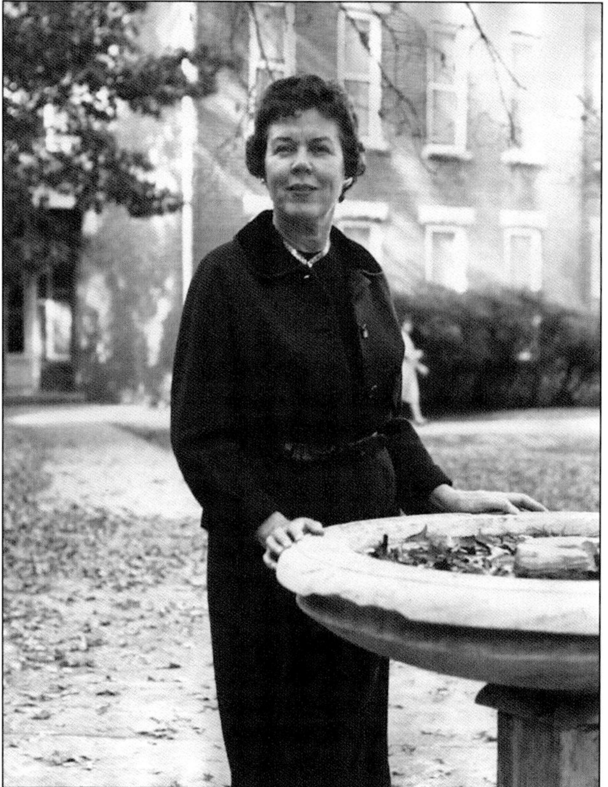

Until retiring in 1978, Iva Gibson was Winthrop's Dean of Students for 17 years. Miss Gibson earned a B.A. degree in English and education from Winthrop in 1934. She was the 1976 recipient of the Mary Mildred Sullivan Award, the highest honor Winthrop can bestow on an alumna.

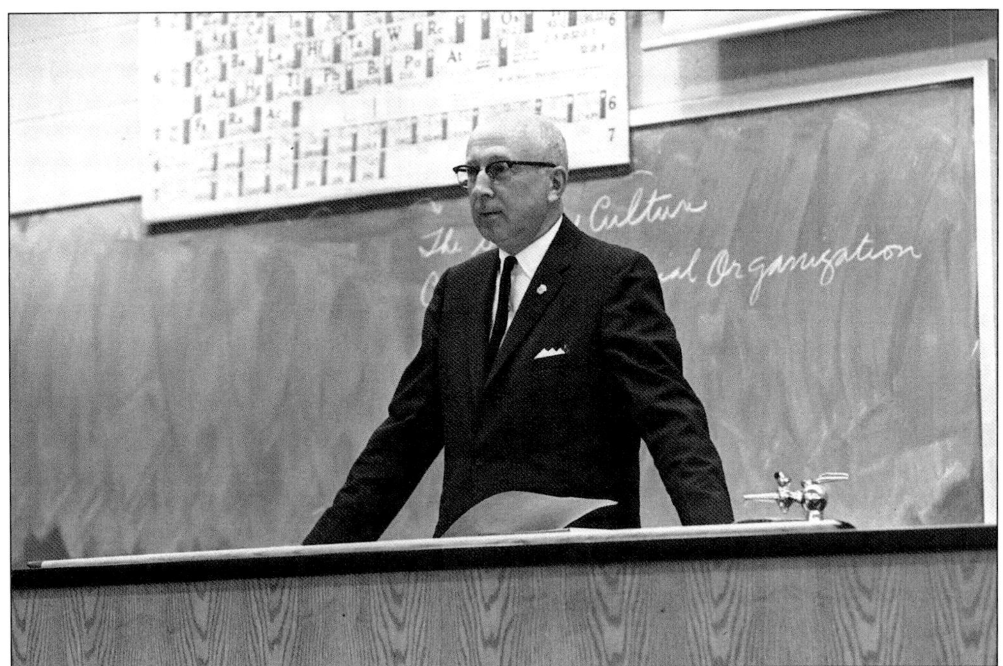

Dr. Allan Edwards is seen here in 1969 teaching a class. Professor Edwards was chairman of the Sociology Department for 27 years. In 1983, he was appointed the state director of the South Carolina chapter of the American Association of Retired People, and in 1995 he was named "Outstanding South Carolinian" for his lifelong service to others.

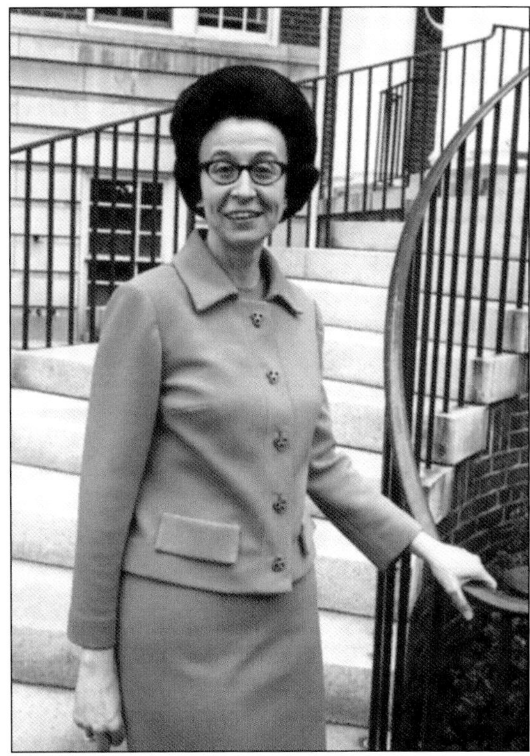

Dr. Ruth Hovermale served as Winthrop's first Dean of Home Economics from 1966 until her death in May 1978. In 1975, Dr. Hovermale was honored as South Carolina Career Women of the Year by the state's Business and Professional Women's Club organization.

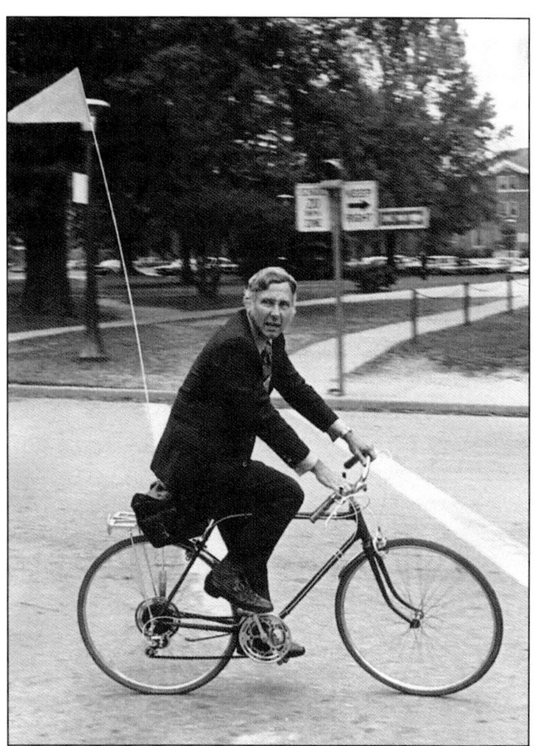

Dr. Rondeau Laffitte takes a spin in 1973. Dr. Laffitte joined the Winthrop faculty in 1959 as a member of the Psychology Department and later became its head. He retired in 1995.

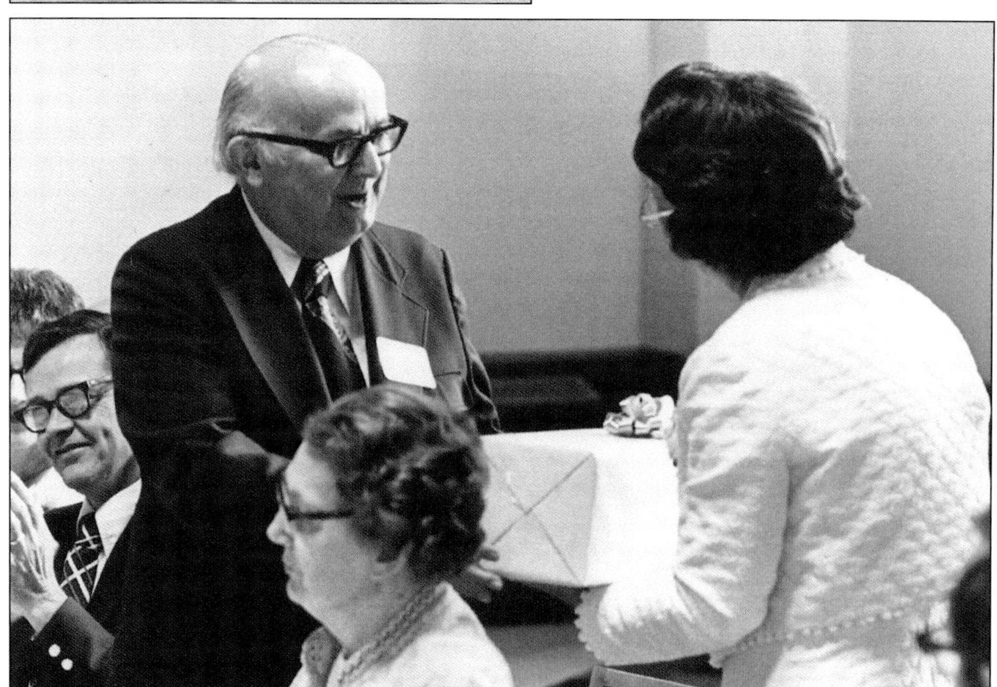

Dr. Harold Gilbreath, seen here at Alumni Day in 1974, helped develop Winthrop University's business school and was presented the institution's first Distinguished Professor Award in 1961. He served Winthrop for more than 37 years, retiring in 1974. After his retirement, Dr. Gilbreath became executive secretary of the Winthrop Foundation. He died in 1988.

On the Winthrop faculty from 1954 to 1974, philosophy professor Nolan Pliny Jacobson was one of the university's most distinguished scholars. An expert on Buddhism, Dr. Jacobson was author of *Buddhism: The Religion of Analysis*. He received Winthrop's Distinguished Professor Award in 1963.

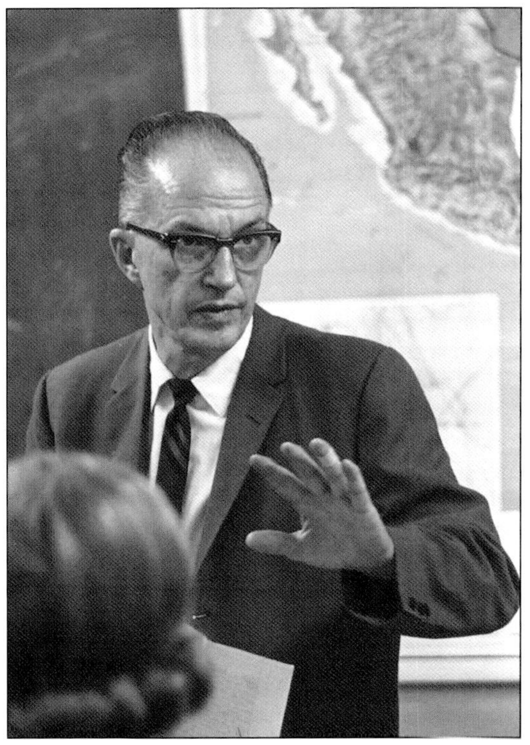

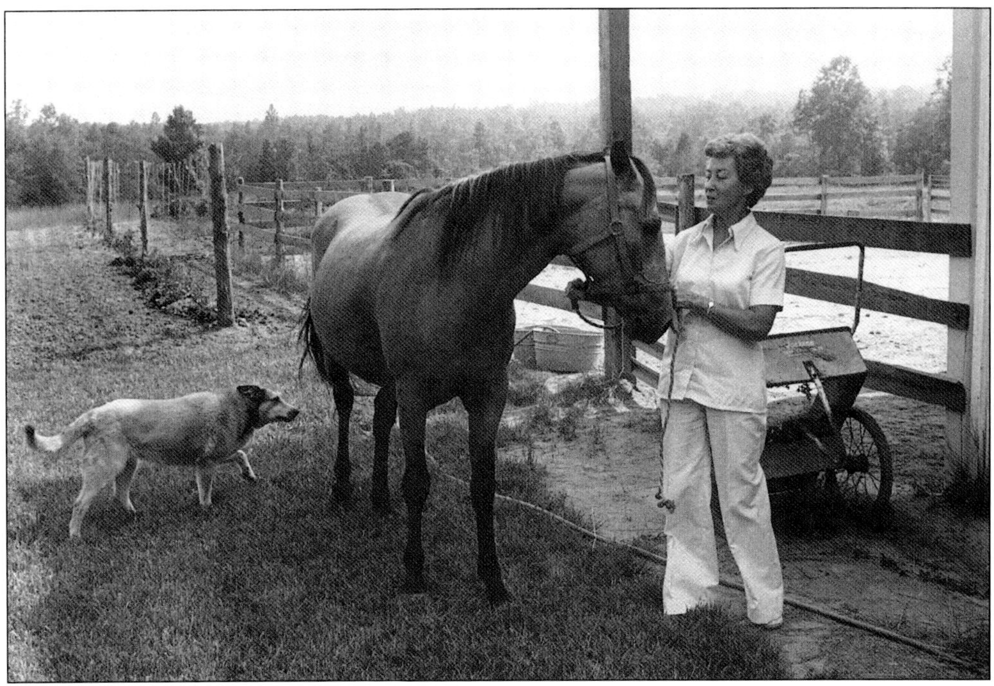

Pictured in 1975, Dr. Mary T. Littlejohn, vice president of academic affairs, came to Winthrop in 1965 as an instructor, and when she retired in 1982, President Charles B. Vail praised her for the creation of Winthrop's Student Affairs Division, which "played a pivotal role in increasing enrollment."

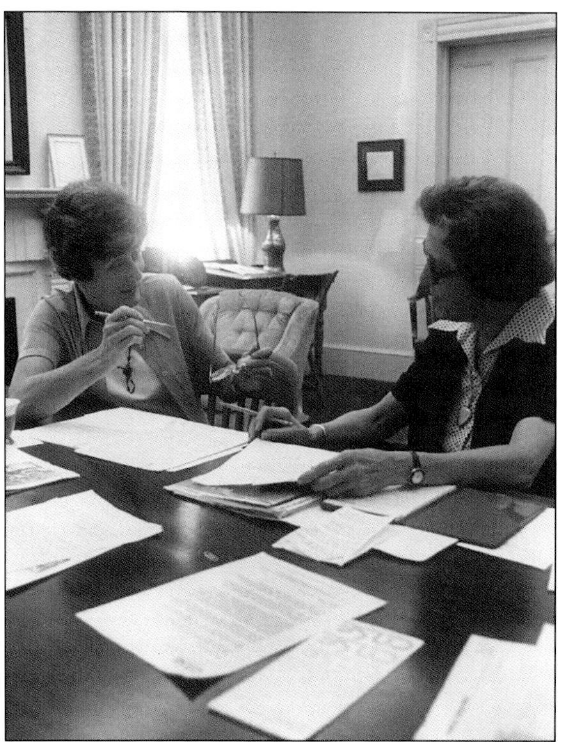

Seen here in 1977, Dr. Connie Lee (left) and Dot Rauch were two longtime and devoted employees of Winthrop University. At the time, Lee was vice president for development, and Rauch, director of Alumni Affairs.

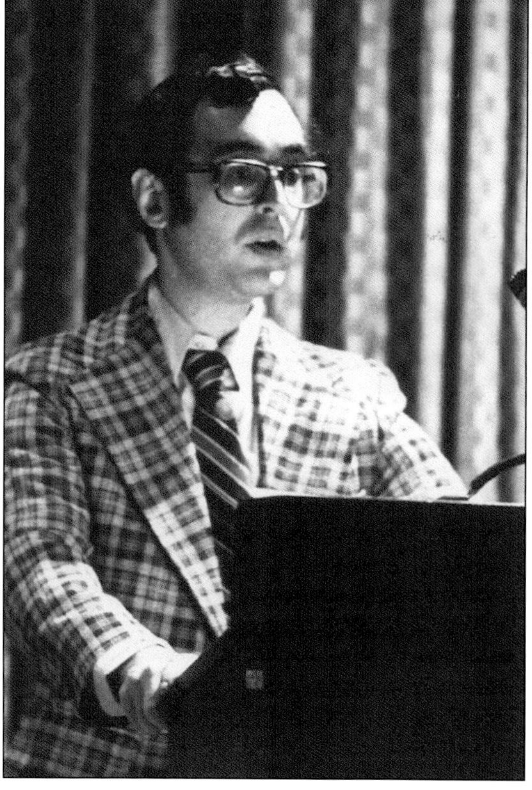

Dr. Arnold M. Shankman speaks on March 26, 1980, at a Winthrop Archives-sponsored program, "Preserving the Past for the Future: Local History and the Community," which was held in York, South Carolina. From 1975 until his death in March 1983, Dr. Shankman was one of Winthrop's most outstanding scholar-teachers. He was a highly regarded authority on U.S. history and wrote numerous books and articles on the subject. Among his many honors was the Winthrop College Presidential Citation for Library Service in 1982.

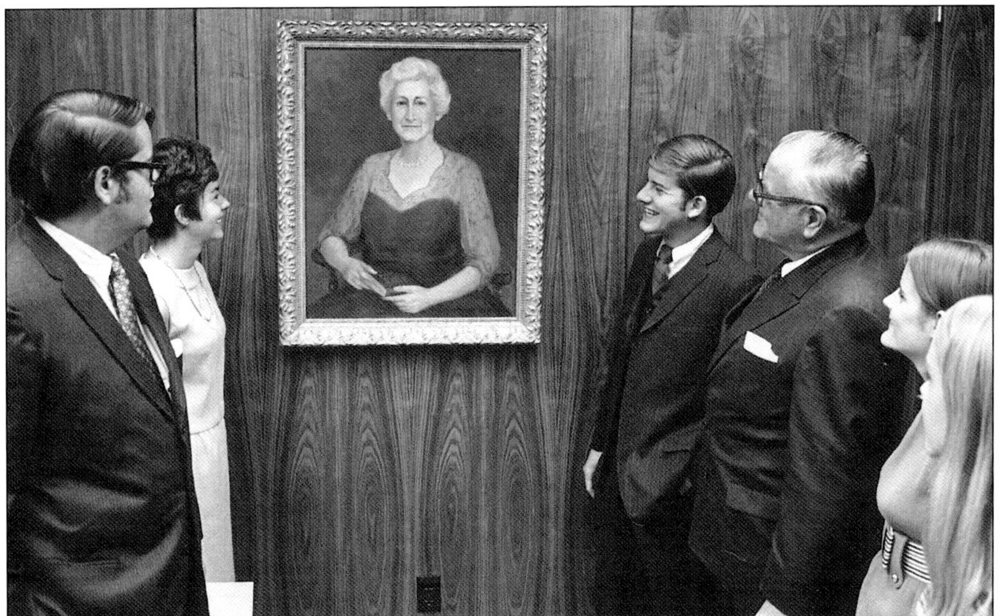

Attendees at the dedication of the Dacus Library in October 1969 look at the portrait of Ida Jane Dacus, the first head of the Winthrop library, serving from 1898 to 1945, and the first certified librarian in South Carolina.

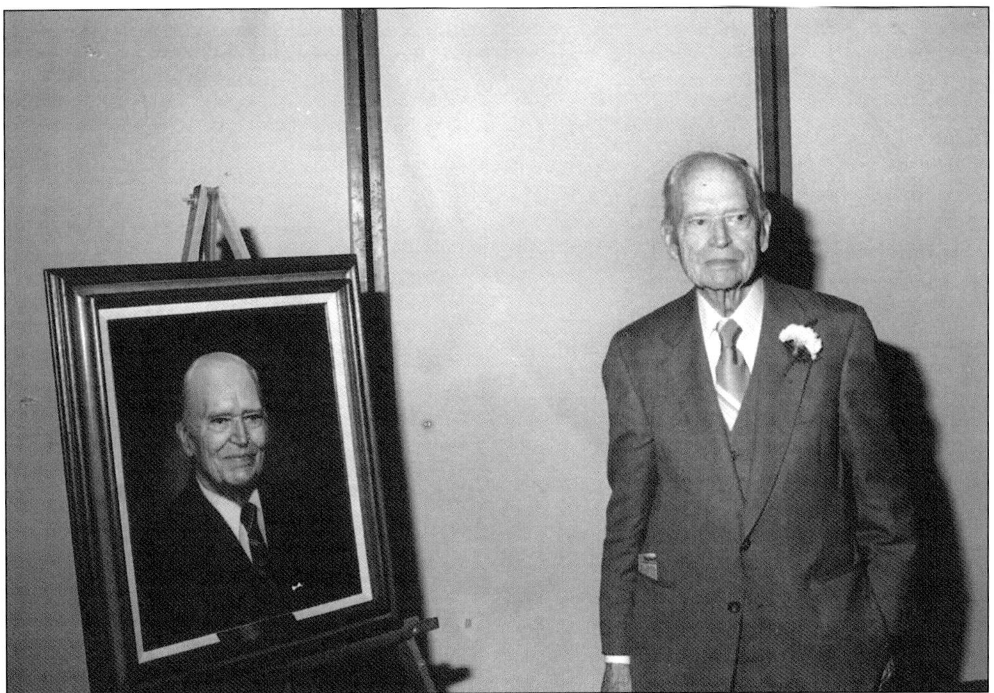

A beloved faculty member, Dr. Walter Roberts served Winthrop as chairman of the school's music department and was a faculty member from 1925 to 1958. He founded the York County Choral Society, and the Walter B. Roberts Music Scholarship is named in his honor. Dr. Roberts died in 1992 at age 99.

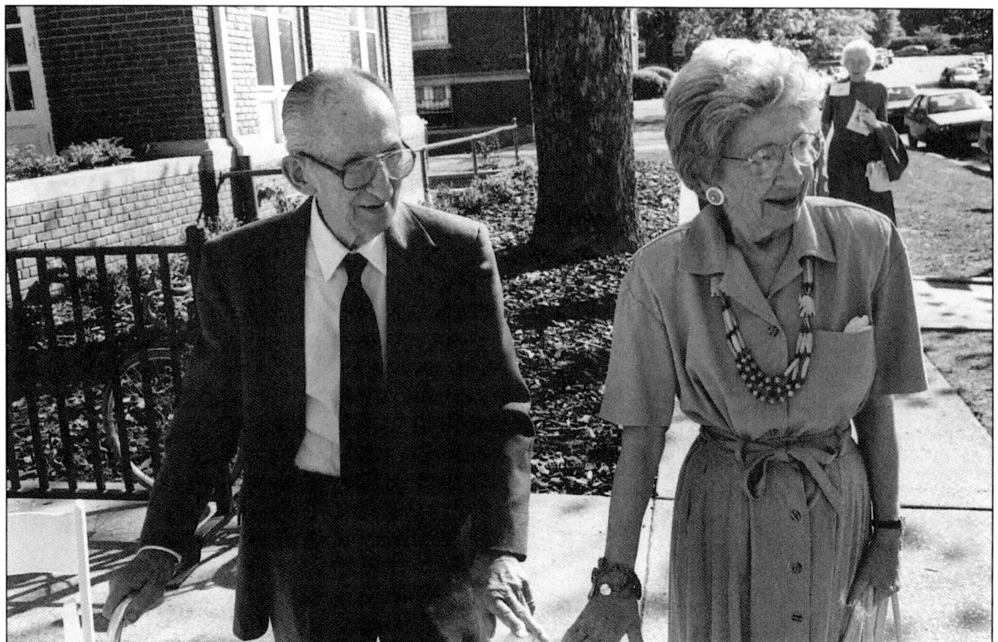

Bill and Mary Long are photographed here in 1994. Bill Long established Winthrop's theater program and the Palmetto Drama Association, the University's first high school drama festival, which now draws student actors from 22 schools statewide. Mary Long was a longtime Rock Hill High School drama teacher, who touched lives through drama and television.

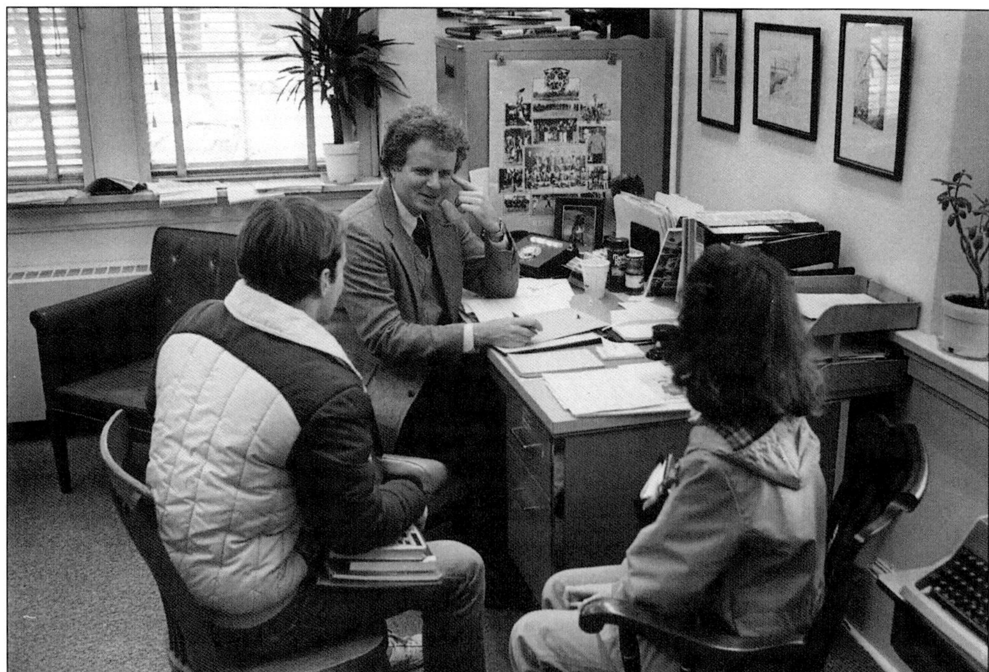

Dr. John Anfin, a faculty member in the School of Education, meets with his students in his office in February 1983. Dr. Anfin is a noted cartoonist whose cartoons have appeared in numerous publications at the local, state, and national levels.

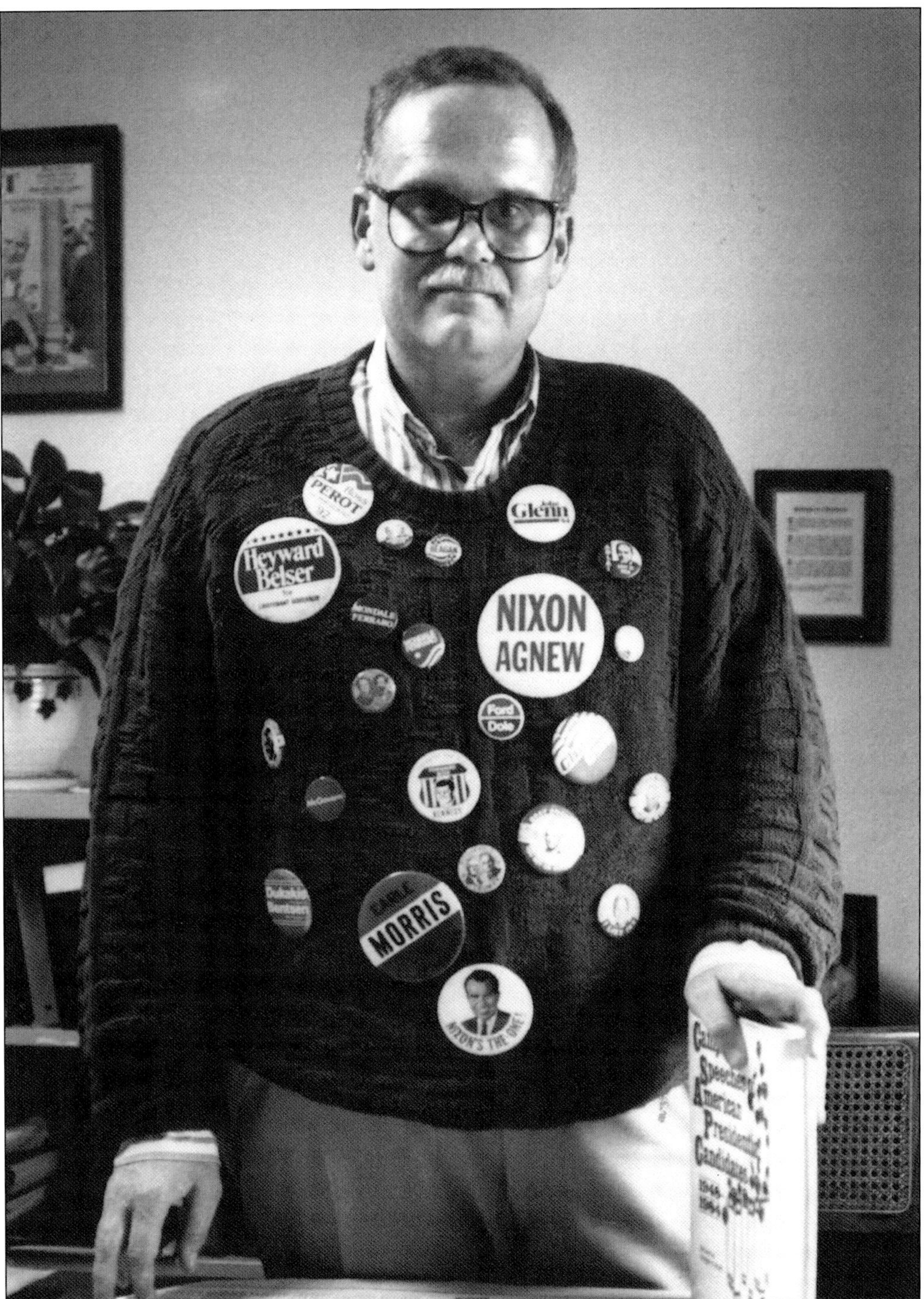

Dr. Edward Lee, currently a member of the History Department and a charter member of the Archives Senior Research Association Program, is one of the university's most dynamic professors. He has served as president of the South Carolina Historical Society, and his book *From Yorkville to York* won the 1999 South Carolina Confederation of Local Historical Societies award for best publication.

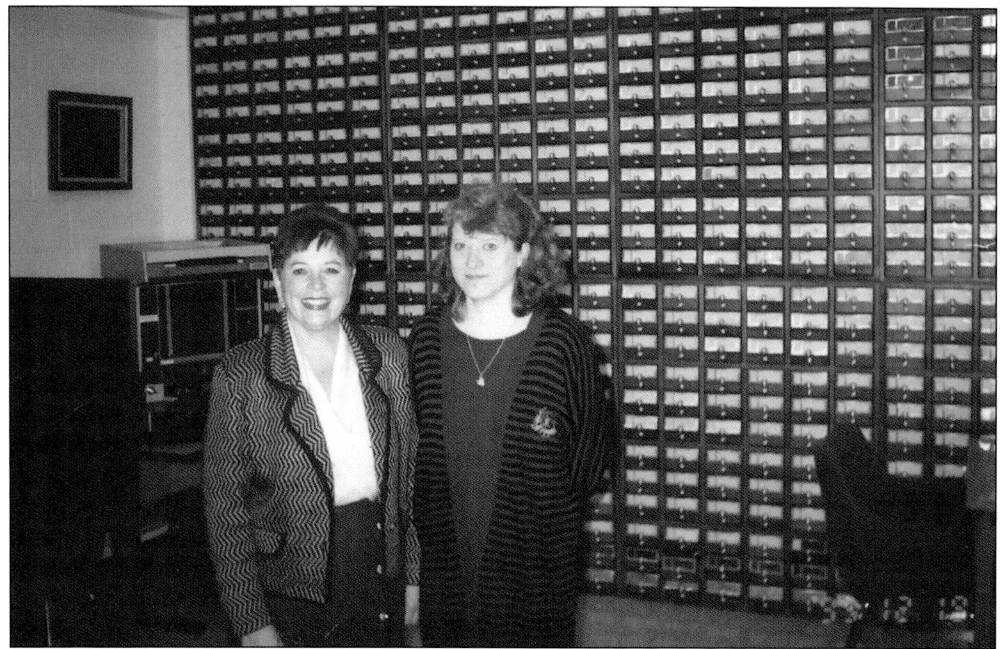

Dr. Patricia Cormier, vice president for academic affairs from 1993 to 1996, and Gina Price White (right), assistant archivist, get together in the Winthrop Archives.

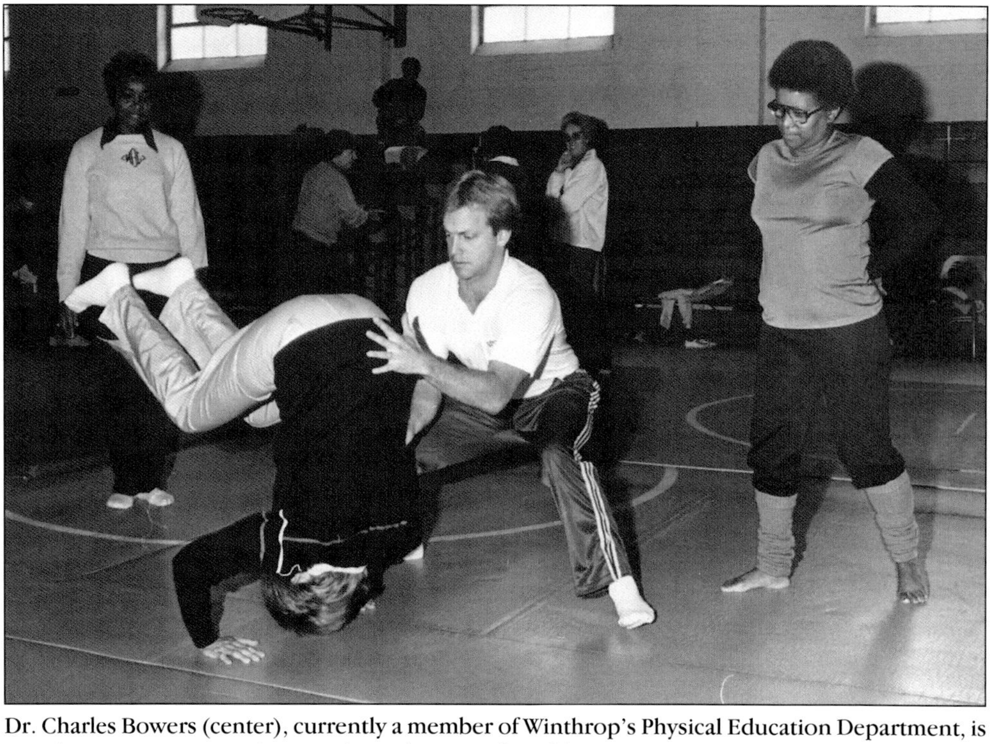

Dr. Charles Bowers (center), currently a member of Winthrop's Physical Education Department, is seen here instructing students in the technique of tumbling. Dr. Bowers has published numerous articles on physical education, and in 1996 he was a local winner in "The Most Loving Coach" contest, which was part of a national search conducted by "USA Weekend."

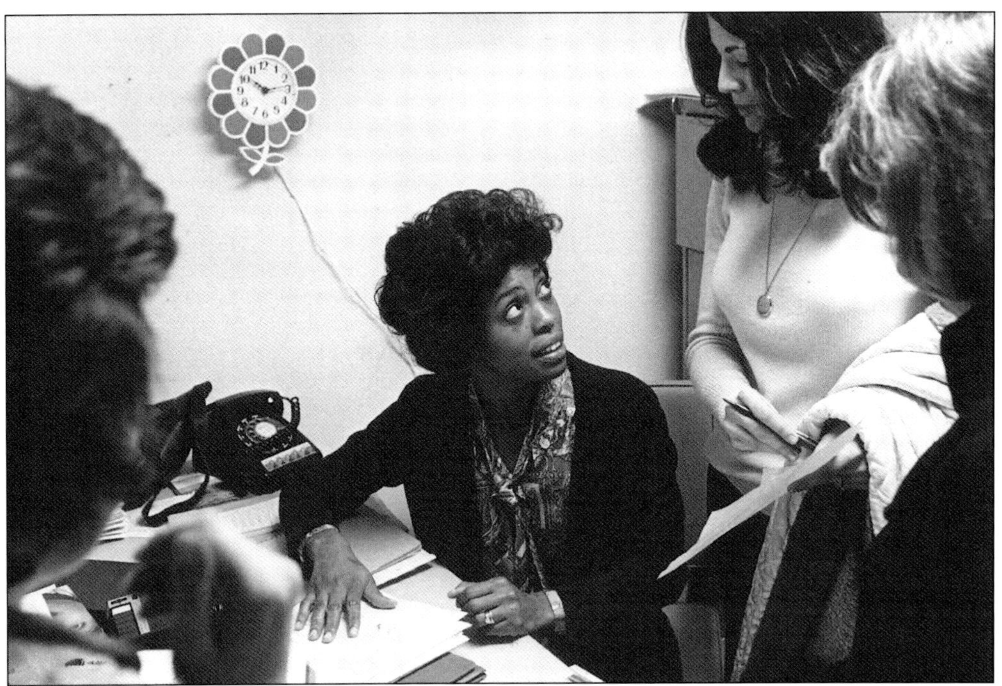

Students confer with education professor Bessie Moody-Lawrence in 1974. In addition to her teaching duties, Moody-Lawrence is currently serving her fourth term in the South Carolina state legislature as a representative from House District #49.

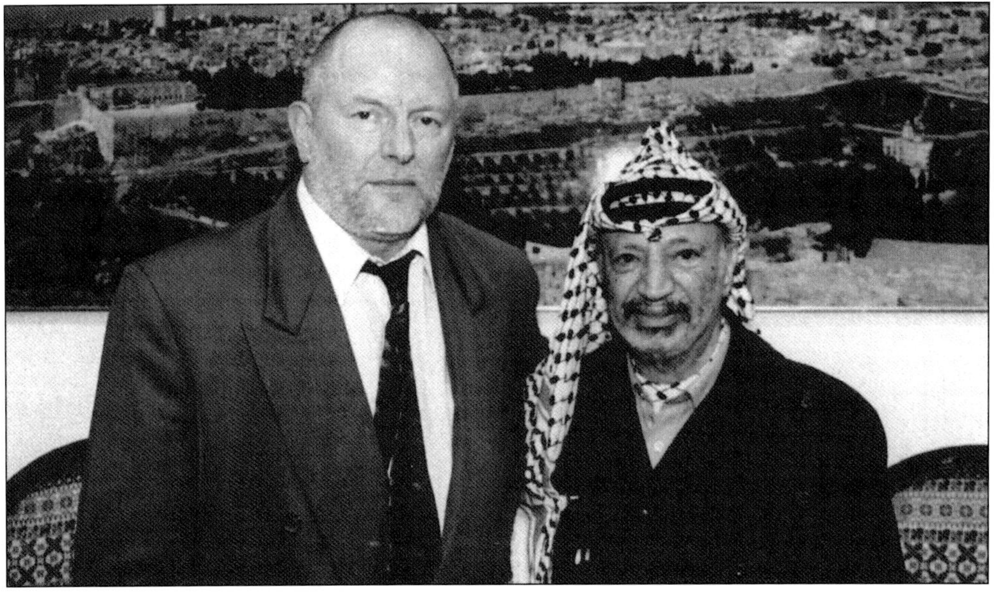

Ron Chepesiuk, head of the Winthrop University Archives from 1973 to the present and founder of the department's Senior Research Associate Program, is seen here with Yasser Arafat in November 1997. At the time, Chepesiuk was serving as a consultant to the Palestinian Authority on the construction of a Palestinian National Library. In 1999, he received the American Library Association's Humphrey-OCLC Forest Press Award for significant contribution to international librarianship.

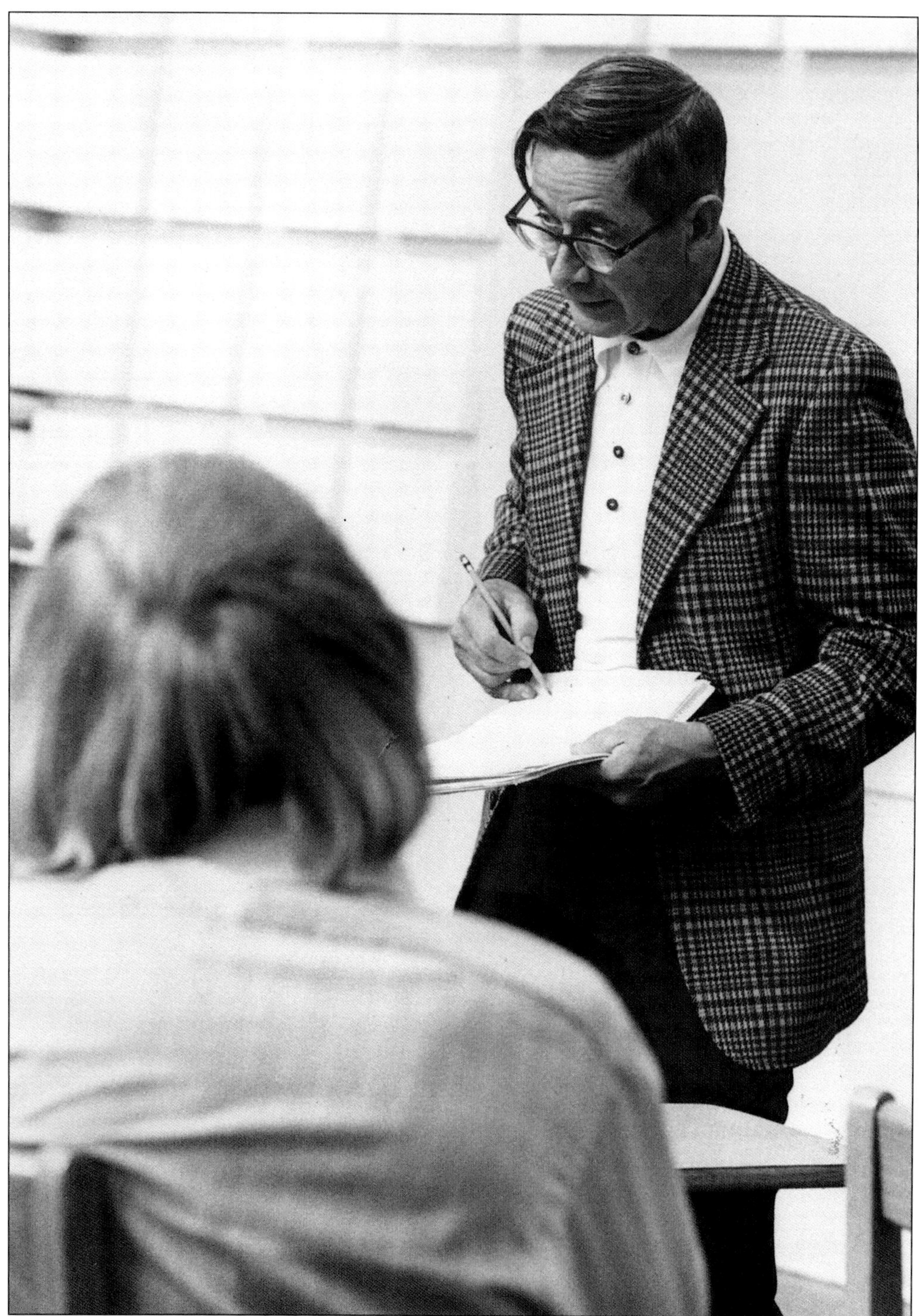

Dr. John A. Sargent, seen here teaching in September 1975, served as chair of Winthrop's Department of Communications from 1965 to 1975, began the university's program in speech pathology, and helped develop the speech and hearing centers of York and Chester Counties. He died in 1999.

Five

The Alumni: A Tradition of Service and Distinction

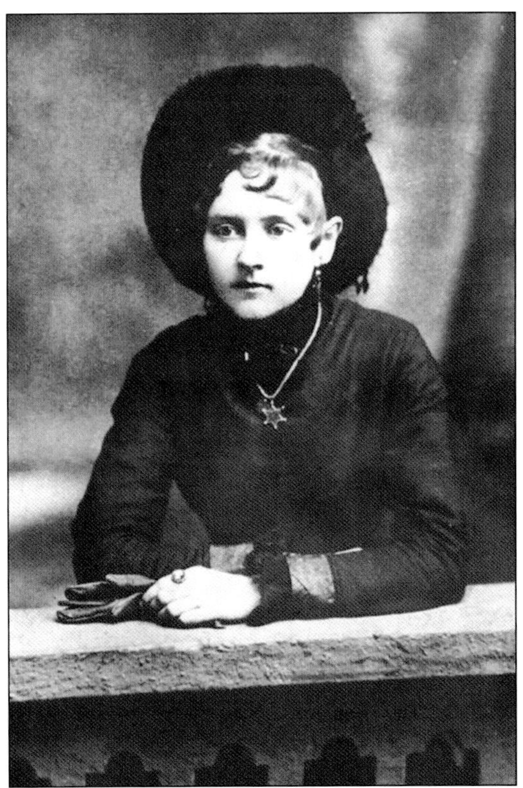

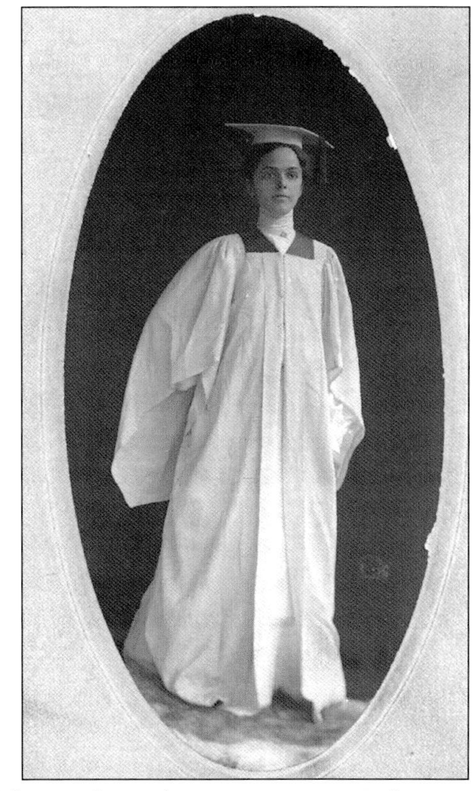

Left: Miss Julie Bonham was the first president of the Winthrop Alumni Association. *Right:* Inez Felder, president of the Winthrop Literary Society, is pictured when she received her degree at the 1900 commencement.

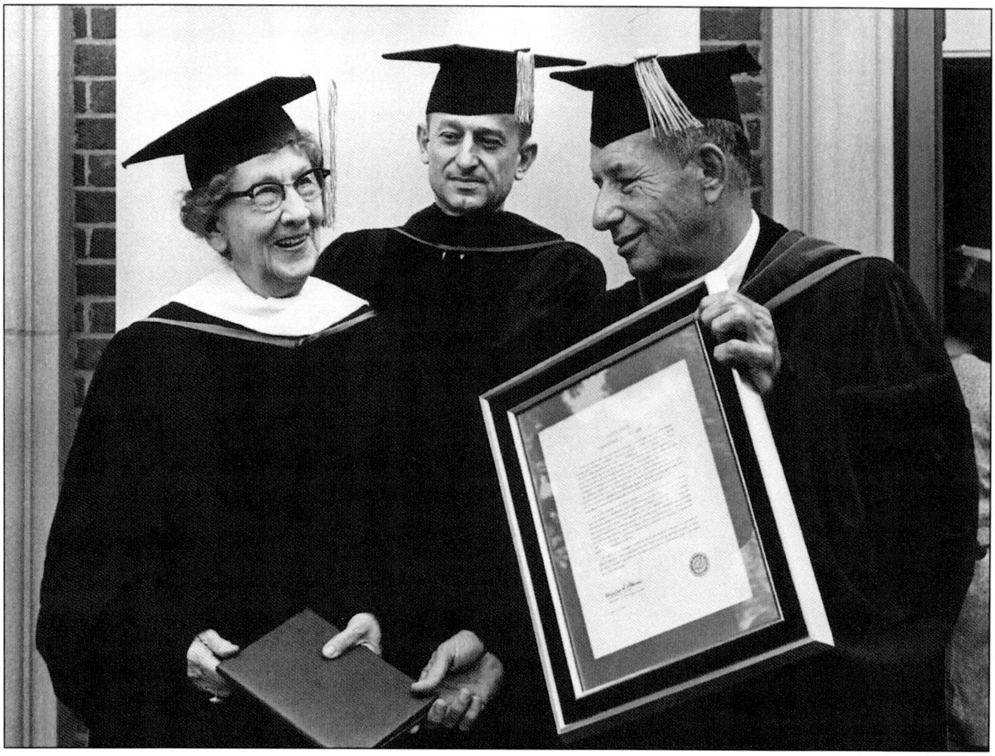

In 1921, Christine South Gee, Class of 1903, organized the first Council of Farm Women in the United States. She was a state home demonstration agent from 1918 to 1923, when she married Dr. Nathaniel Gist Gee and moved to China for the next ten years. She served as a trustee of Winthrop University from 1944 to 1962. In 1966 Winthrop gave Mrs. Gee its first honorary doctorate. From left to right, Mrs. Gee, Thomas Henry Jr., and Winthrop president Charles S. Davis are pictured here at the ceremony.

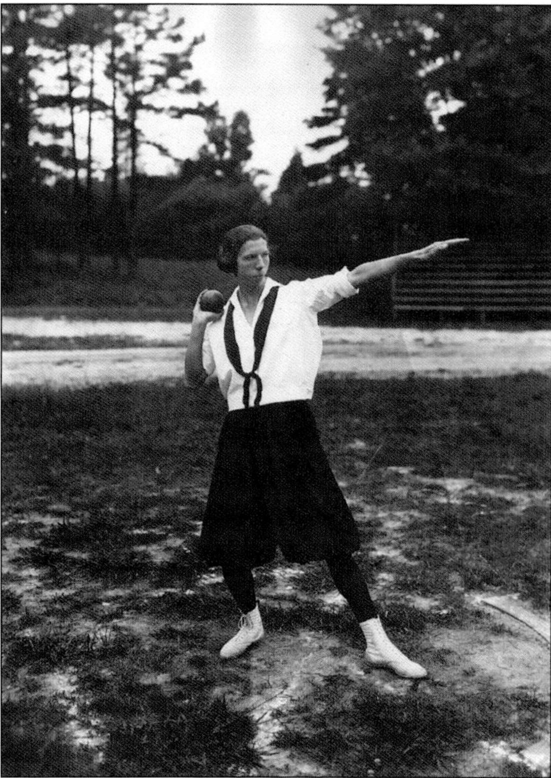

Lucile "Ludy" Godbold, Class of 1922, won two gold medals and four other medals in Paris in 1922 in the first International Track Meet for Women. The medals were for the shot put and hop-skip and jump. At this time, women were banned from Olympic competition. The meet was considered the forerunner to women's participation.

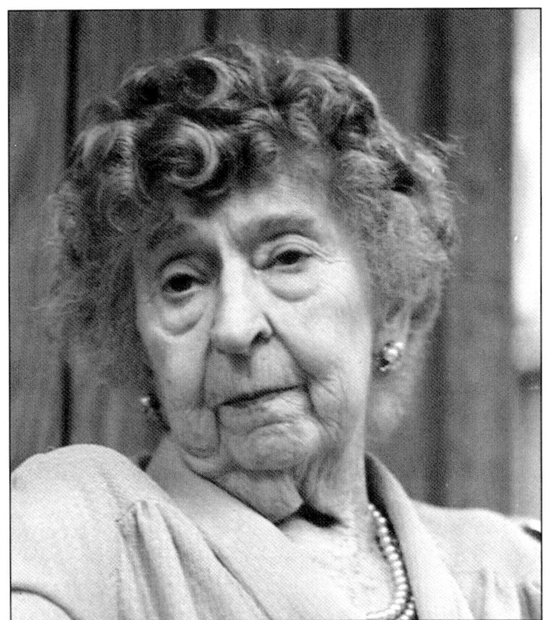

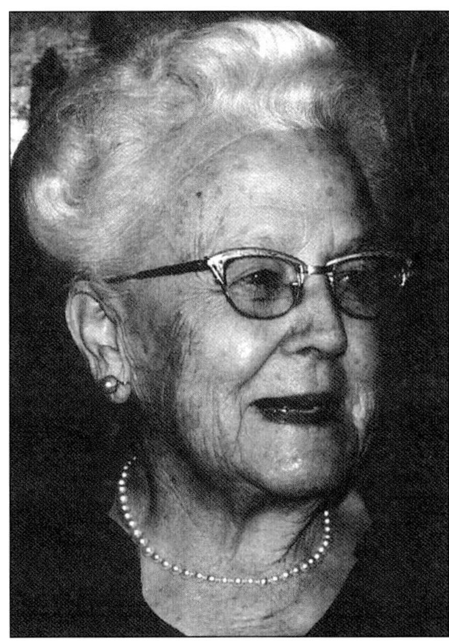

Left: Marguerite Tolbert, Class of 1914, had a big impact on South Carolina education in various capacities. She worked as state supervisor of adult education in the South Carolina State Department of Education, assistant director of the South Carolina Opportunity School, and founder and operator of Camp Jr., a school for delinquent boys that was set up during World War II. *Right:* Martha Franks, Class of 1922, became one of South Carolina's most noted missionaries, serving in China from 1925 until the communist takeover in 1949. She continued to serve her calling in Taiwan before retiring in South Carolina. Ms. Franks died in 1988 at age 99.

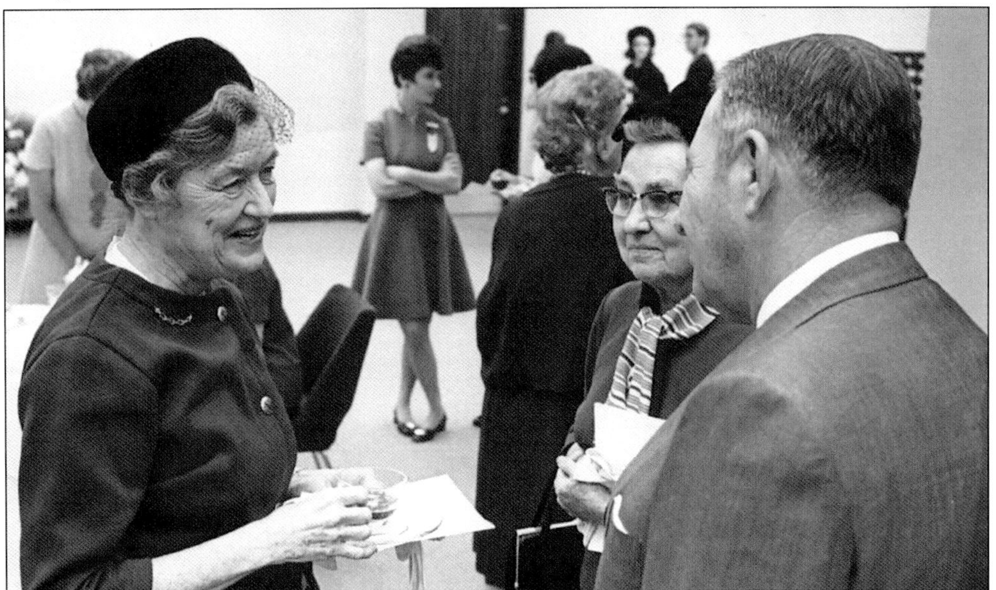

Frances Lander Spain, Class of 1925, used her skills and experience as a Fulbright Scholar to establish the modern library movement in Thailand from 1951 to 1952. Dr. Spain served as president of the American Library Association and was a longtime children's librarian at the New York Public Library.

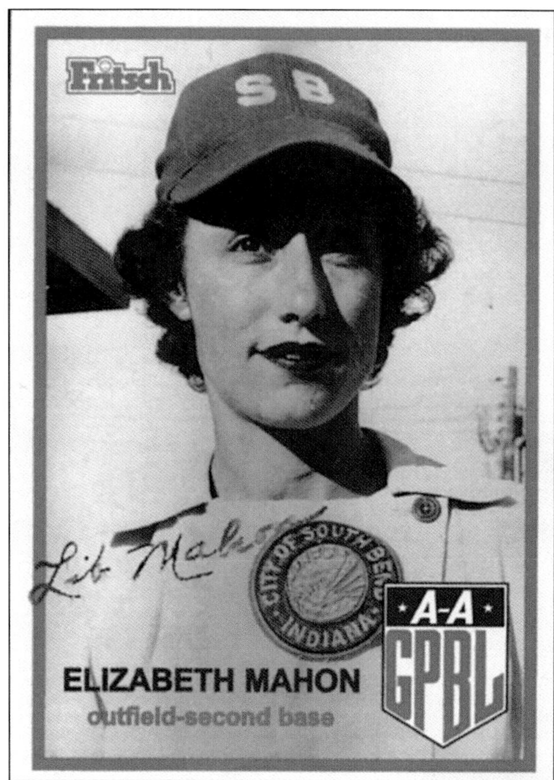

This baseball card features Elizabeth "Lib" Mahon, Class of 1942, who graduated with a degree in physical education and played professional softball for several years. In her stellar career, Lib averaged a .248 lifetime batting average, batted 2,903 times in 837 games, amassed 721 hits, and scored 432 runs. After earning a Master's degree at the Indiana University in 1960, she became a guidance counselor. Lib Mahon retired in 1991 and lives in South Bend, Indiana.

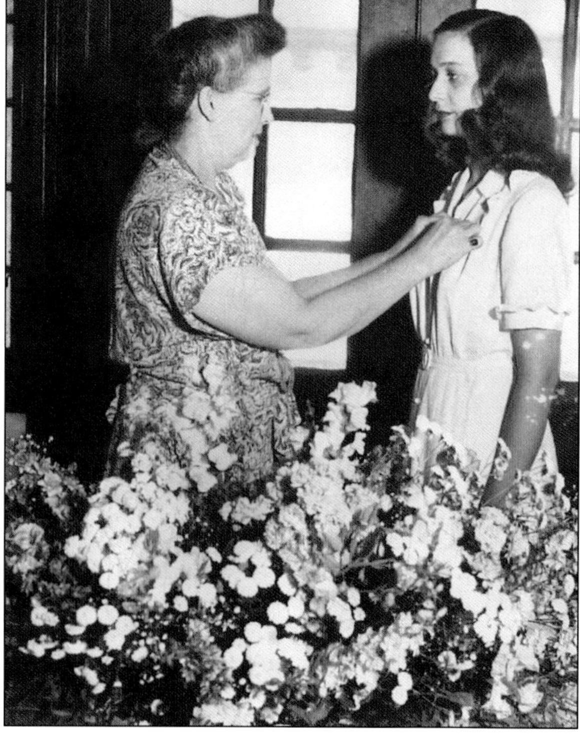

In this Senior Induction Ceremony during the 1946–47 term, Mrs. Rosa B. Guess (Class of 1911), on the left, pins Jean Crouch (Class of 1947), who married current Senator Strom Thurmond in 1947. The senator's proposal of marriage was contained in a letter he dictated to her. As the couple later revealed, she typed out her affirmative reply. Mrs. Thurmond died in 1960 at age 33.

Barry Jean Wingard was Miss South Carolina in 1949. She was a junior at the time.

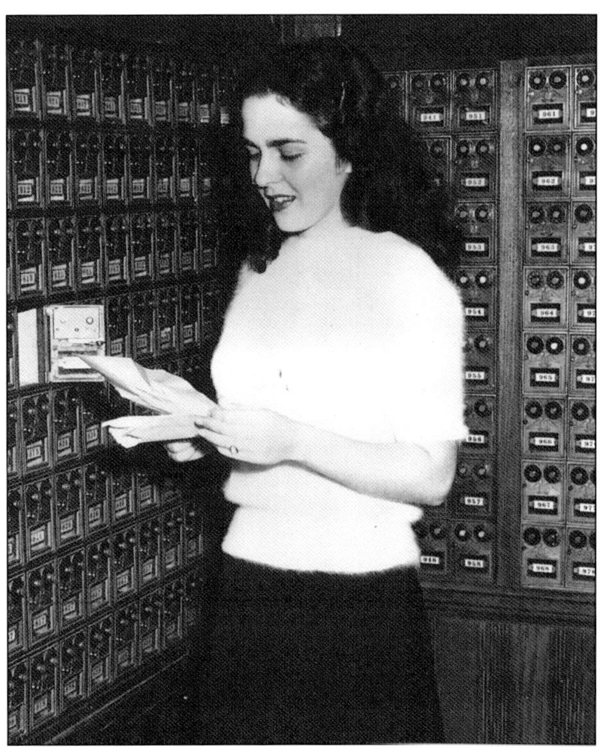

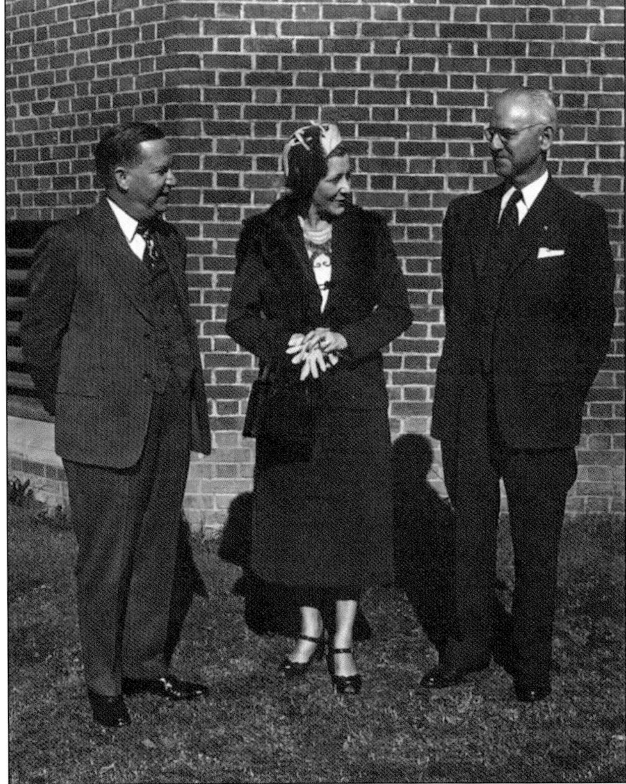

Martha Thomas Fitzgerald (1895–1981), Class of 1916, became the first woman elected in a general election to the South Carolina House of Representatives. She represented Richland County from 1950 to 1962, when she decided to run for Congress and lost. Ms. Fitzgerald was an advocate of many causes, including women's service on juries. Here she is pictured with Winthrop president Henry R. Sims and J.M. Fitzgerald.

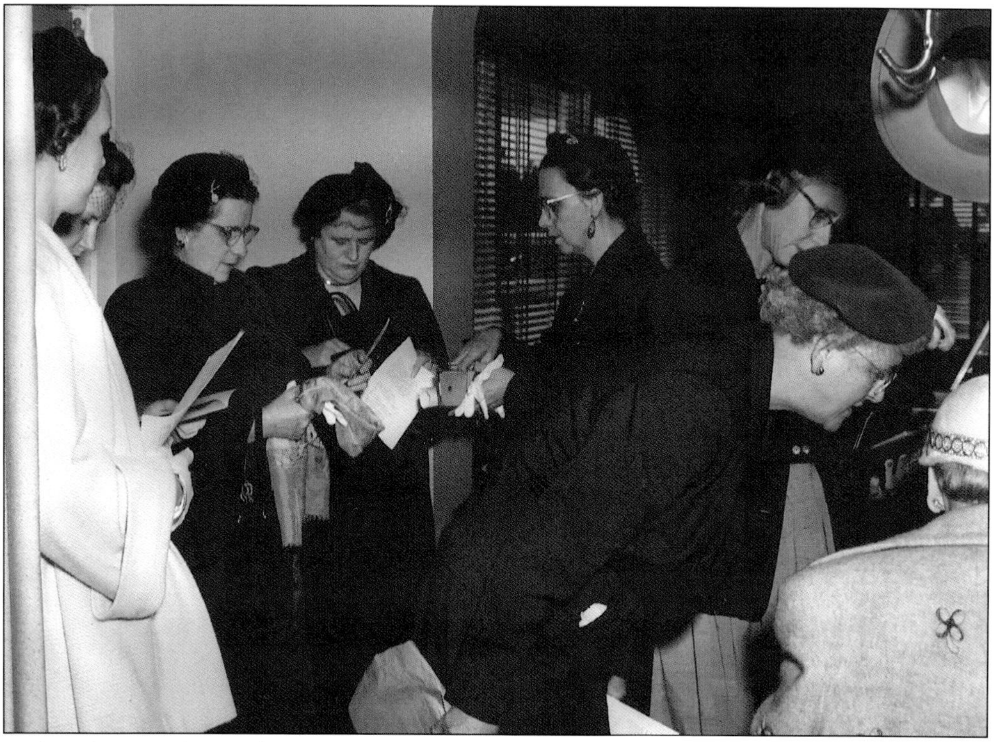

In this photograph, members of the Southern District of the Winthrop Alumni Association meet in November 1954.

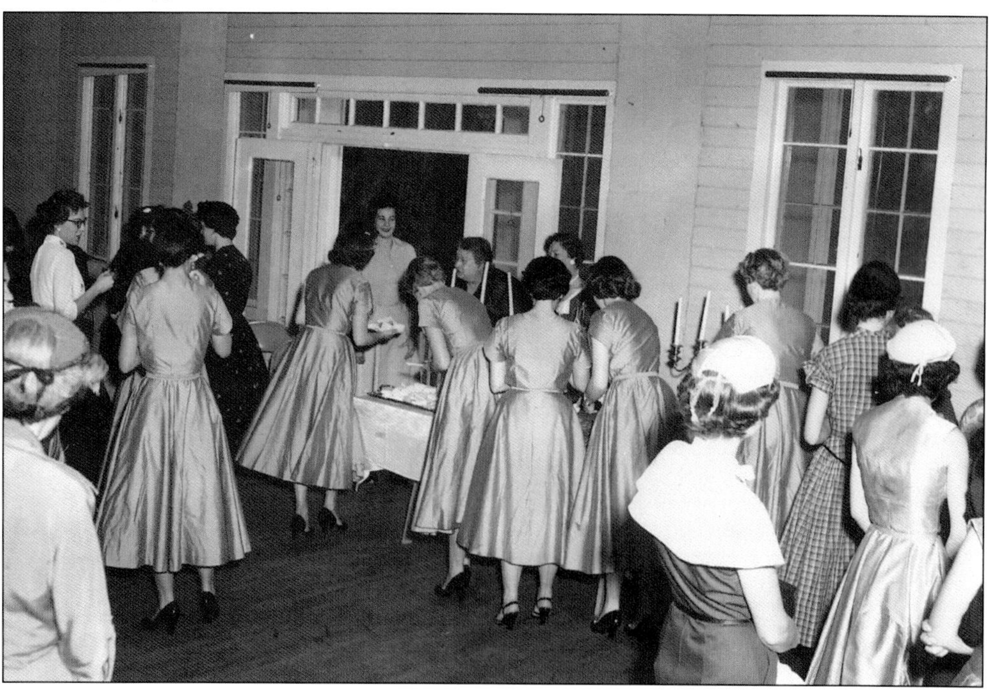

Members of the Orangeburg chapter of the Winthrop Alumni sponsor a tea for local high school girls in March 1955.

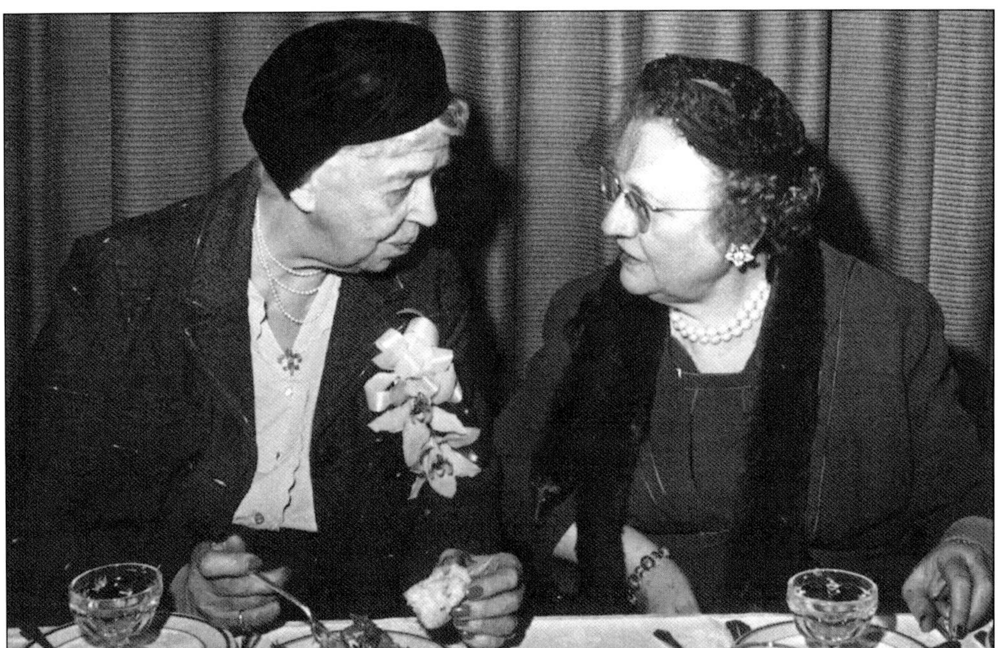

Dr. Margaret Bryant, Class of 1921, became a noted linguist specializing in American usage, folklore, and proverbs. She was the first Winthrop alumna to receive a Ph.D. degree. In this 1959 photograph, Dr. Bryant is seen here dining with former First Lady Eleanor Roosevelt (left).

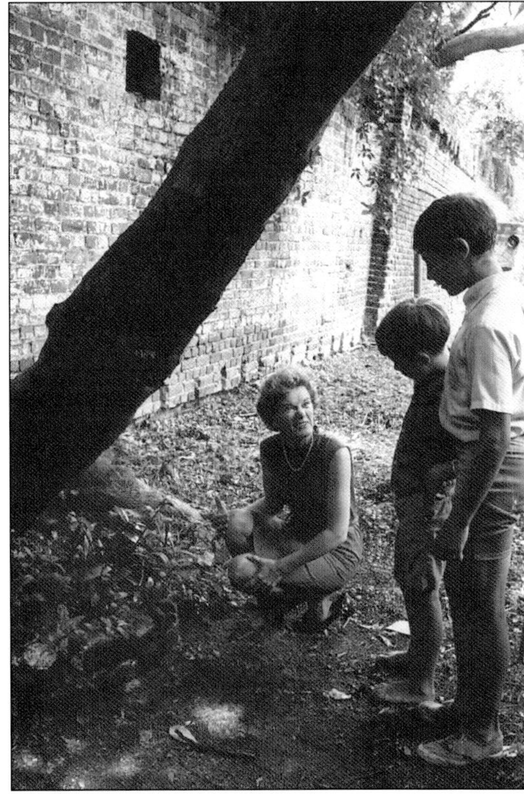

Ruth Marshall Williams, Class of 1919, served Winthrop as its alumnae secretary from 1944 to 1954. Mrs. Williams had taught in the Rock Hill school system, and then after leaving Winthrop, she served as executive secretary of the South Carolina Federation of Women's Clubs. She was the first classroom teacher and the second woman ever elected president of the South Carolina Education Association.

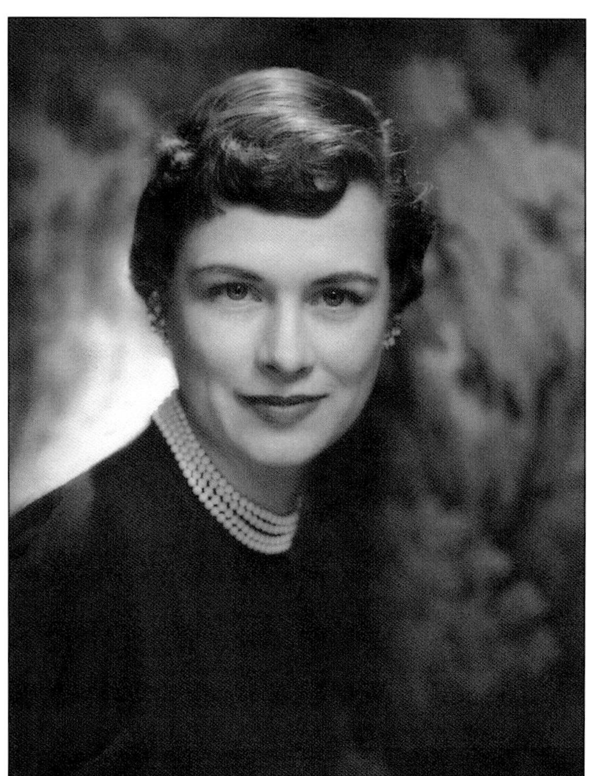

Ida Crawford Stewart, Class of 1943, left South Carolina and found success in the world of cosmetics. Beginning in 1961, she became a close advisor of Estee Lauder, serving the entrepreneur's company as vice president of marketing.

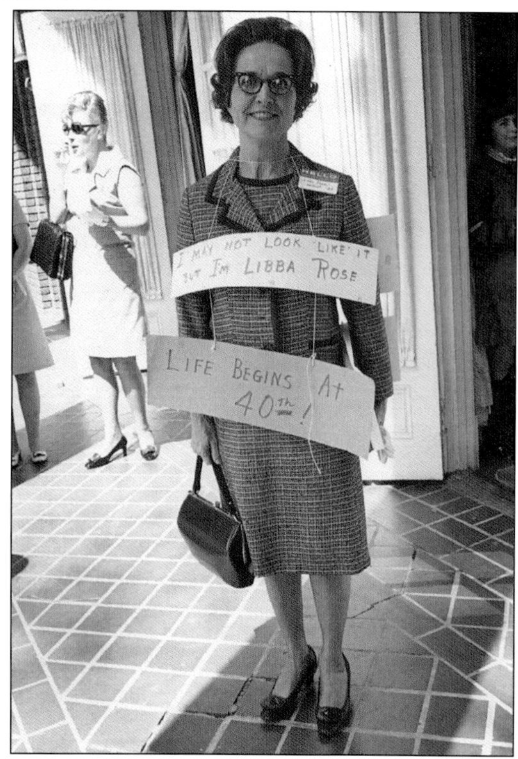

A Winthrop alumna shows her sense of humor at Alumnae Day in April 1969.

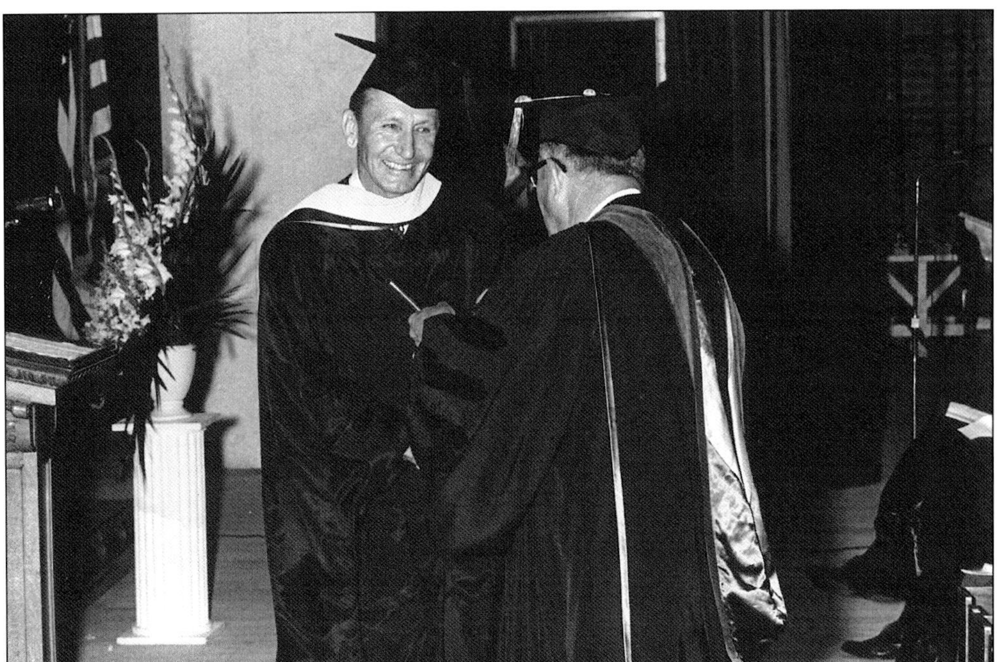

In 1969, Walter Schrader became the first male student to be awarded a Winthrop degree, graduating with a Master of Arts in Teaching in Biology.

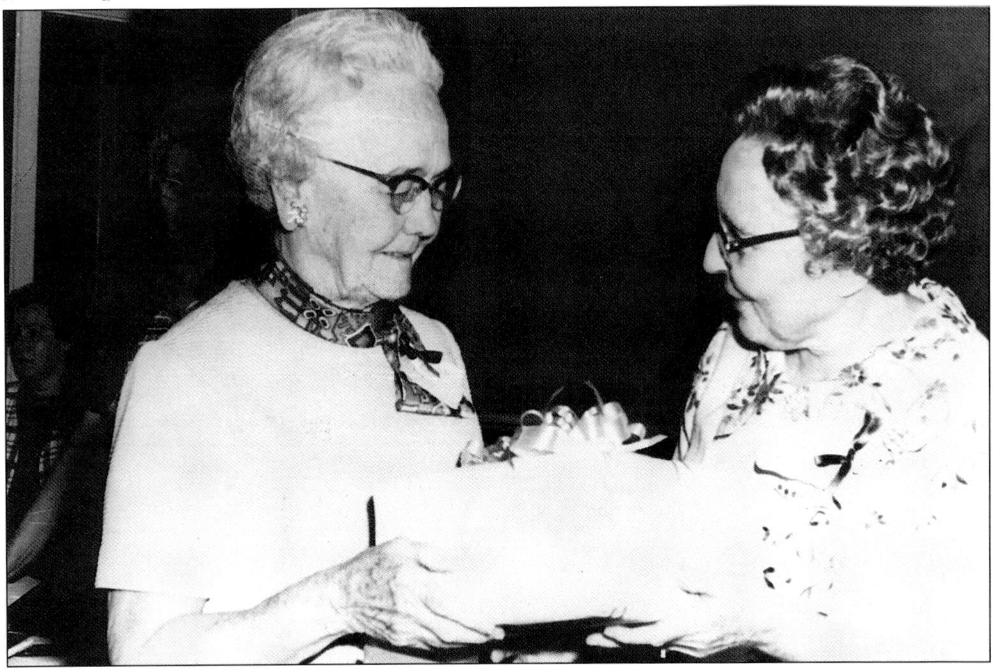

In 1970, Elise Altman (right) presented a plaque to Mary Eva Hite, Class of 1908, as Business and Professional Women's Clubs Woman of the Year. Mrs. Hite served as supervisor of teacher education for South Carolina from 1942 to 1957, executive secretary of the South Carolina Legislative Committee on Aging, division president of the AAUW, and a delegate to the 1961 White House Conference on Aging.

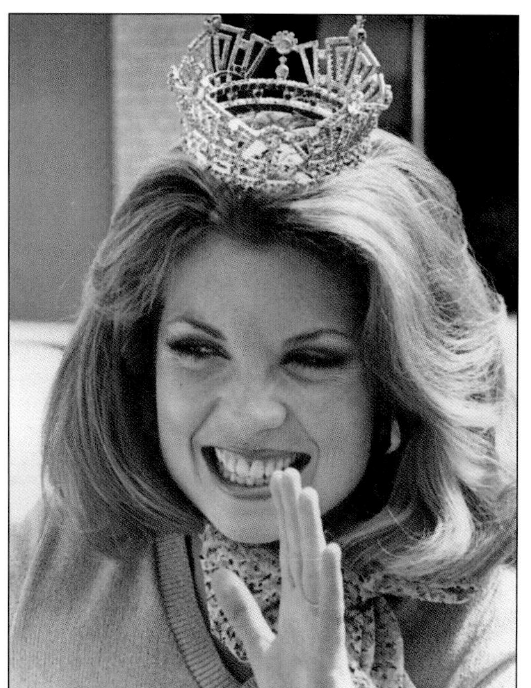

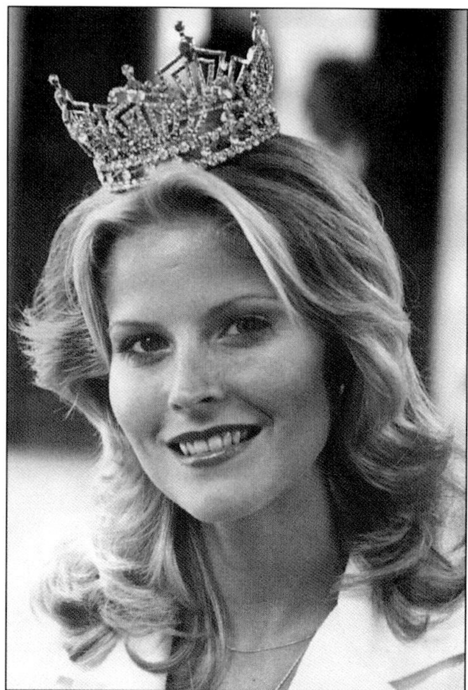

Two Winthrop students became Miss South Carolina in consecutive years: Lavinia Cox (left) in 1976 and Kathy Hinson in 1977.

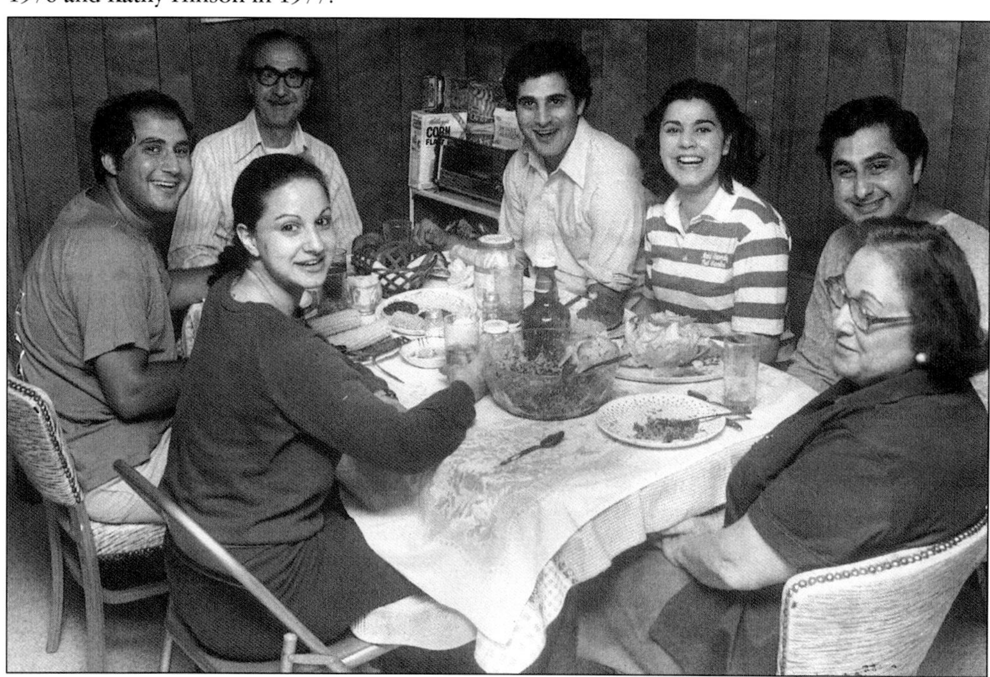

In 1979, the Louis Raad family of Rock Hill, which sent several of its members to Winthrop, was named Regional Family of the Year, one of ten such families in South Carolina. Members of the family are from left to right as follows: Rose; Joey; Louis Raad; George and his wife, Patricia; Tom; and Mrs. Raad.

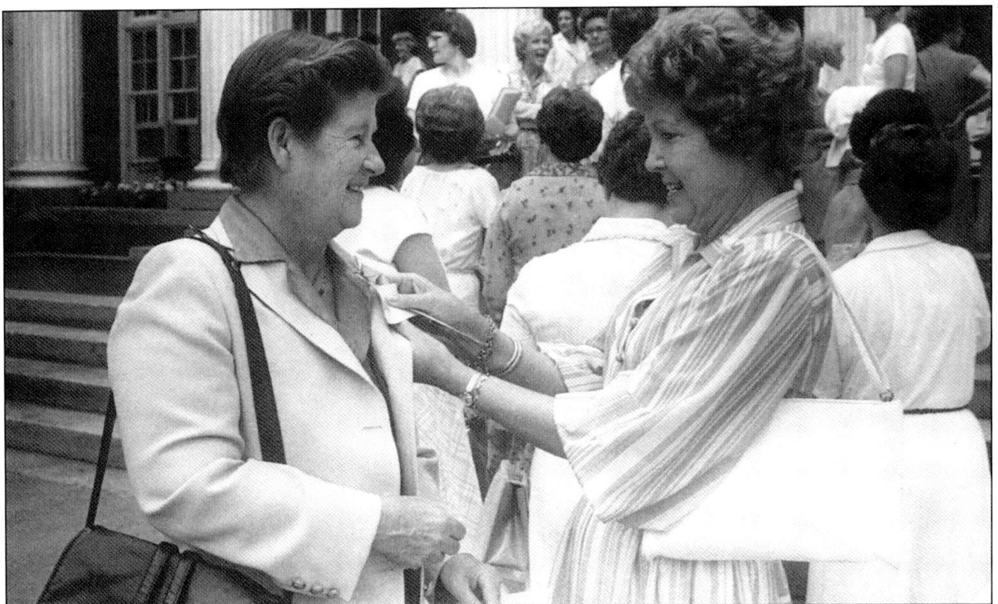

Two longtime friends and loyal supporters of Winthrop, Lois Rhame West (left) and Mary Sue McElveen enjoy the 1980 Alumni weekend. Both are 1943 graduates of Winthrop. Mrs. West, the wife of John C. West, former governor of South Carolina, received a honorary doctorate degree from Winthrop in 1984. Mrs McElveen is a former member of the Winthrop Board of Trustees and the Winthrop Foundation.

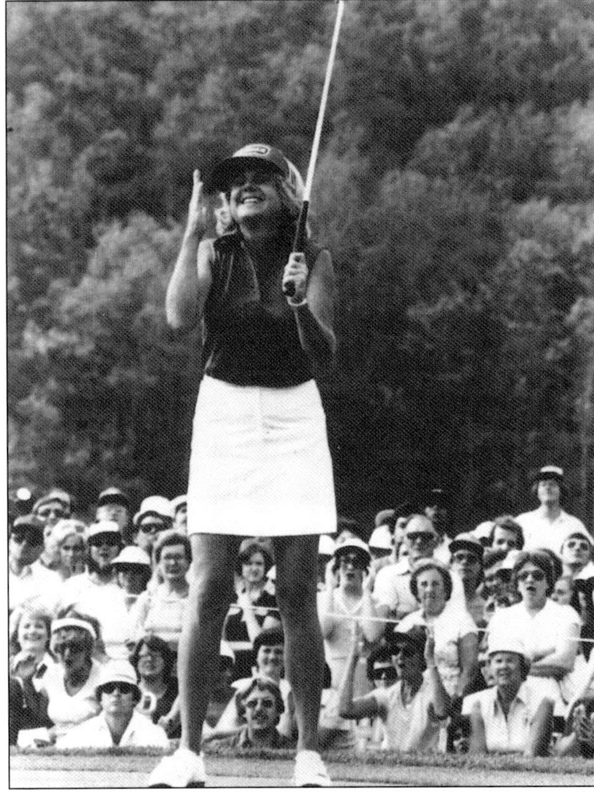

Kathy Hite, Class of 1970, played for many years on the Ladies' Professional Golf Association (LPGA) tour.

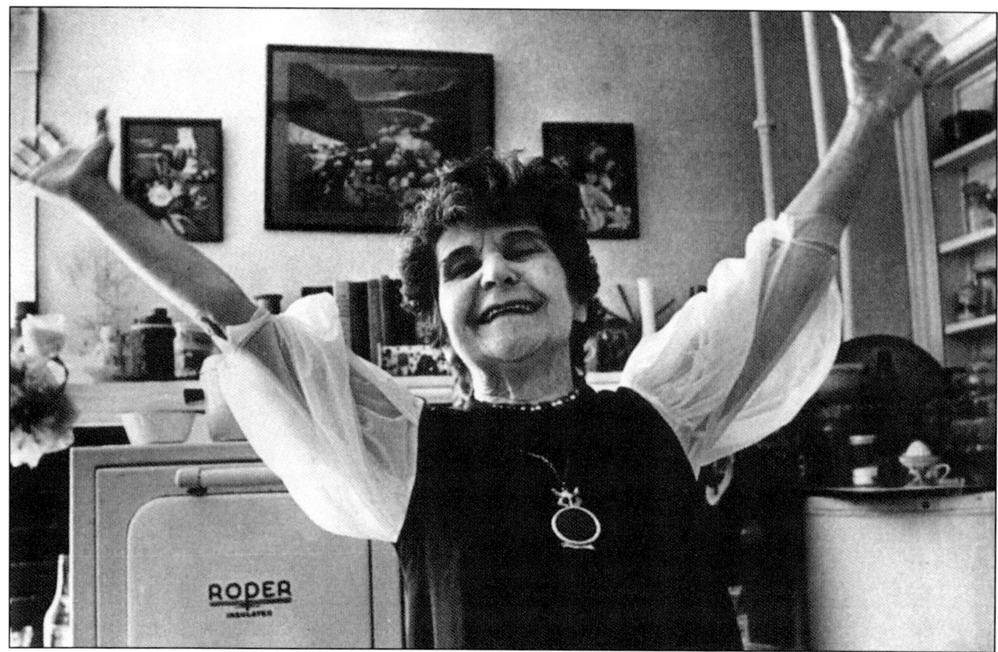

Mina Surasky Tropp, Class of 1918, was known as a collagist and painter with flora. Her artwork is an intriguing mix of paint and preserved plants and flowers.

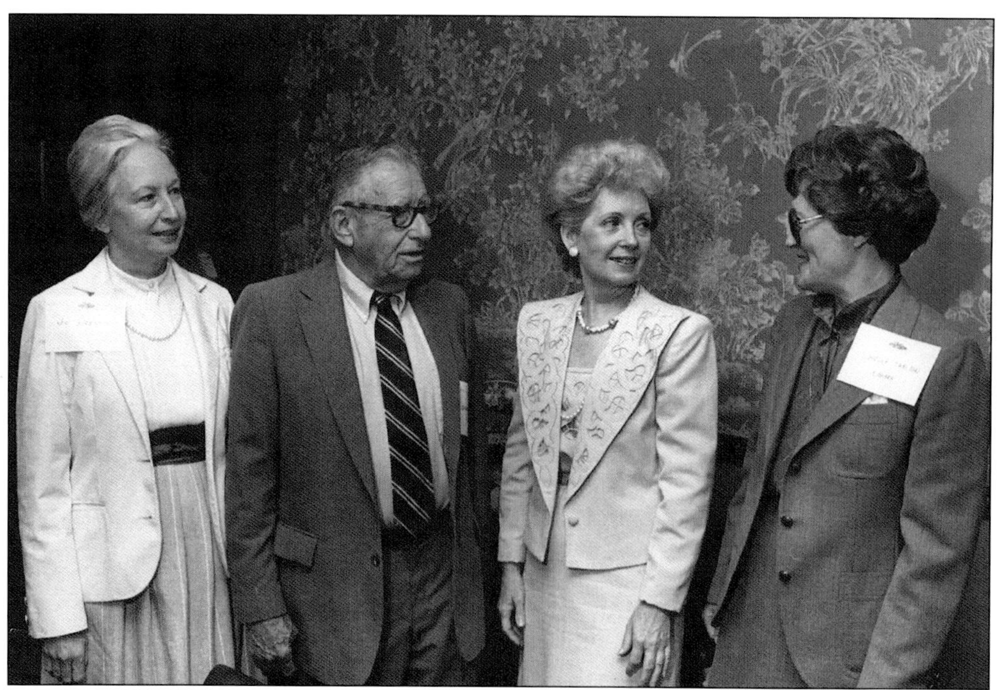
From left to right, Mrs. Charles S. Davis, President Charles S. Davis, Frances Patton Statham (Class of 1951), and Dean of the Winthrop Library Shirley M. Tarlton meet in April 1985. A native of Rock Hill, Statham is a best-selling novelist; her 1986 novel, *To Face the Sun*, won the National Review's Choice Award for best World War II novel. She presently resides in Georgia.

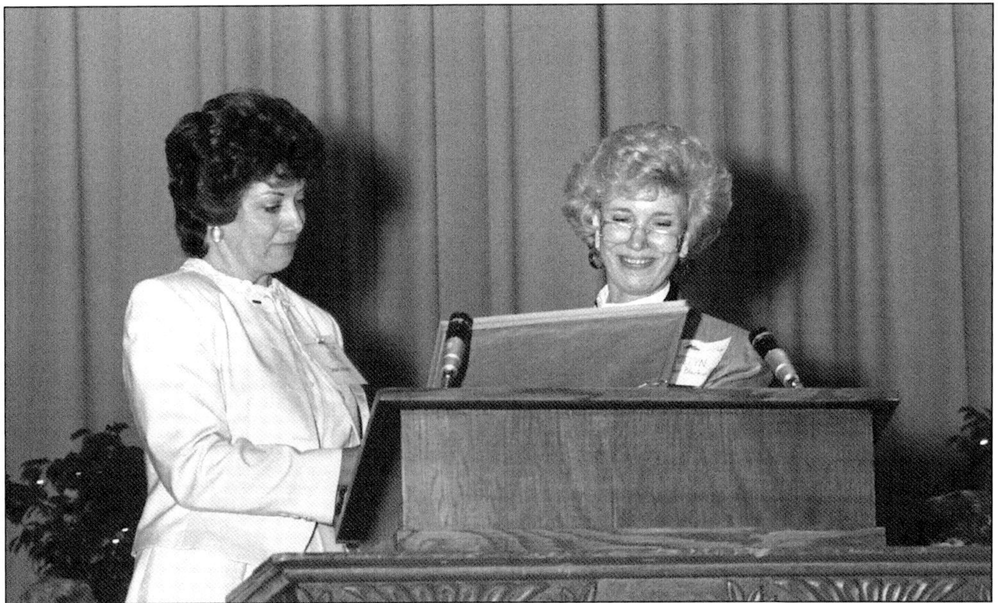

In 1989, Angela Brown Burkhalter, Class of 1968, of North Augusta was recognized at Winthrop University during Alumni Weekend for being named South Carolina Teacher of the Year. At the time, Mrs. Burkhalter was also a member of the Winthrop Board of Trustees. Here, she is being presented with a certificate of achievement by Dr. Evelyn M. Berry, Class of 1961, of Columbia, president of the Winthrop Alumni Association.

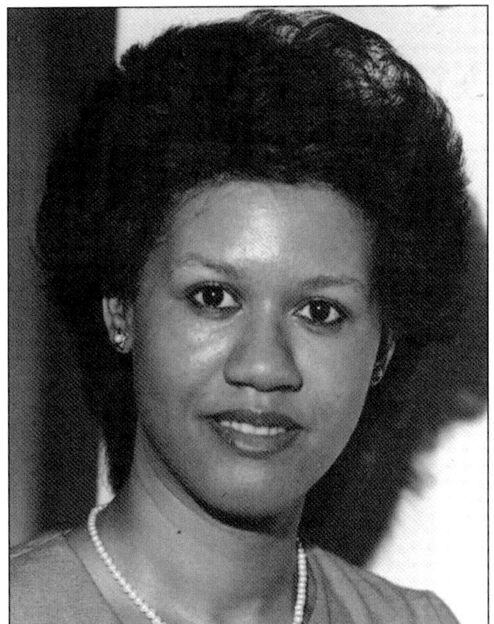

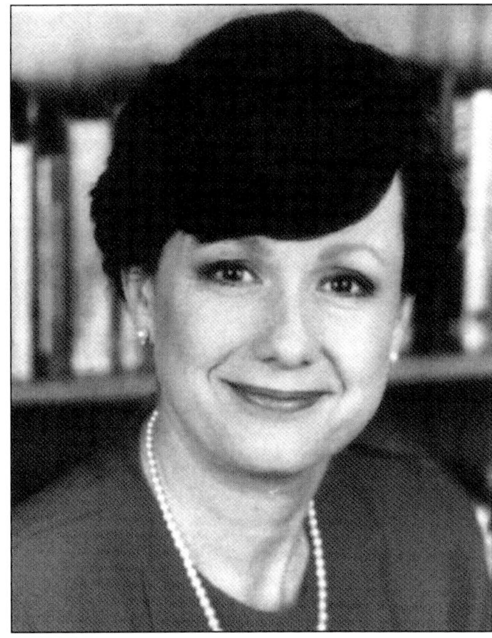

Left: Sheila McMillan, Class of 1974, is an attorney, a former member of the Winthrop Board of trustees, and a prominent figure in South Carolina political circles. *Right:* Cecily Truett, Class of 1971, is one of the creators of the PBS show *Reading Rainbow* and the *Puzzle Place*. *Reading Rainbow* has focused on encouraging reading by school-age children for more than 16 years. It has won 13 Emmy awards and more than 150 total broadcast awards.

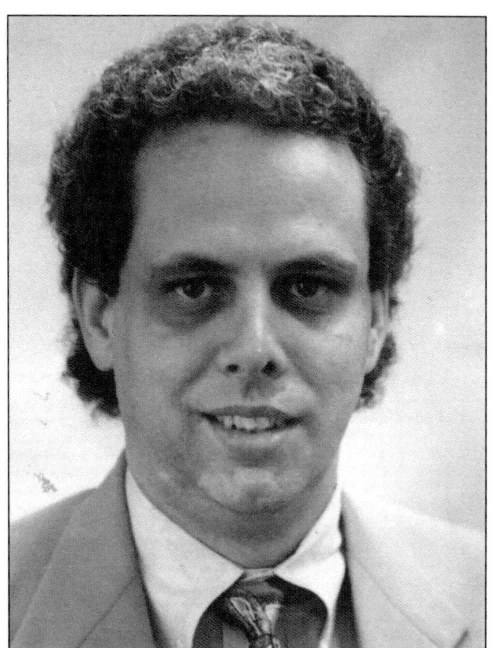
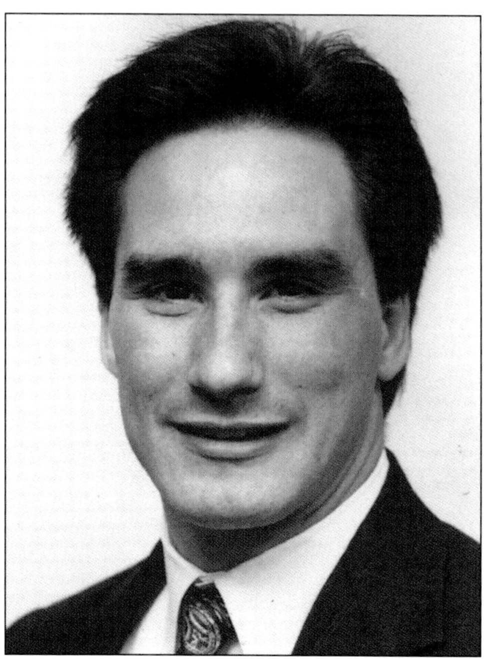
From left to right, Karl Folkens, Class of 1978, and Watts Huckabee, Class of 1989, have served as members of the Winthrop Board of Trustees in the 1990s. Folkens, an attorney from Florence, was elected to the board in 1994 and served as its chair until 1998. Huckabee has served on the board from 1995 to the present.

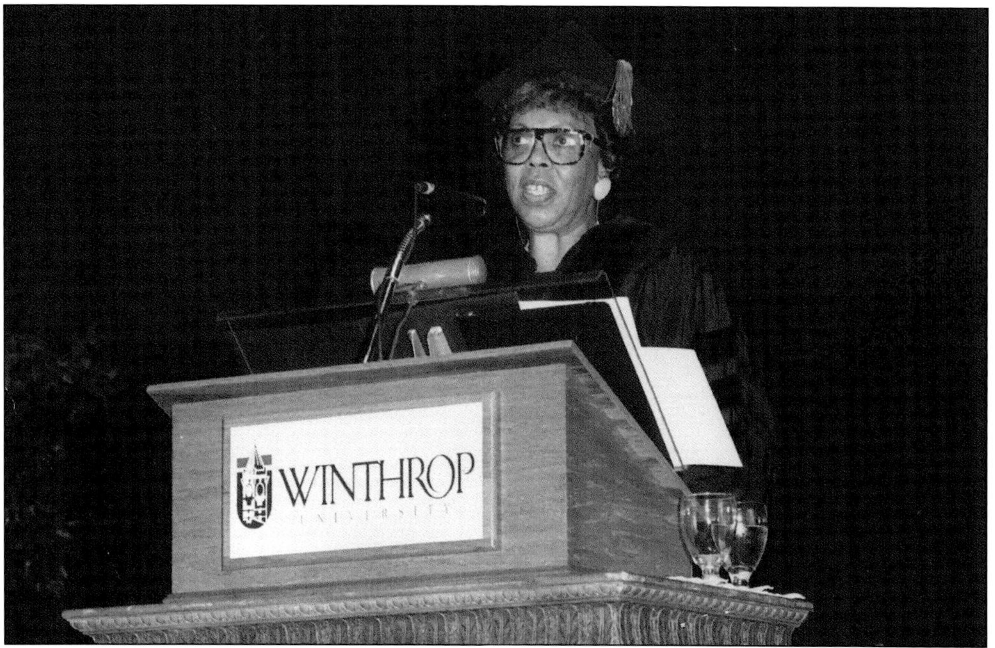

In August 1994, pioneering Winthrop graduate Cynthia Plair Roddey returned to Winthrop as the convocation speaker. A native of Rock Hill, Ms. Roddey integrated Winthrop in 1964, when she became the institution's first African-American student. She graduated with a Master's of Arts in Teaching degree in 1967.

Six

Town and Gown

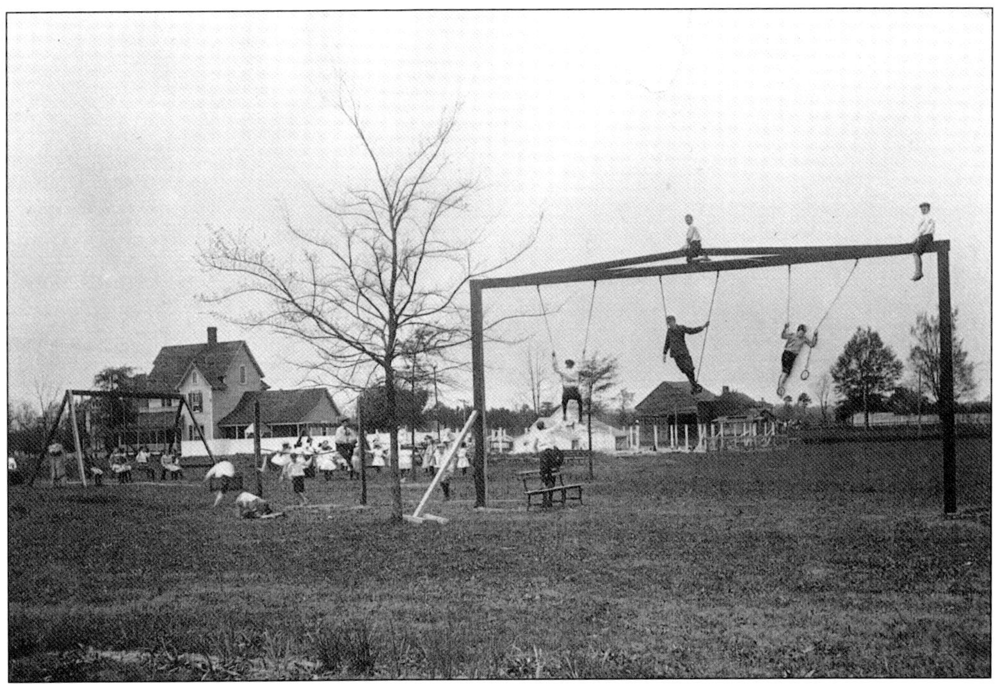

Children from the Winthrop Training School can be seen playing in this 1917 photograph, four years after the school's official opening. The school's purpose was to provide training for South Carolina teachers.

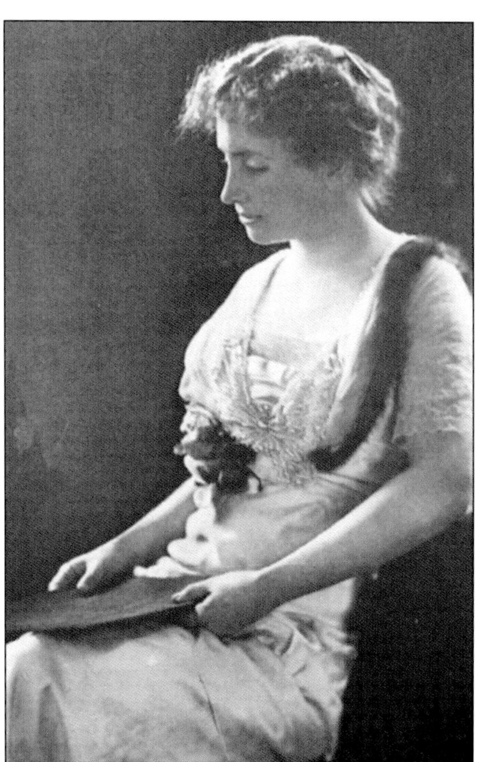

Helen Keller appeared at Winthrop in 1917 as part of the school's Artist Series program. Over the years, many famous people have come to Winthrop, including Will Rogers, Amelia Earhart, Martha Graham, and Gloria Steinem, among others.

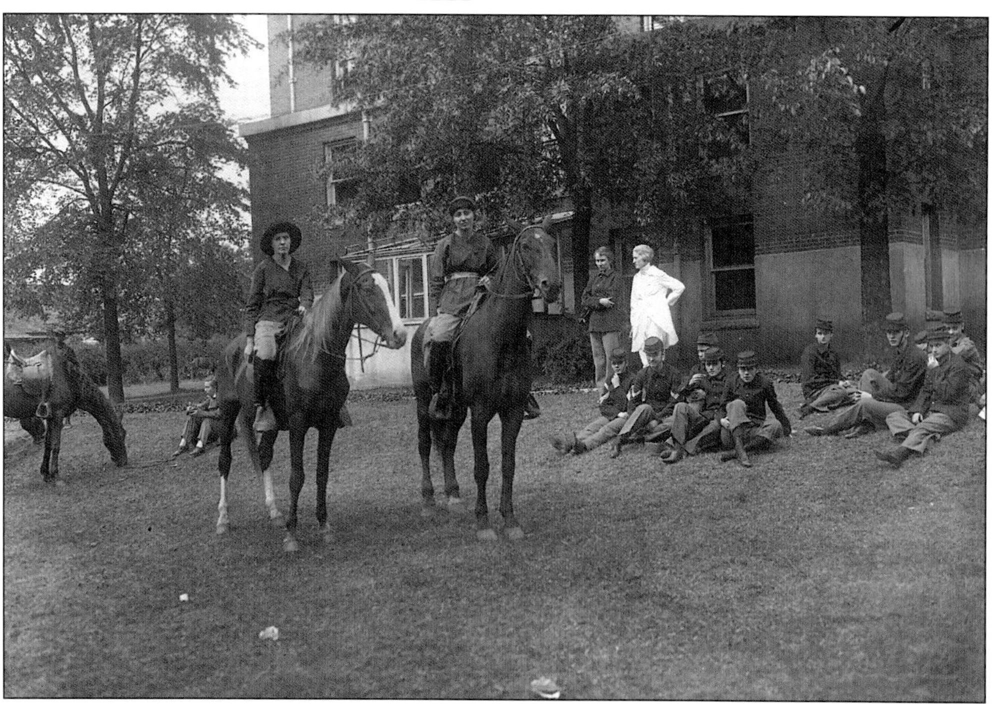

This is a scene from the "Making of South Carolina" pageant, which was held at Winthrop in 1921. The pageant was a popular activity at Winthrop in the early 1920s, and thousands of people from all over South Carolina attended the event.

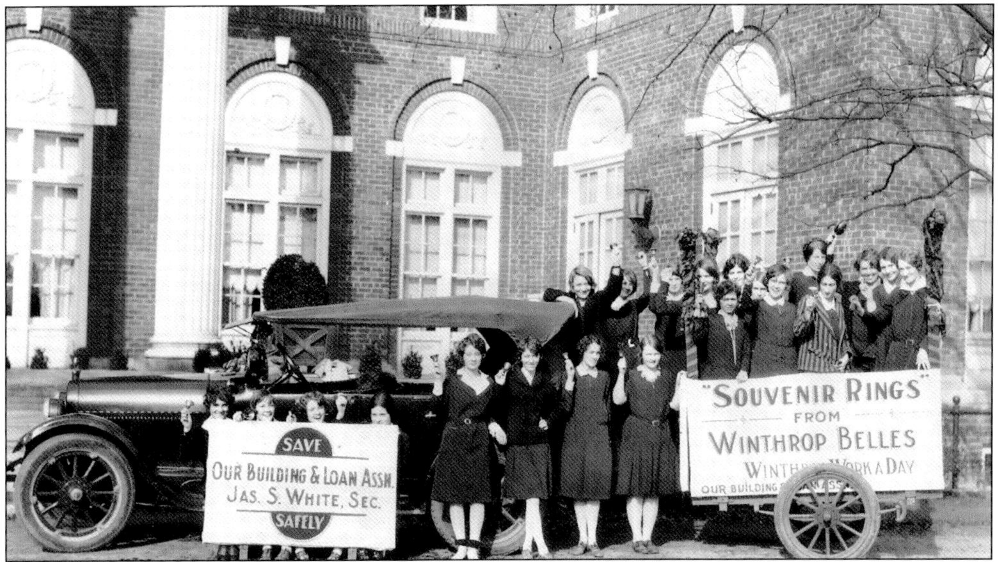

This photo from the December 17, 1927 issue of the *Johnsonian*, Winthrop's student newspaper, had the following caption: "Blue skirts hold reins of labor and business for the day." According to the article, the event was sponsored by the YMCA in cooperation with the Rock Hill Chamber of Commerce, and Winthrop students were "to be found in nearly every business house in many homes doing everything from acting as city mayor to shining shoes and washing cars."

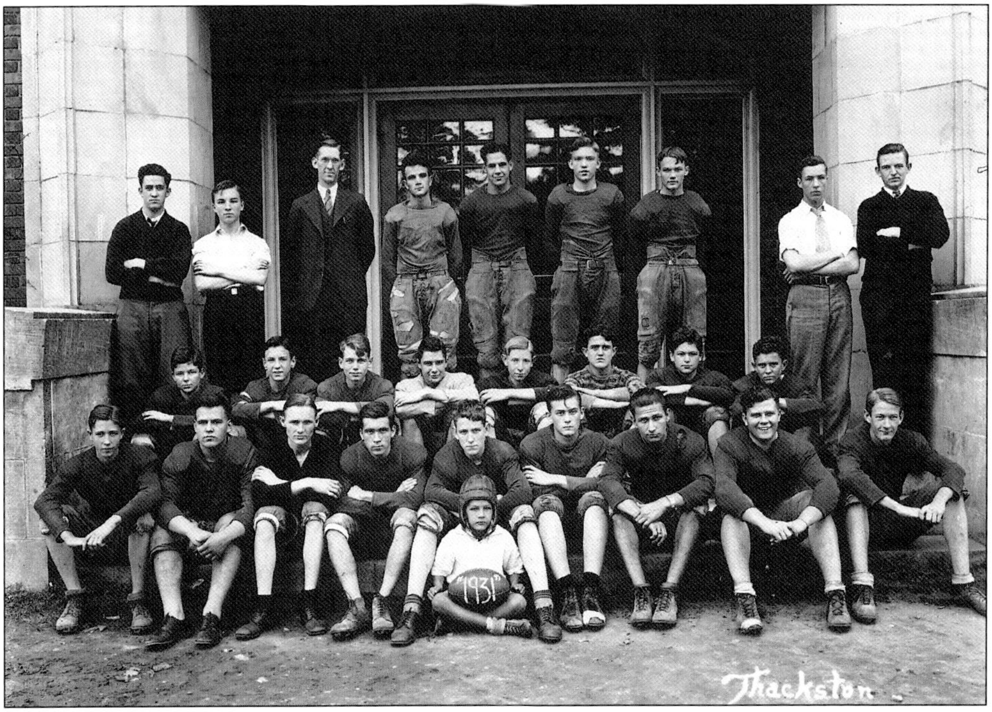

This is a portrait of the 1931 Winthrop Training School football team. The Winthrop Training School was a part of the Rock Hill School System, although it was operated by Winthrop College. The school had grades from kindergarten through the 12th grade, which was added in 1948–49. The Training School closed in 1968 and was converted into a classroom building.

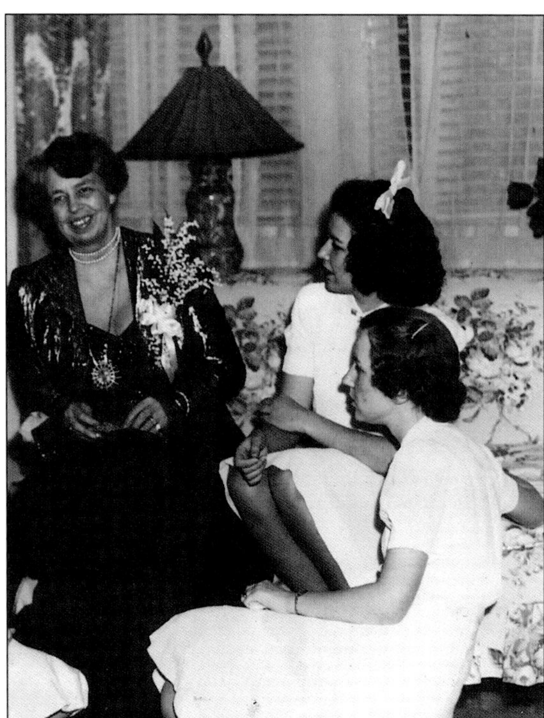

Mrs. Eleanor Roosevelt chats with students in the Winthrop President's House. Mrs. Roosevelt spoke at Winthrop on April 27, 1940.

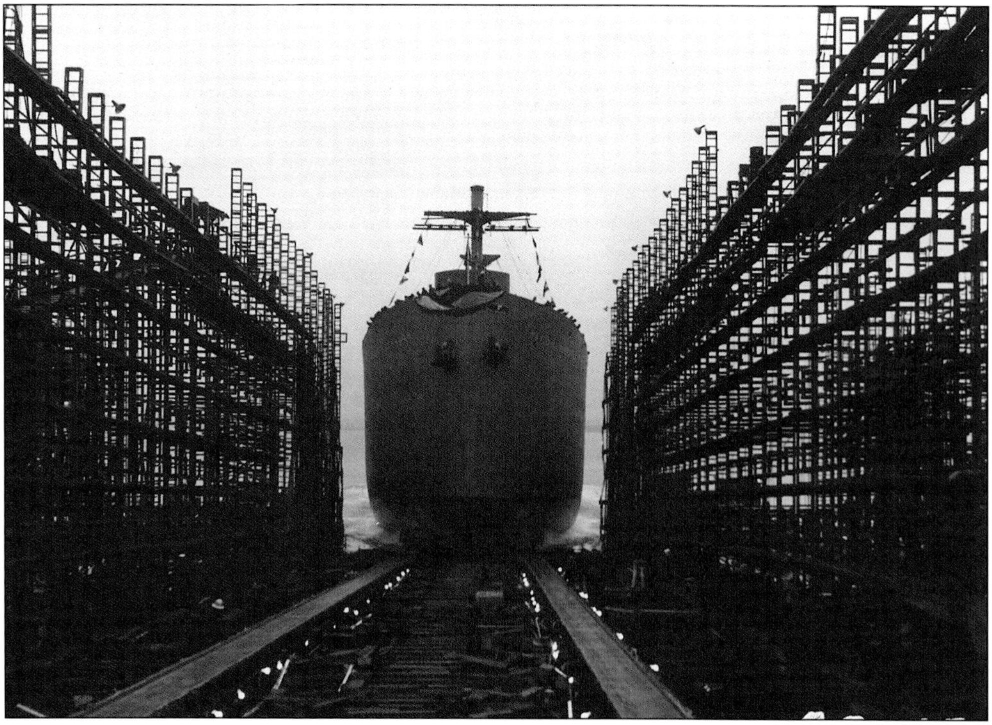

During World War II, a liberty ship was named after David Bancroft Johnson, Winthrop's first president. Liberty ships were special cargo ships named for outstanding Americans, and they delivered badly needed supplies to the Allies.

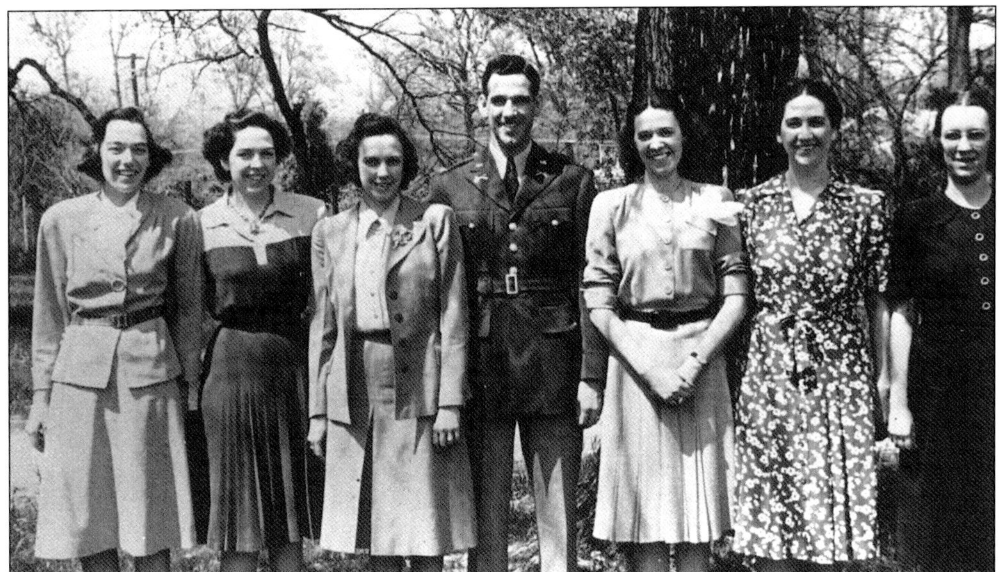

Edward Holman Smith (center) was a part of the Civilian Pilot Training Program, which operated at Winthrop from 1942 to 1944 and was designed to prepare World War II pilots, both physically and mentally, for pre-flight and flight school training in other parts of the country. This 1942 photo includes, from eft to right, the following: Meta Smith, Hettie Smith Carter, Blanding Smith, Edward Holman, Rebecca Smith, Anne Smith Cook, and Grace Smith Harrison.

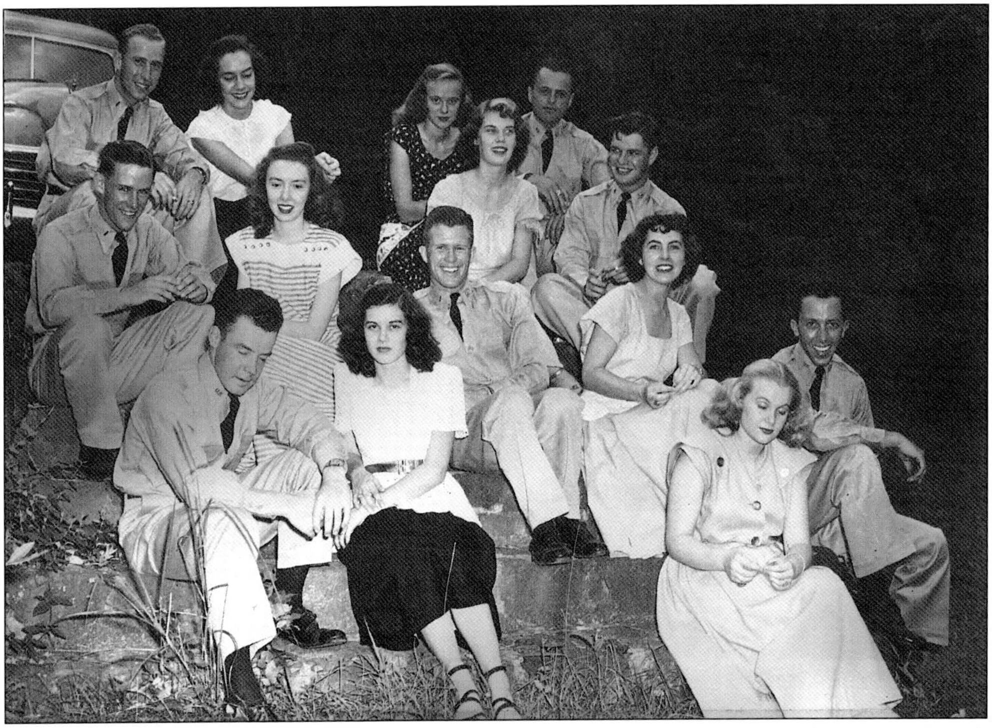

West Points cadets visited Winthrop on July 24 and July 25, 1948, and socialized with Winthrop students.

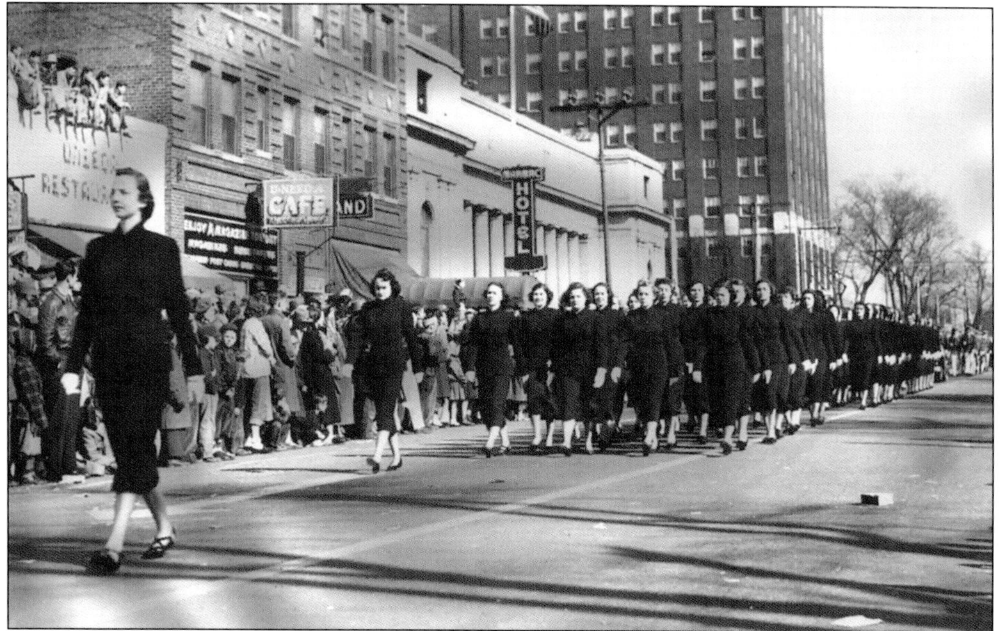

Winthrop students march proudly and smartly in their uniforms during Gov. James F. Byrnes's inaugural parade in Columbia on July 16, 1951.

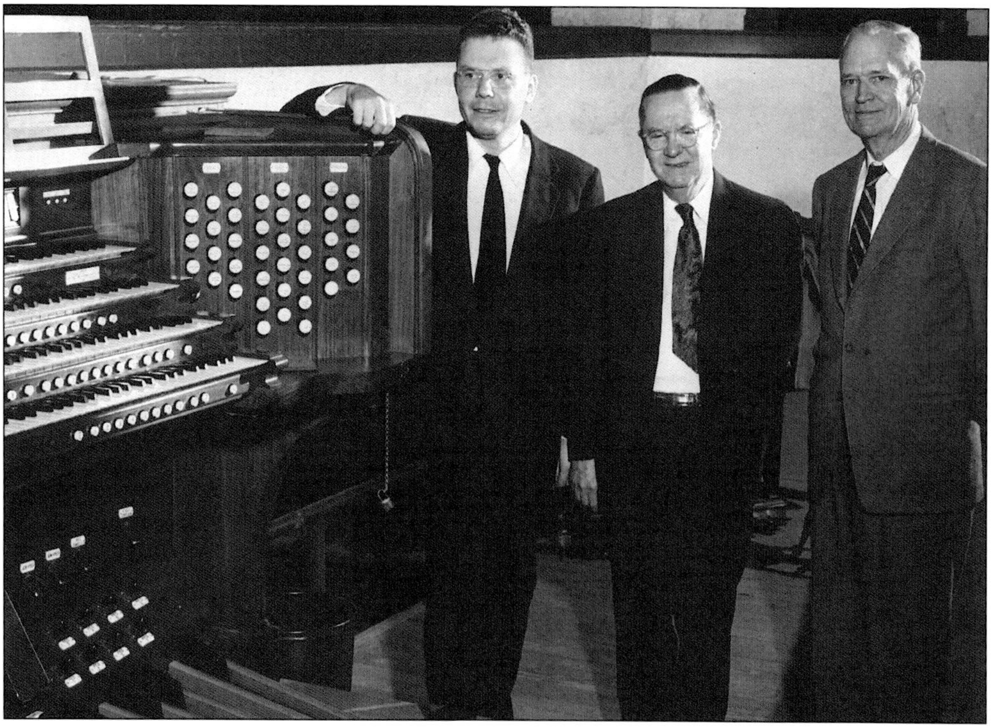

From left to right are Virgil Fox (organist), Henry R. Sims (Winthrop president), and Walter B Roberts (Winthrop professor of music from 1925 to 1958). Famed organist Virgil Fox dedicated the Memorial Organ in Byrnes Auditorium in November 1955. Since then, the organ has brought musical enjoyment to thousands of South Carolinians.

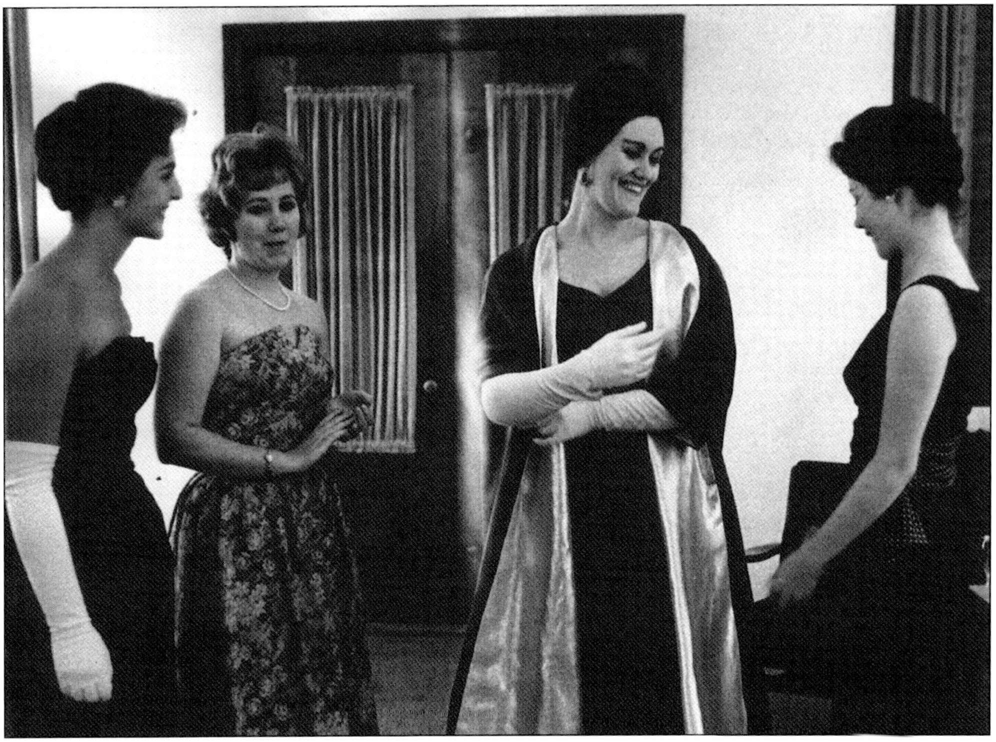

Winthrop students meet with one of the most famous personalities in the music world when soprano Joan Sutherland (second from right) made her U.S. concert debut at Winthrop in early 1961. They are, from left to right, as follows: Paula Newman of West Palm Beach; Phyllis Smith of Shaw Air Force Base; Ms. Sutherland; and Susan Griggs of Conway.

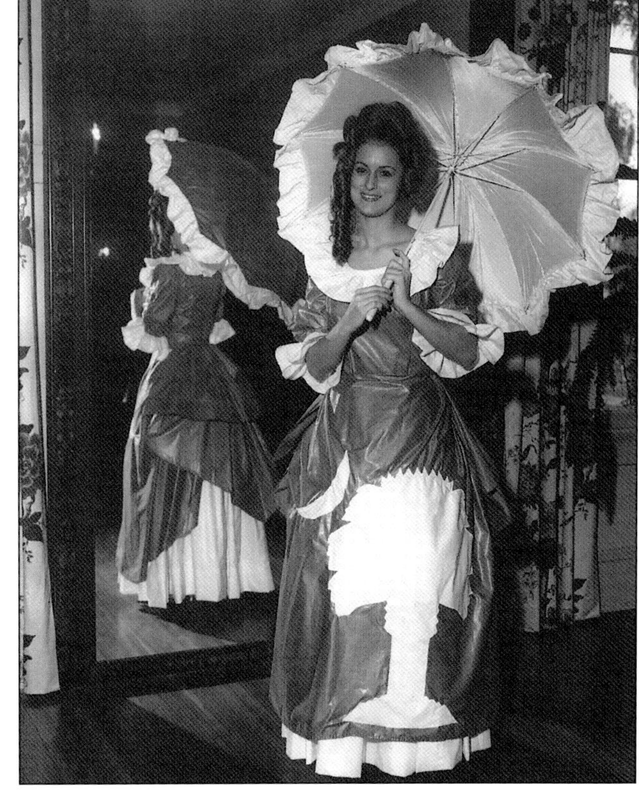

Invoking images of the Old South, Maree Marchette was Winthrop's Cherry Blossom princess in 1969.

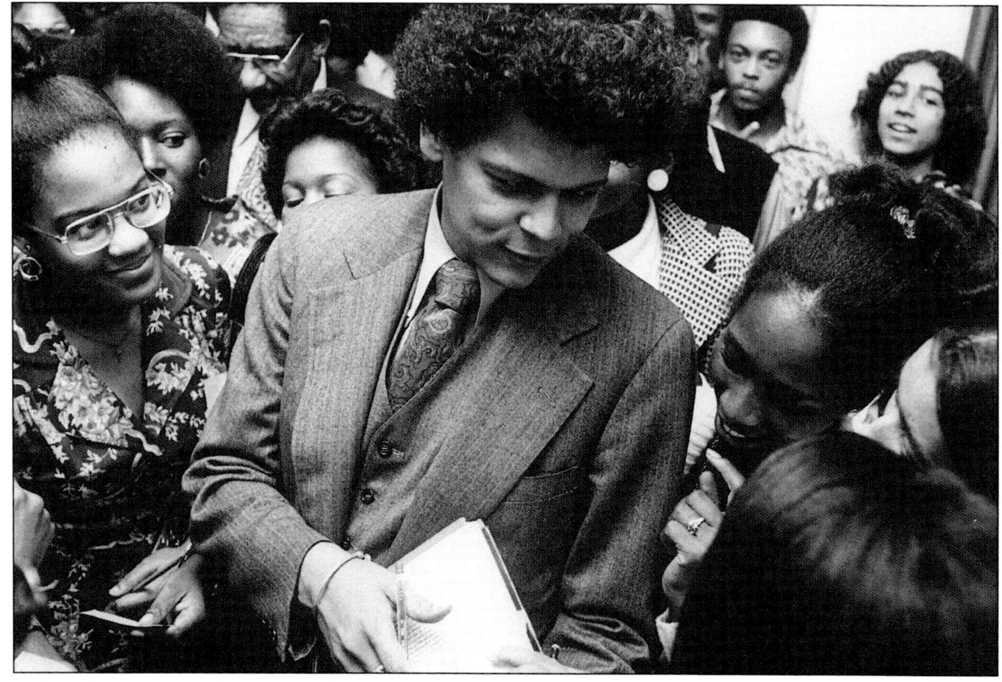

Political activist Julian Bond meets with members of the Association of Ebonites in February 1975.

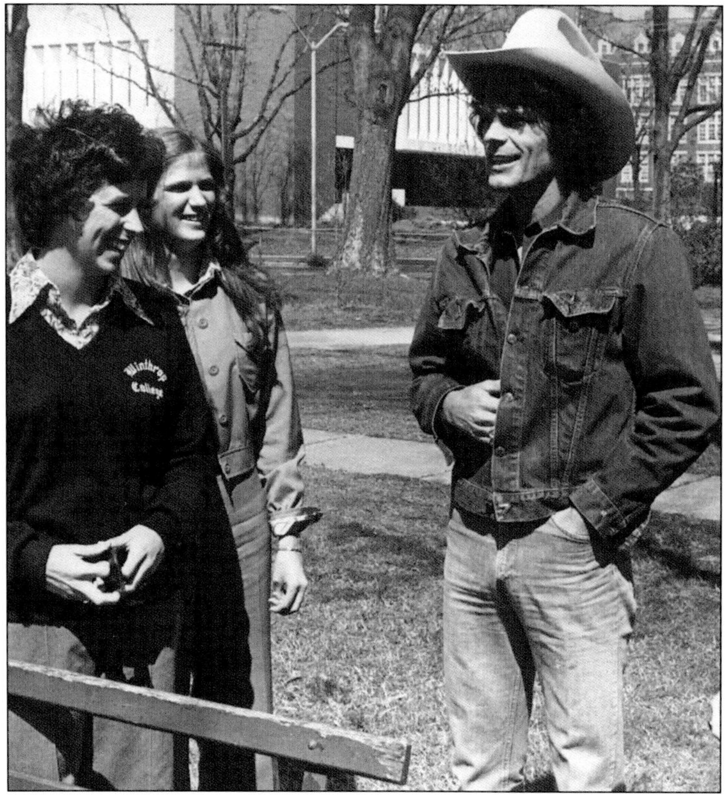

In April 1975, popular singer B.J. Thomas enjoys a moment with Winthrop students when he appeared at the school.

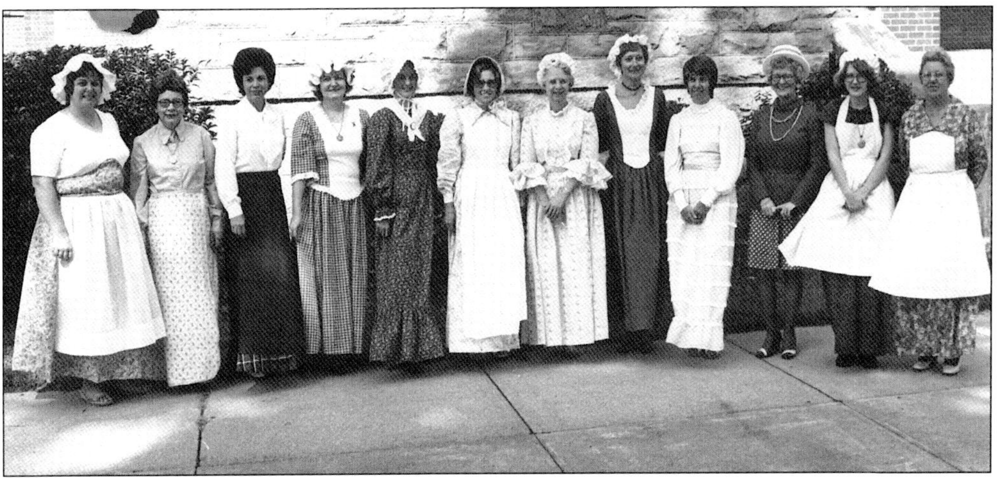

Winthrop employees celebrate the U.S. Bicentennial in July 1976, donning outfits that reflected a patriotic theme.

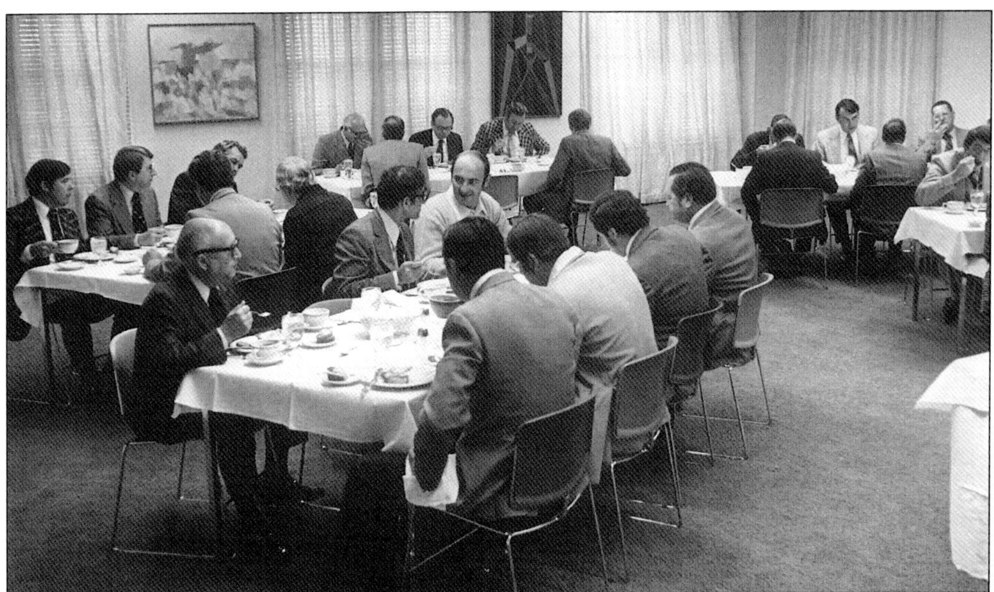

The Eagle Club sponsors a booster club breakfast in November 1976. The official booster club for all Winthrop athletics, the Eagle Club has been a big factor in the growth and development of the Winthrop athletic program.

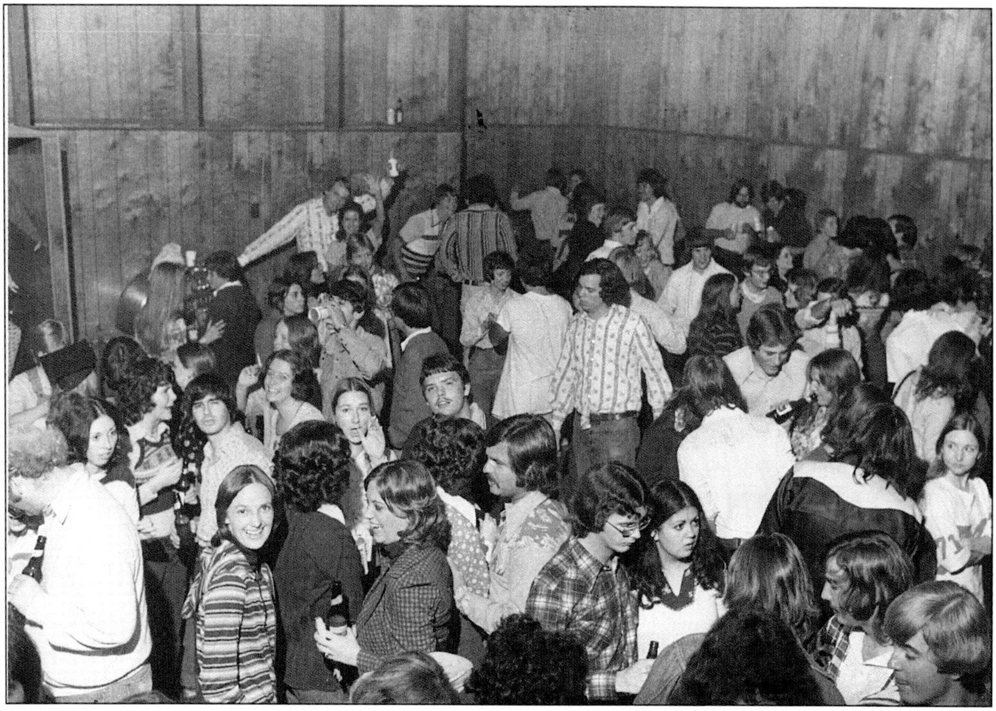

Located on the outskirts of Rock Hill, the Barn was a popular gathering place for Winthrop students in the 1970s.

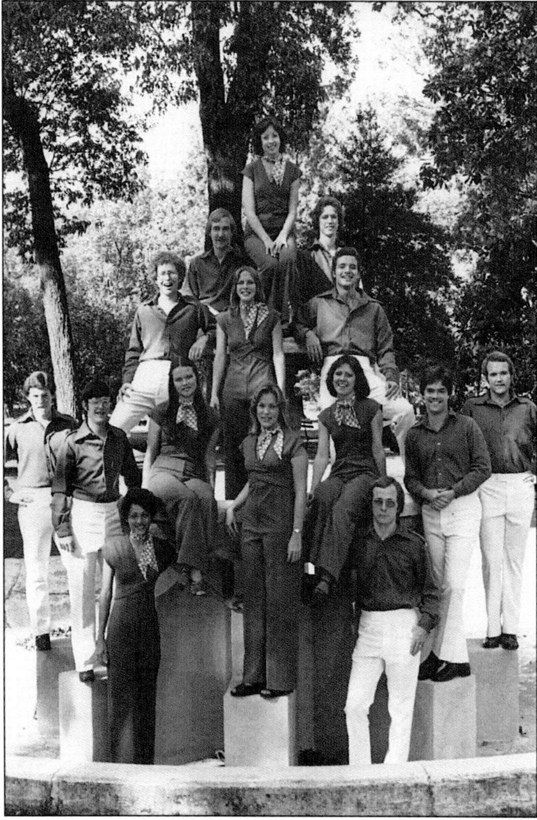

The Winthrop Singers, seen here in October 1977, is a dynamic musical group that has been an ambassador for Winthrop for more than two decades.

The Winthrop-sponsored Model United Nations is seen here meeting in April 1979. The Model U.N. was established in 1977 as an effort to increase the student body's interest in international affairs while providing leadership training. The event has always included talented high school students.

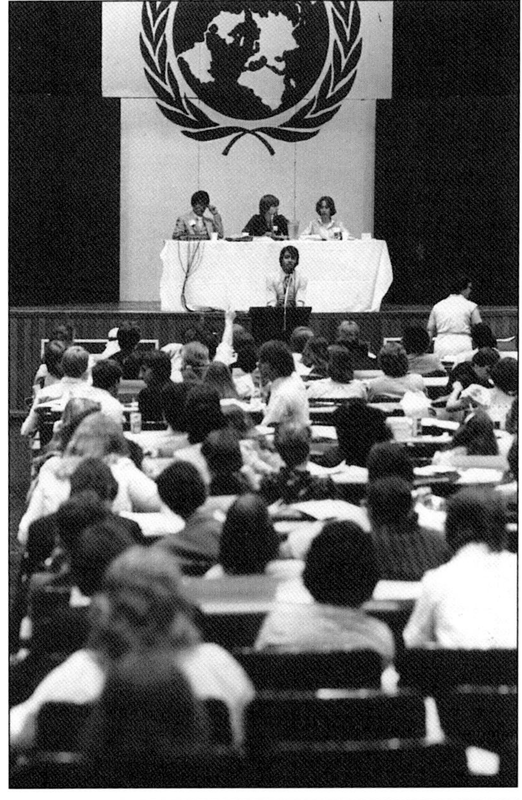

Winthrop students Johnny Schwartz (center) and Gerry McAlister (right) participate in the 1979 Eagle Run. Since its founding in March 1977, the Eagle Run has become a Winthrop tradition.

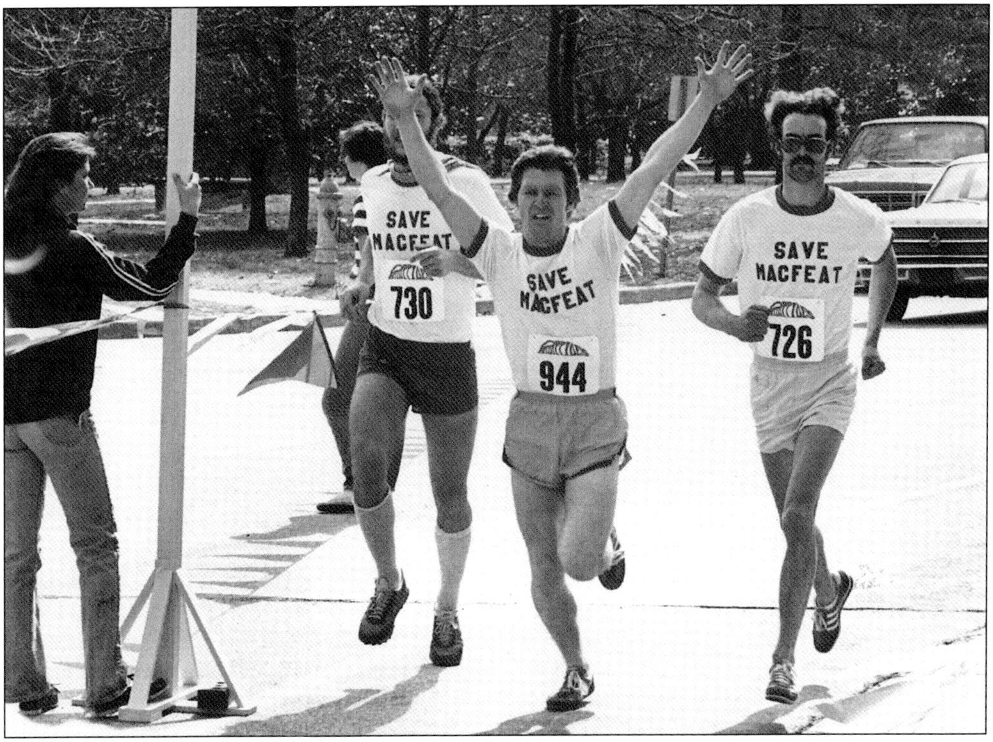

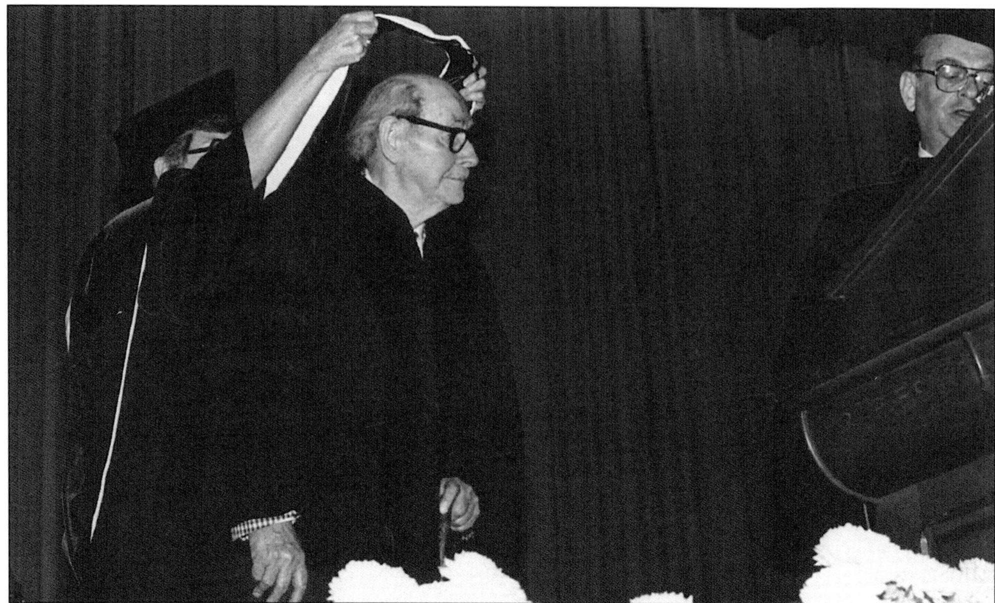

Marion Allan Wright, noted South Carolina civil rights activist, receives an honorary degree from Winthrop in 1980. Wright was strong opponent of the death penalty and a champion of civil rights and civil liberties.

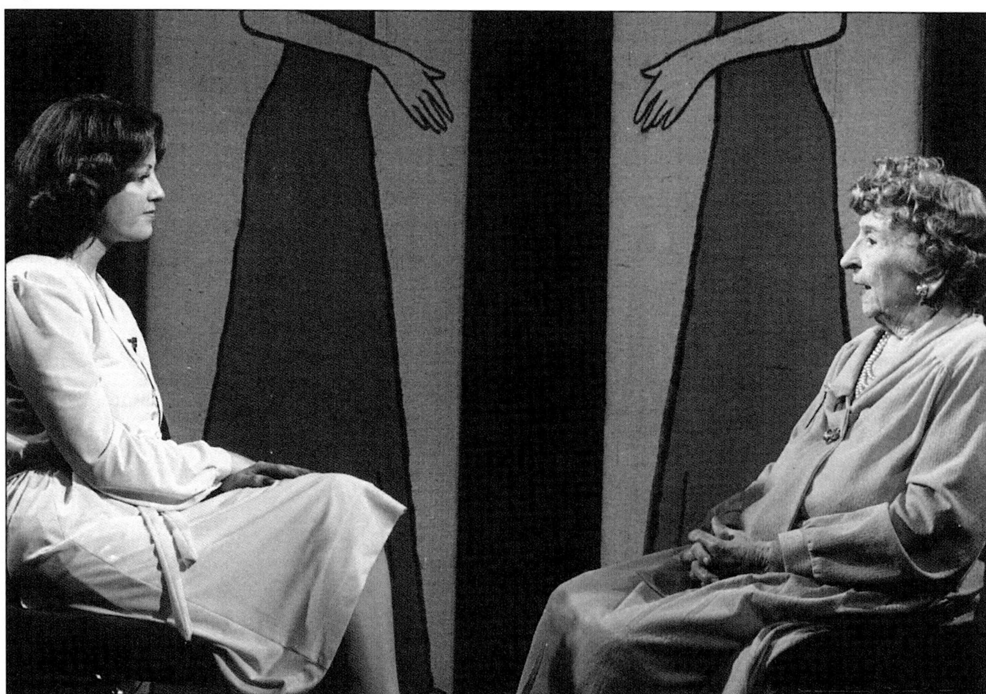

Ann Evans, assistant archivist, interviews educator Marguerite Tolbert in September 1981 for a 13-part television series on "Women Leaders in South Carolina." The program was co-sponsored by South Carolina ETV and the Winthrop Archives and also included interviews with such notable women as Rosamunde Boyd, Estellene Walker, Sara Vandiver Liverance, and Agnes Hildebrand Wilson.

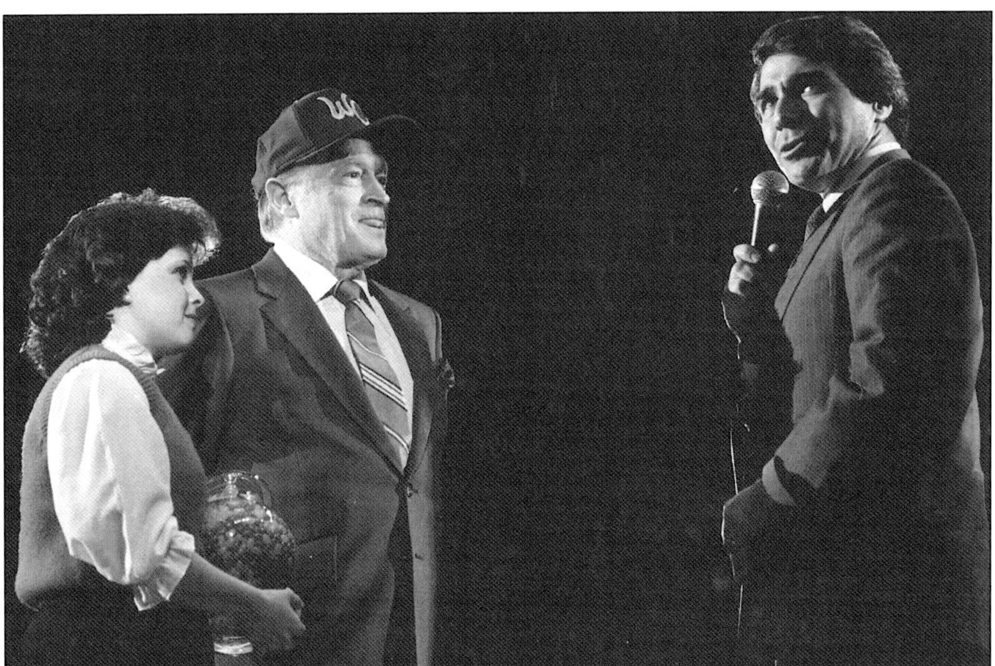

To Winthrop students' delight, President Philip Lader named Bob Hope an honorary Winthrop student in November 1984, when the legendary entertainer visited the university.

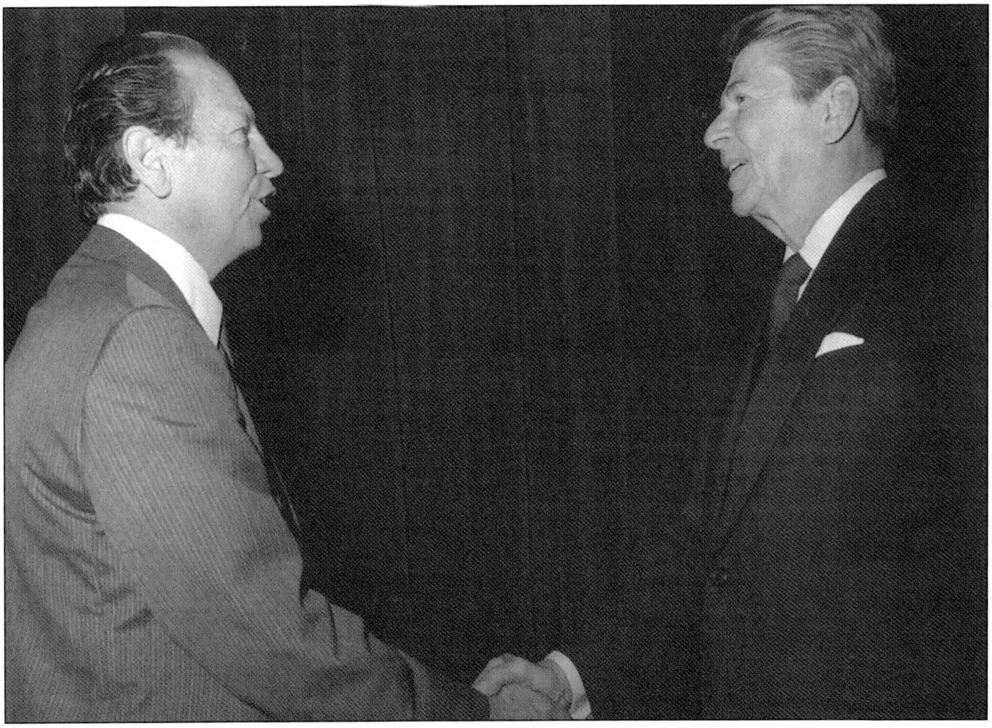

John Hardin, chairman of the Winthrop Foundation Board, meets President Ronald Reagan in March 1986. A former mayor of Rock Hill, Hardin has been an instrumental factor in strengthening the bond between Winthrop and the Rock Hill community.

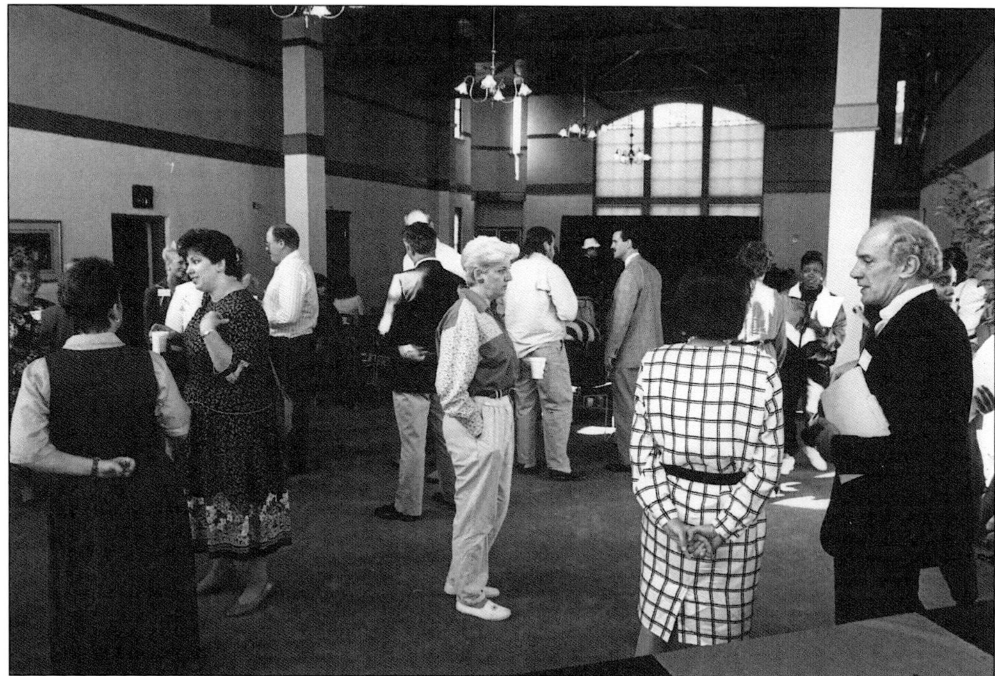

Participants in Winthrop's New Start program gather in October 1992. New Start is a service program that helps adult students with admissions and registration and also gives them support and information.

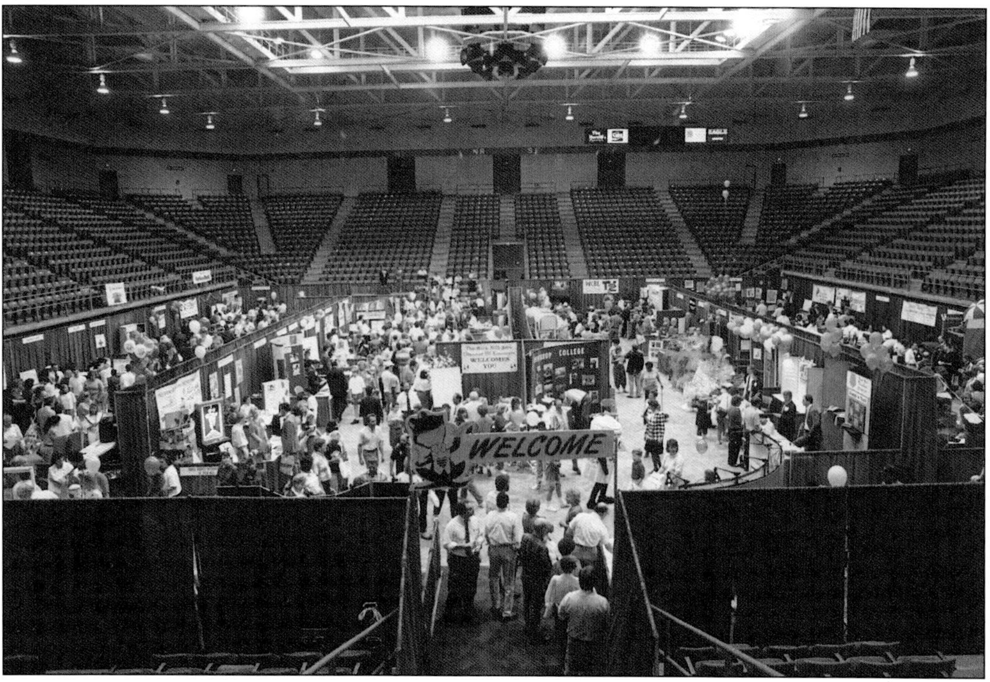

A "Business Bazaar" was held at Winthrop Coliseum in April 1992. During the 1990s, Winthrop has been active in teaching the public about the new global economy.